the
post-
adoption
blues

KAREN J. FOLI, Ph.D., and
JOHN R. THOMPSON, M.D.

the
post-
adoption
blues

overcoming the unforeseen
challenges of adoption

RODALE

Mention of specific companies, organizations, or authorities in this book does not imply endorsement by the publisher, nor does mention of specific companies, organizations, or authorities imply that they endorse this book.

Internet addresses and telephone numbers given in this book were accurate at the time it went to press.

Disclaimer
In order to protect privacy and anonymity, the names of the parents, children, and family members in this book—with the exception of the authors' family and our panel of experts—have been changed.

Printed in the United States of America
Rodale Inc. makes every effort to use acid-free ∞, recycled paper ♻.

Book design by Judith Stagnitto Abbate / Abbate Design

Library of Congress Cataloging-in-Publication Data

Foli, Karen J.
    The post-adoption blues : overcoming the unforeseen challenges of adoption / Karen J. Foli and John R. Thompson.
        p.   cm.
    This book is intended as a reference volume only. The information given here is designed to help you make informed decisions.
    Includes bibliographical references and index.
    ISBN 1–57954–866–0 paperback
    1. Adoption—Psychological aspects.   2. Adoptive parents—Psychology.   3. Adopted children—Psychology.   4. Parenting.   I. Thompson, John R., M.D.   II. Title.
HV875.F59   2004
362.734'01'9—dc22   2004005949

Distributed to the book trade by St. Martin's Press

2 4 6 8 10 9 7 5 3 1   paperback

RODALE
WE **INSPIRE** AND **ENABLE** PEOPLE TO IMPROVE
THEIR LIVES AND THE WORLD AROUND THEM

FOR MORE OF OUR PRODUCTS
WWW.RODALESTORE.COM
(800) 848-4735

This book is for our children:
Ben, who taught us faith;
Peter, who taught us patience; and
Annie, who taught us kindness.

contents

part I: expectations of yourself as a parent

part II: your expectations of your child

part III: expectations of others

part IV: a closer look

preface

A baby is born and the birthmother agrees that you will parent her newborn child.

A court halfway around the world signs the documents that finally allow you to bring your child home.

After a year in the court system, the judge terminates parental rights and declares that the foster child you've been caring for is legally yours.

Your 20-year-old daughter gives birth to a healthy son, which she leaves in your care.

Loving a child, any child, is an ongoing act of astounding beauty. Our emotions, our unconditional, tenacious, relentless love of a child not born to us is what sets us, the adoptive parents, apart from many others in the world. This book is about that love. During our interviews with parents, we—Karen and John—were awed, humbled, and honored by what these parents so generously shared with us. They shared their hopes and dreams, their heartbreaks and struggles. But what they ultimately shared were their triumphs as a family. They were motivated by the thought of helping others on their journey of adoption or kinship parenting. We believe that what they've shared truly will help. They have changed our lives, and we are forever grateful to them.

These dedicated parents offered us the chance to glimpse their personal lives—flawed, human, and beautiful. The most important gifts they offered us were proven, home-tested strategies learned through trial, error, and the experience of forming a new family. Reflecting on what they had found to be the most helpful ways to cope when faced with unexpected emotions and overwhelming events, these parents shared with open hearts.

In addition to the generosity of these parents, we were moved by the commitment and intelligence of the adoption professionals we contacted to better understand the many ways in which adoption creates and changes families. Almost a dozen experts in the field of adoption from throughout the country—experts with hands-on, day-to-day experience with adoptive and kinship families—contributed their ideas to our work. These folks do not live in ivory towers. They help, advise, and counsel parents who need objective insight and feedback as they stabilize themselves and their families after adoption. Some of our experts are adoptive parents themselves; one is an adult adoptee. We chose these extraordinary people because they don't just think about adoption as an intellectual enterprise, they live the adoptive experience.

This book blends the experts' counsel and advice with the wisdom of parents. We share with you what our experts, through years of their own research and heartfelt efforts, have found to help families. Our experts also recommended many of the "Selected Readings" found on page 230. These readings will help fill in parts of the adoption story that are beyond the scope of this book.

Our book is designed to do two things. The first is to explain the common issues that face most, if not all, families during the post-adoption period; and the second is to provide simple, effective help for you, the adoptive or kinship parent. We define post-adoption as the time after placement of the child in the home and onward. For our purposes, post-adoption encompasses the "post-placement" and "post-finalization" periods (see "Glossary" on page 226).

As authors, we speak not only from our research and study, but also from experience with both the joys and the unforeseen challenges of adoption. We are the parents of two children by birth and one child by adoption. We met our daughter for the first time in an airport, when she was carried off a plane from Kolkatta, India. That memory will stay as close to our hearts and as vivid as the births of our other children. We saw a tiny baby—almost 5 months old—in a thin pink sleeper, her small hands clinging to her escort's shirt. As she was gently jostled up the jetliner's ramp on a dark, warm March night, our daughter came closer and closer to us for the first time.

That moment marked a new beginning for our daughter and our family, the symbolic birth of Annie. What we didn't know that night was that we were meeting an infant who carried the effects of an early life without consistent care, a life that had already endured so much stress. Her challenging behaviors—and more notably, our lack of preparedness—led us to struggle as a family. Karen was particularly susceptible to the mass of contradictory post-adoption emotions that we address in these pages. Karen felt shame, guilt, and the fear of being judged by others. All these toxic emotions kept her, for a time, from embracing her role as Annie's parent and showing what was in her heart.

After so many months of longing for this child, Karen wondered how she could be so unhappy. Shocked by her own emotions, Karen tried to deny them and silence them, to handle them on her own. But they wouldn't go away. Slowly, she began to trust her friends and her husband.

John, concerned about his wife's sadness and anxiety, felt unsure how to help. He offered Karen support and his belief that, with time, she would be able to bond with Annie. Above all else, he continued to love both his wife and his daughter unconditionally.

For Karen, the journey toward bonding with Annie was confusing and difficult. She actively sought information and found what little there was on the Internet. Suddenly, she realized she wasn't alone. There were others who had felt this way. No, it didn't mean that she didn't love Annie. One by one she was able to confront the emotional secrets that were putting distance between her and her family. As these feelings were resolved, understood, and overcome, she and Annie fell in love.

We want this book to bring those unspoken emotions into the open and to mark the start of a new era of open conversations about post-adoption feelings. For too long, these emotions have been viewed as disloyal to the world of adoption. Some people seem to believe that if we talk about post-adoption difficulties, we might somehow discourage others from adopting. This old belief does a disservice to families who need help. Harboring these secrets perpetuates isolation and endangers family functioning. We believe the post-adoption transition period is *normal;* a certain amount of stress is to be expected. Denying that these feelings exist seems to imply that confronting your emotions is futile—and that ignoring your emotions will make them go away. The coping strategies in this book strongly contradict this belief. When you use these techniques, we believe you can transform your feelings into actions that will positively influence you and your family.

We view parents' post-adoption emotions on a continuum—from a twitter of anxiety to a devastating sadness. Even a small but lingering uneasiness has to be acknowledged and a support system put into place. Without these interventions, post-adoption stress can evolve into the post-adoption blues—a kind of depression discussed openly in this book.

Like so many other adoptive journeys, our story continues to evolve and change. Karen is forever changed by being Annie's mother. Annie is forever changed by calling Karen "Mama." And the family is forever changed because of these experiences. We believe we're stronger, closer, and more appreciative of the love we share as a family. As we live this journey, we've learned to embrace our children for who they really are: infinitely precious beings.

In the pages that follow you will find a path that leads you to an even deeper appreciation of your adoptive family. Together, we will explore how you can consciously acknowledge the expectations that may be contributing to your struggles, make sense of the nagging emotions that can keep you from the joy you deserve, and help you move forward confidently and happily as parents and as a family.

acknowledgments

This book grew out of our own leap of faith as parents, as well as our struggles and day-to-day triumphs as parents. Although this journey of parenting is ongoing, we knew the need for this book was urgent. The people behind the voices you'll "hear" in this book shared this urgency, all united in the mission we hoped to accomplish with our words: helping post-adoptive families become stronger and happier.

Parents spoke to us after their children were in bed, on weekends, while the other parent was watching the children, or cautioned us that their child may be out and about while we chatted. They spoke to us in person and on the phone, and they allowed us to tape record what they said so we could accurately convey their messages of hope and help. They thanked us for writing about post-adoption stress and depression, and they only asked that they be notified when the book was published. These parents took a risk with us. They opened their hearts and homes, sharing with us information normally entrusted to only the closest friends. We are in their debt.

Professionals carved time out of their busy schedules to offer their expertise and wisdom: Cheryl Tatano Beck, June Bond, Dottie Boner, David Cross, Jerry Dillon, Dana Johnson, Debbie Joy, Regina Kupecky, Harriet McCarthy, Karin Price, and Barbara Rila (to whom we owe special thanks for hosting our trip to Dallas). All of the professionals offered their expertise with grace and humility. Secure in their own commitment to adoption, they voiced their learned observations and strategies so that future and present adoptive parents would not have to struggle as others had in the past.

To the people who offered us commentary on the draft of the book, Alfreda Singleton-Smith, Leanne Malloy, and Karin Price, we extend our heartfelt thanks. Their comments helped us to be as accurate as possible about this wonderfully quilted-together piece of American culture we call adoption. Jodie Rhodes, our agent, has our gratitude. She captured the essence of our message when it was only a seed and made it possible for that seed to transform into a real book.

We would also like to thank the staff at Rodale: Erana Bumbardatore, our copy editor, who skillfully clarified and corrected, and our editor, Lou Cinquino, for helping make this project the best it could be. His insightful guidance in shaping the text during the concept phase and his sharp feedback during the final stages of completion were invaluable. But most of all, Lou made this book possible by his passionate belief in its message. We felt his editorial direction was always rooted in this passion.

laying the foundation
for stronger families

Parents who adopt come from many different circumstances. We have been asked many times, "Why did you adopt?" However, no one has ever said us, "Why did you get pregnant?" Somehow parenting through adoption mystifies people, as if the experience is only for the foolish or the flawed. Yet increasingly, adoption is the first choice for many: during courtship, many couples discuss adoption as a natural way to have a family together.

Still others come to the adoption community after infertility. Adoption, while not a second choice necessarily, isn't an option that people anticipated. Still others come to adoption after having birth children. Perhaps secondary infertility has become an issue, or a preference for a child of a specific gender drives a couple to adopt. Same-sex couples often grow as a family through adoption.

However, the parents we met while researching this book told us in no uncertain terms that the reason they chose adoption is simply the desire to parent a child. Please leave off, they've asked us, the "adoptive" part of adoptive parent. They voiced a longing to parent, a gap in their lives, a feeling of not "being finished" with their families.

Therein lies a paradox: *We* see ourselves as parents first, adoptive parents second. *The world* sees us as adoptive parents first, parents second. Yet our joy and our sadness are no less real than that of other parents.

Kinship parents, parents who take over the primary care of a relative's child, come to adoption (or an informal arrangement of parentage) under different conditions. Looking to become a parent again is often the furthest thought from their minds. They may have limited funds, be physically impaired, or have medical conditions that make caring for a young child extremely challenging. However, for whatever reason, the immediate family member is not parenting the child. The kinship parent is asked to step in—rendering care so intense that their role gradually grows into Mom or Dad. Friends often ask, "How can you raise this child?" The kinship parent's heart answers, "How can I not? If not me, then the system would have to." No other decision is possible for these parents.

While not an overt decision to parent, all of the kinship parents we spoke with cherished, adored, enjoyed, and were committed to their children. Tough times had indeed come for many, but a child's colored picture brought home from kindergarten, an unexpected speech about them at a high school graduation, or being called "Mom" was enough to erase any doubts they had about the path they had chosen. Strikingly, many kinship parents felt that they had been given a second chance at parenting and that the child gave them "purpose in life."

the many paths to adoption

As heterogeneous as the adoptive parent population is, so too are the paths to adoption. According to the U.S. Census Bureau, there are 1.6 million adoptees under age 18, making up 2.5 percent of all American children in that age group. Adoption is an American tradition, a non-translatable cultural phenomena woven into our history and heritage.

Adoptive parents look a little different, too. Adoptive parents of children under 18 tend to be older, on average, than birth parents, at 43 versus 38 years old—with higher incomes, as well as more education, than birthparents.

One type of adoption, special needs adoption or public adoption, occurs when a child is adopted through the child welfare system. These children have been in and out of home placements (residential settings or foster homes). For our purposes, we will use the term "public adoption" for clarity. The placement occurs through a government-operated agency or through a contracted private agency. Societal assumptions abound about the children who wait in foster care; many people believe that the children who live in this system are damaged, older, and have special needs. And the parents we spoke with agreed that they had been challenged by their children's unknown and unexpected needs. Certainly while these children tend to be at high risk, no child—birth or adopted—is without unique needs. Risks are inherent in any parenthood situation.

Private adoptions are arranged through a myriad of professional agencies and individuals. Agencies range from nonprofit to for-profit, and from licensed to unlicensed. Independent or nonagency adoptions place children in nonrelative homes directly through birthparents or through licensed or unlicensed facilitators, medical doctors, members of the clergy, or attorneys.

The Internet has forever changed the adoption triad's—that is, the child, the birthparents, and the adoptive parents—ability to connect and reconnect. However, when the Internet is used to facilitate an adoption, resources can be very thin and the risks very high. The cyber age has also meant easy access to information that used to be difficult to obtain. Prospective adoptive parents can now read articles, schedule seminars, read about adoption agencies, and scan pictures of children. Adoption providers (public and private agencies, attorneys and therapists, etc.) might not be equipped to manage the increase in adoptions that this level of access has made possible. For example, the Interstate Compact system, which oversees where the child resides pre- and post-adoption, is sometimes left out of the loop in these cases. Through the Internet, families are able to access information on available children outside the states where they live. They begin the adoption process with out-of-state agencies, and in many cases, the proper state entities are not aware of the placement plans until *after* the child is in the state with the family. This can create Interstate Compact violations and threaten the placement.

Historically, private adoptions have been "closed." Information about birthparents, medical history, and heritage haven't been available to adopted children. Parents are left with questions that cannot be answered. But the trend over the past decade has been toward open adoption. Many experts view this type of adoption as natural and healing. Certainly, it seems there is no going back to closed adoptions, as more and more birthparents and adoptive parents are seeking to provide a more complete family life for their children and themselves.

Children who are citizens of other nations and are adopted by American families are classified as internationally adopted children. Due to the decrease in infants available for adoption in the United States, many parents are deciding to adopt a child from abroad. Approximately 20,000 children are adopted this way every year; 14 percent of adopted children under 18 were born in other countries.

Kinship parents assume parentage of a relative's child with or without the help of a public agency. According to the U.S. Census Bureau, there are approximately 2.4 million grandparents who are responsible for raising one or more grandchildren. These figures do not include aunts, uncles, or other relatives acting as kinship parents. In kinship parenting, a formal adoption may or may not have taken place. Termination of parental rights by the birthparents can be difficult to obtain, or may be unwanted by the kinship parent for many reasons, such as loyalty to family members and the need for financial support.

shared experience
of the post-adoption period

While the above discussion may be review for many of you, it's striking how little we adoptive parents know of other adoptive paths once we've chosen ours. Many kinship parents legally adopt their children, yet they may not see themselves as adoptive parents. At times, you may have found yourself speaking to another adoptive parent who has chosen a different path of adoption. You may see the differences before you see the similarities of your experiences. Yet the parents of a little girl adopted from China may have more in common with the parents of a foster child adopted at age 3 than may at first be apparent.

No one path of adoption is "better" than another. Often the parents of an internationally adopted child will be asked why, when there are so many children in this country who need homes, did they choose to go outside their own country? We find these questions do not serve any purpose and tend to divide the adoption community. We must respect our fellow adoptive parents' choices.

One thing we discovered as we spoke to families and experts was that no matter what path was chosen, the post-adoption time was a vulnerable time. The period after the child came home was full of potential crisis. We must recognize our opportunity to avoid these crises. We must accept this vulnerability as a reality and stop worrying about what may be the politically correct thing to say when we discuss adoption.

Who better to understand, to empathize with what you are feeling, than a person who has already experienced similar emotions? Widen your view, your circle of adoptive parents, and you will find support.

post-adoption expectations

The adoption triad—the child, the birthparents, and the adoptive parents—come together at a point in time, at a specific place, and their lives are changed forever. The adoptive parents realize that they did not give this child life, but they desperately want to give this child *a life.*

Although the joining of parent and child is spectacularly memorable, the post-adoption period—whether that time is days, weeks, months, or years—has been neglected. On the pages that follow you will hear from adoptive parents, often the adoptive mother. She will speak of how it felt to become a parent through adoption and what she experienced after the adoption. She will talk about the highs and lows and what she has learned in the process about herself, her spouse, her child, her child's birth parents, and society.

As we've discussed, the paths to adoption differ, and along those paths an adoptive parent creates expectations. Those expectations come from a variety of places: her family of origin, her past experiences as a parent, her past experiences with infertility, her experiences with the process of adoption, the media, her hopes and dreams, and so on. She imagines the interactions that may happen as she embarks on this journey called adoption. She imagines what kind of mother she will be. She expects instantaneous love, an inseparable bond with this desperately wanted child. She imagines what her spouse will do once he becomes a father to this child.

The adoptive mother thinks about the birthmother and imagines what that mother went through in making her adoption plan for that child. The birthmother may be a stranger—a person who lives in a neighboring state or even a country halfway around the world. In some instances, the birthmother becomes a new extended family member who will be part of the child's life forever. The birthmother may even exist in an intimate role. She may be a daughter or daughter-in-law, having given birth to the grandchild who is now adopted.

The adoptive mother considers how her extended family and friends will react to her news of adoption and how they will treat her child. She imagines how the child will act and what the child's needs might be. Finally, she expects society to accept the role she has undertaken. She expects that neighbors, acquaintances, and strangers will respect the intimacy of her family.

Instead of having her expectations met, she is hit with mixed, tepid responses and with intrusive "explain your life and its decisions" type questions. These queries wear her down. Suddenly, what she thought were private decisions are open to public discussion. Reality differs greatly from what she has imagined, and this difference creates stress and, sometimes, great sadness. These emotions can be intense, difficult to understand, and they may take her completely by surprise. It is their suddenness that makes the emotions especially challenging.

The father's critical role in the life of the family will also be explored in this book. Recently, the National Institutes of Mental Health (NIMH) have concentrated on examining the special features of men and depression, an underreported problem. How men report stress and depression, how their bodies react to stress and depression, and how they frame it in their daily existence varies considerably when compared with women. Gender differences in parenting roles exist. Yet the father's role cannot be minimized or made secondary in this discussion. Fathers help foster a family's identity, pride, and nurturing for one another, and they shape the children's parenting experience for generations to come. We will look at both the birthfather and adoptive father roles during our discussion, and in detail in chapter 11.

our mission

This book is the first in-depth attempt to understand the challenges of the post-adoption time. It is our strong belief and conclusion from researching—and living through—the post-adoption blues that discussing this subject, once considered taboo in the adoption community, will lead not to fewer successful adoptions by scaring people away, but rather to a greater number of successful adoptions by helping more adoptive families overcome the emotional challenges that adoption brings. Our basic premise in examining these challenges is a belief that an open discussion of post-adoption stress and depression can help alleviate these feelings and in so doing, strengthen family functioning.

As much as we all wish that every aspect of adoption were painless and joyous, the challenging and sometimes negative emotions described in these pages do exist for many parents who adopt. We didn't invent the feelings of stress and depression that some couples wrestle with, but we have set out to help us all understand them—not feel ashamed of them—and ultimately, to overcome them.

Research has repeatedly shown that maternal depression influences child development. A depressed mother often begets a depressed household. A mother's functioning ripples throughout the family, like a stone that sinks into a lake, the cause of the disturbance buried deep under dark water. Hesitant to admit the need for help or confused about how to seek support, an adoptive parent is often stuck in an emotional tornado that feeds upon itself.

In this book, coping strategies and advice from experts and from adoptive parents who have "been there and done that" will outline the steps to break the vortex of hopelessness. In this way, the mother, father, siblings, and child can begin to heal. We have a few goals we'd like this book to accomplish:

■ Narrow the differences between what is expected during the adoption process and what is actually experienced in order to lessen stress and depression.

The expectations of an adoptive parent often differ considerably from what is experienced. This difference creates stressors that may be chronic and severe. When these stressors create anger, guilt, sadness, and futility, depression often results. In the same way that talking about labor pains isn't meant to convince women not to give birth, this "reality check" is not meant to dissuade couples from adopting. Rather it will ensure that those who can prepare for the ups and downs of this wonderful path to parenting will be prepared.

▪ Teach adoptive families to confront stress and depression by allowing them to express the very real pain they're feeling; this will create opportunities for growth.

Many of the parents we spoke with were able to resolve the corrosive emotions that were souring their experience. As they did this, through techniques we'll share with you in this book, almost every aspect of their lives improved: Their marriages were strengthened, they found more meaningful connections to their communities, and they became better parents by understanding their own strengths and vulnerabilities.

These results were not achieved quickly or without pain. It wasn't easy to admit their own shortcomings, to express that they weren't able to bond with their child, or that they were angry at how society viewed them. We want to emphasize that while this kind of growth may not be easy, the pain and unease will be worth it. It will take courage to get there and that's why we wrote this book—to give you the strength and tools you need to succeed.

▪ Open the dialogue on post-adoption emotions in order to contribute to better-prepared adoption experiences.

One of the parents that we spoke with made it very clear how discussing these emotions will help other adoptive parents:

If I had had a book that covered this stuff when I was struggling, it would have been so wonderful. I felt afraid to express my feelings to anyone. You just don't want them to know that you can be depressed after you've received this child, a child you've waited so long for. You don't want to even admit that you're a normal mom and you don't have all the answers. The stress and depression have nothing to do with how much these children are loved. In some ways, it's harder because you do love them so much.

When a family decides to adopt a child, considerable energy is put forth during the preplacement time. Seemingly endless and intrusive paperwork, government agency requirements, advertisements to birth parents, and so forth, drain adoptive parents' financial and emotional resources. There isn't much left when the child finally arrives.

Indeed, often the mother and father experience a letdown of the adrenaline that has fueled the rigorous and public steps of adoption. They have attained a major life goal: parenting. Instead of understanding that the journey has only begun, some adoptive parents feel that the goal has been accomplished. Because the preadoption process can be all-consuming, the precious time that needs to be used to prepare for parenting is stolen because so much energy has been put into the process itself.

New research found that preadoption education and preparedness increases prospective parents' desire to adopt. These findings parallel our own: The more prepared the parents were about the issues they might face after adoption, the better able they were to process the post–adoption experience.

∎ Concentrate on securing for adoptive parents the care and help they need.

The adoption literature has concentrated on the child and the birthparents, and their decision to allow another person to parent. Often, the adoptive parents' needs have been skipped over or lost. We believe this focus on helping adoptive parents is necessary to balance the adoption circle, to complete its beauty and wholeness, and ultimately, to strengthen the families that are created through adoption.

One psychologist we spoke with stated that in addition to providing therapy, she also acted much like a social worker, helping families connect with healthcare, financial, educational, and social resources. She provides these services long after the initial placement of the child. In fact, she sees her clients as "clients for a lifetime," providing reality-based parenting

Our Panel of Experts

Cheryl Tatano Beck, D.N.Sc., is a professor of nursing at the University of Connecticut. She has worked for the past 20 years toward understanding the theoretical makeup of postpartum depression. She is the coauthor of the Postpartum Depression Screening Scale and an adoptive mother.

June Bond is the executive director of Adoption Advocacy of South Carolina and a certified adoption investigator who has published numerous articles on adoption. She coined the term "post-adoption depression syndrome" in 1995. She is mother to six children, four of whom are adopted.

Dottie Boner, L.I.S.W., A.C.S.W., M.S.W., has over 30 years of experience working as an adoption professional. Trained as an adoption mediator, Dottie counsels parents on issues surrounding open adoption.

David Cross, Ph.D., is an associate professor of psychology, the director of the Developmental Research Laboratory, and the director of Camp Hope at Texas Christian University. His research focus is international adoption and special needs adoption.

Jerry Dillon, M.S.W., co-founded Dillon International, Inc., over 30 years ago. He pioneered international relations and laws that continue to affect international adoption today. Through education and preparation, Jerry advocates for fathers to be heard and supported as they take on their parenting role.

Dana Johnson, M.D., Ph.D., is professor of pediatrics, director of the Neonatology Division, and director of the International Adoption Clinic at the University of Minnesota. Dr. Johnson commands a global reputation in evaluating and treating the needs of post-institutional children.

Debbie Joy, M.S., is a psychotherapist who has been in private practice for 20 years specializing in treating children who were adopted and/or in foster care. She is also an adoptive mother to three children.

Regina Kupecky, L.S.W., coauthor of *Adopting the Hurt Child* and *Parenting the Hurt Child,* has worked in the field of adoption for over 25 years. A national and international speaker, Ms. Kupecky treats children with attachment disorders at the Attachment and Bonding Center of Ohio.

Harriett McCarthy is the administrator of the Parent Education and Preparedness List, part of the Eastern European Adoption Coalition. She has three adopted sons and was first to research post-adoption depression.

Karin Price, B.S.W., is the regional coordinator of Dillon International, Inc. A 20-year veteran in the field of adoption, Karin is also the mother of two children, including one daughter who was adopted from Haiti.

Barbara Rila, Ph.D., is a licensed psychologist whose private practice specializes in adoption. Through the North American Council on Adoptable Children, Dr. Rila hosts a monthly support group for parents. With 20 years experience with adoptive families, Dr. Rila is also a national speaker on adoption issues.

support and individual support for years. We applaud her work. In life, it is often the tangible benefits of support that help us move forward.

■ Increase awareness and usage of effective coping strategies to help deal with stress and depression.

We made countless encouraging discoveries in our research, not the least of which was that each expert and each parent we met offered proven ways to cope with stressors. To put it bluntly, "You don't have to feel that way!" You are not alone in facing these challenges anymore.

■ Describe and better understand the specific vulnerabilities of each type of adoption, be it domestic (open or confidential), international, foster parent, or kinship.

The paths to adoption are varied. Many themes are shared, and support and comfort can be gained from parents who have followed other paths. However, different adoption paths result in different issues that need to be understood. For example, the kinship parent who has adopted a grandchild seeks to understand her role as mother. This is complicated by her trying to understand her birthchild's decision to relinquish parentage to her. This book will explore the many faces of adoption.

the many dimensions of expectations

When we take a close look at our expectations, we can understand our post-adoption emotions. The cognitive construct of expectations emerged as part of social cognitive theory (SCT), conceptualized in the 1960s. This theory viewed the creation of expectations as forethought capability, or our ability to evaluate anticipated outcomes, and that this anticipation, more than the actual outcome, influenced our behavior.

Today, cognitive theory, derived in part from SCT, maintains that how we interpret our experiences determines how we feel and behave. Sadness (one of the four emotions, along with elation, anxiety, and anger) is felt when there is a perception of loss. This loss is created when what we expected is met with defeat or failure, or is unfulfilled or not confirmed. We also feel loss and grief when our personal relationships are disrupted. These losses, we believe, can lead to depression.

Anxiety is felt when there is a threat to self or valued attachments. In response to these losses or threats, we withdraw, try to appease others, or become offensive (as when we feel anger). Expectations and perceived threats drive our emotional responses to our real experiences.

In understanding post-adoption emotions, we examine expectations along several dimensions: our expectations of ourselves, of our child, of our family and friends, of our child's birthparents, and of others (including our adoption professionals and society). By doing so, we will help you manage, refocus, and understand your expectations— or in hindsight, help you identify what expectations were not met— and help you build new expectations that are more realistic for your situation. By more realistically anticipating what you believe your future experiences will be, you will be better able to manage your emotions and build more successful relationships.

More than any other goal, we want to help you experience that fourth emotion—elation—as you and your family move forward.

We firmly believe that post-adoption stress and depression are under-diagnosed and under-treated. We also believe that the proven coping strategies and support systems presented in this book will not only help us to identify those parents who are struggling, but also provide a blueprint for parents and professionals alike in overcoming these challenges. This is our passionate mission.

expectations of **yourself** as a parent

the adoption process

In all facets of our lives we have expectations that are shaped by our cultural, societal, and biological worlds. Our expectations help form our vision of the future and enable us to successfully prepare. They are an inescapable, normal part of the way we live our lives.

However, unless we're careful, we can build our expectations on shaky assumptions. Maybe because we're in denial or simply because we don't have sufficient or reliable information about a situation, we create unrealistic expectations that doom us despite our best efforts.

Many adoptive parents don't even realize that our expectations prevent us from seeing that certain possibilities exist. We didn't. And maybe that's not all bad. The truth is, our decision to parent is not entirely rational. If we ever became obsessed with a realistic study of all the difficult things that could "go wrong," many of us would never have followed our hearts' calling. Maybe a certain amount of denial— or faith—is necessary.

Having high expectations and trusting your heart is one thing, but being unprepared is another. This is something echoed by all the experts we spoke with: Adoptive parents who were prepared, who educated themselves, and had ties to support services, were better equipped to deal with the adoption and had less stress and depression.

Let's begin with how we evaluate and perceive ourselves as parents.

The parents we spoke with confessed to an assortment of unmet expectations of themselves as parents, imposed from many internal and external forces in their lives. In the pages that follow, we take a look at these unrealistic expectations as they relate to the adoption process; the feeling that you need to be the world's best parents; and parent-to-child attachment issues, which are the least explored yet the most central concern for many adoptive parents. More importantly, we look at how we can use these expectations to fuel changes in our lives.

your expectations
of the adoption process

"I will have control over this process."

The adoption process is more about unpredictable, unavoidable, exasperating snafus than about control. So for those of us who enjoy a certain amount of certainty in our lives, adoption can be quite stressful. The preadoptive parent realizes how little control she has, and she tries to compensate by exerting influence over the things she can control, such as gathering the necessary paperwork. One self-professed "control freak" tried unsuccessfully to exert her influence during a very long adoption process that had gone from months to years of waiting. After she had requested numerous documents that kept expiring, the State of Pennsylvania refused to send her additional certified birth certificates without a complete explanation of the purpose of the document request. They were fearful she was selling them to illegal immigrants.

Anger at adoption agency workers and bureaucratic agencies (both abroad and domestic) can surface, as well. Documents get lost, cultural events close courts for weeks, and governments change adoption

thoughts from an expert

control

The mother who needs a high sense of control in her life may rush through the adoption process only to find that lack of control exists once the child is home. The mother may have a strong need to show the world she can handle the new situation without admitting to weakness or need. The need for control outweighs the need to ask for help.

June Bond,
executive director of Adoption
Advocacy of South Carolina

policies. All of these can cause frustration and a sense that the process is out of your hands. But once the child is placed with you, you believe control returns. Reality soon whispers otherwise.

Parents often experience a panicky feeling once the child is home and control has been lost—again. You blame yourself. Somehow, you should have known about all this and how you would feel. Yet, you and your life seem totally out of control.

"I have resolved all of my emotional pre-adoption issues."

Infertility can leave traces, small paths in frayed pastures that you think have been left behind. Yet adoption can reopen some of those wounds, and how we react when this happens can impact how we parent and how we feel as a parent. Leftover or unresolved grief can surface unexpectedly when a child is received. Experts agree that those whose goal was parenting, not pregnancy, cope better as parents of a child by adoption.

Veronica struggled with infertility for 5 years. For months on end, her body experienced the bloating, sickness, and emotional roller coaster caused by the infertility drugs. She said, "You feel like you're pregnant, but with no baby at the end." She and her husband, who was in military service, decided to take a 2½-year break from trying to get pregnant before they adopted—a decision Veronica feels was a healthy one. Yet the effects of the experience lingered. While planning for the baby and the nursery, Veronica shared these feelings:

> *Everyone kept saying, "Don't let people spend money on you." I think the counselor ingrained this fear in our minds a lot—that the adoption may not happen. I can remember the first time I walked into the baby department alone and started to*

thoughts from an expert

infertility

I think a lot goes back to the stages of grieving. Where is the parent in the cycle? There are layers of grief. That grief over the child's needs triggers the grief over infertility, which triggers more grief. You have a part of your body that does not work.

Adoption is the final admission that you're never going to have a baby of your own. It's okay. People go on. Yes, adoption is wonderful, but there is loss. You're mourning things you can't put your finger on. You may be mourning the fact that you adopted a child, and it's not the child you wanted or expected.

Regina Kupecky, L.S.W., coauthor of Adopting the Hurt Child *and* Parenting the Hurt Child

look for sleepers. I kept thinking that at any minute, when I picked up
a sleeper, an alarm was going to go off and repeat: "Infertile woman!
Infertile woman!" The sound would warn the public that I had no
business here. I was worried that if I touched the baby clothes, I would
be told to get out!

"The adoption process is complete once my child is placed."

Once your child is home, you believe she is your daughter, or he is
your son. In your eyes, there is no difference between the love you
feel for this child and the child who would have or did come to
you by birth. And this is true. The intensity of the love and the passion you feel toward this child is strong and everlasting. But there is a
difference.

Accepting this Forever Child into his Forever Family means that
your family has become a Forever Adoptive Family. Generations will
be affected by this decision. New extended family in the form of a
birthparent may be added to the family tree. Cultural heritage issues of
countries around the world may change your diet, your clothing, and
your decisions. In-family adoptions or kinship adoptions will change
the family dynamics: your grandchild, your son's son, is now simply
your son.

Yet after the public nature of adoption, after the exhausting
years of infertility, after the years of wondering if this child will be
yours, your first reaction may be to disappear into the folds of society. To silently, gratefully, and blissfully become one of the
everyday American families that blend seamlessly into a nondescript
family unit.

Yet there will be questions in your child's mind, and in a later
chapter we'll speak to the points of vulnerability that arise in your
child's life . . . the teacher who asks the child to write his family
tree or the Mother's Day card made at school. You need to be prepared for these questions that may have been just under the surface
and now have arisen with enough strength to be spoken.

Martha, a 52-year-old adoptive mother, confessed she was caught
off guard when her 8-year-old son began commenting on his place in
the family:

*Yesterday, I was taking Collin to his karate class and he said some-
thing about feeling like we wanted to get rid of him. He said, "I was
in the pantry listening to you talk." I said, "Collin! I never said anything like that. What are you talking about?" He said, "Well, I have
a real mom if you don't want to keep me." I said, "That's not true at
all. You're our real son. People come to families in different ways.
Daddy and I weren't a family, but we met each other and got married,
and then your sister wasn't a part of our family until she was born.
Then you came into our family. You were born to somebody else, but
you are a permanent family member. You're forever." He's heard that
before: Forever Family Member.*

*He is processing adoption information. He thinks about it some-
times and then forgets about it. He thinks about it again. It concerns
me a little bit that he doesn't feel as secure in his home and situation.
But we really try to let him know.*

*I'm not sure where it's coming from. It's hard to pursue an idea
with him because he'll say, "I don't want to talk about it." Or he
just doesn't know. I left it hoping that I had reassured him. Then
we talk about adoption or read a book about a duck that was really
a swan, the Ugly Duckling story. He loves that story, the Ugly
Duckling. So we got a couple different versions of it and read it
to him.*

*We really try to embrace it that way and not pour it on him,
"Oh, you're adopted." We try to do it low-key, to just make it part
of his life story.*

Part of our family identity now is being an adoptive family. Ideally,
it should be natural and ongoing, but also, a conscious choice in
everyday life. Martha, a warm, articulate, caring mother, loves Collin
dearly and tries to be the best parent she knows how to be. Yet there
are times when the topic of adoption needs to be opened up and feelings discussed. It wasn't always like this; adoption's history is full of secrets and sealed documents.

Today's environment is turning toward understanding more about
the child's needs and using those needs as a guide. We also know
that there are resources in the adoption community that have the
answers.

common **reactions** to unmet expectations

Our feelings about these unmet expectations shape the way we respond, either through "knee-jerk" defense mechanisms or by more positive coping strategies that help us process the feelings and transform them. The coping strategies we present are fluid—they are commonly associated with many of the unmet expectation we discuss in this and other chapters.

Perhaps you'll see some of your own reactions in the defense mechanisms discussed here. If you are using your ways to cope, consider the alternatives we present to get you where you need to go. Sometimes our reactions to emotional distress are helpful in the short-term because they protect us from immediate harm. But in the long run, these defenses can actually make a situation worse or stop us from taking steps toward feeling good about our situation.

We want to stress one overall point: *These feelings are normal and not uncommon.* Expert upon expert agrees that stress, depression, ambivalence, and anger are emotions they see frequently, and part of the assistance they offer to parents is to help them realize these feelings are normal.

withdrawal

You may find yourself shutting down or escaping into a world of silence, too exhausted or panicked to do much else. Friends' calls may go unanswered. Responsibilities as a parent may be neglected. One mother confessed that during her 2 months of depression, she had little recollection of what she did. She only knew that her husband had assumed care of their child.

Withdrawal occurs because of the secrets in your heart. They're too much for you to think about and too much to share, so you become isolated by shame.

Withdrawal can be effective if it is short-lived and helps us regroup. Many people find that "alone" time is necessary to fight stress. However, there is a difference between this regrouping time and continued withdrawal due to guilt and shame.

normalizing post-adoption emotions

The emotional reactions I see from parents run the whole gamut from absolute, utter delight to people who are very circumspect. It really depends on the expectations of the family. We often think of challenges in families with special needs children. But I think there clearly are problems in terms of maternal bonding in reasonably healthy children. It's like having a birth child: One's expectations sometimes aren't met. This may happen a little more frequently in adopting families since there may be unresolved issues that existed prior to the child coming into the family. Some of the transition of the child into the family brings out a lot of issues that haven't been dealt with in the past. Those issues can include infertility—the grief and loss associated with being unable to have your own birthchild.

These are higher-risk kids, so the reality of the situation is often quite different than the parents' expectations. Everyone who has children has fantasies about their kids. I think a lot of families expect their child to immediately love them and be like the toddler that they had 5 years ago or that their sister or a friend down the road has.

A lot of these kids come with behaviors that are unexpected, and without putting those behaviors and additional needs in context, a parent can feel real disappointment.

We do get families that come into our clinic and say, "We've got a problem. We need to talk about this. This isn't what we expected. This is behavior that is way outside what we consider normal, both from our own personal responses and from my child's response." Then we have other families who are stoic and say everything is going fine and it's really not a problem.

For some families, we'll advise, "You know, we see behaviors that could be somewhat problematic and these are things that we think you should do." They'll answer, "Oh no. No, this is just fine." They're in denial—a lot of people are initially in denial. I think that's a normal response. As time moves on, people usually come to the realization that maybe things really aren't going all that well.

The child is a mirror of the parent's success or failure. So if the child is having a problem that relates to mom or dad feeling inadequate as a parent, we try to take the blame away.

*Dana Johnson, M.D., Ph.D., professor of pediatrics, director of the
Neonatology Division, and director of the International Adoption Clinic,
University of Minnesota*

anger

There are many people and things to feel anger toward: ourselves, our spouses, our families, our children, our jobs, our adoption agency, and even society. Yet emotions aren't right or wrong. It's what you do with that emotion that counts. Still, it's easy to let the anger build and go unchecked.

Anger also needs to be explored and articulated, shared with a trusted individual. When anger is not dealt with, aggressiveness can result, and then we risk hurting others emotionally and even physically.

denial

A sense of the surreal, a sense that "this really can't be happening to me" may pervade your life. While denial doesn't accomplish much resolution, it can afford you a little time to get ready to face the situation at a later time.

coping strategies

Realize what you will and will not have control over. Because we adoptive parents put so much of ourselves on the line during the adoption process, a critical step is to employ strategies that make us feel safer and less vulnerable. The first two strategies we offer focus on personal growth; the others relate to seeking and accepting help from the adoption community. Because expectations are future oriented, at first glance we often can't see what is really under our control. But by pausing a moment and taking stock in present day reality, the division becomes clearer.

We control our actions and we are responsible for how we act upon our emotions. But the adoption process is impacted by events and decisions that happen thousands of miles away or 5 miles down the road in a courthouse, events that are truly out of our control and events that are out of our adoption agency's control.

By accepting our lack of control, we can release the energy that has been committed to trying to change the unchangeable. We are not advocating passivity, however, but rather appropriate assertiveness and letting go of those unproductive events that cost us energy and time.

The stakes are high: a child. Sometimes you feel like the bottom of the adoption "food chain." You feel that you are the last to know, the last to have any voice in the process. These feelings need to be shared and discussed, and a balance reached between letting go and paying attention to your emotions.

Allow yourself to grieve past issues. Grief is a process, one that waxes and wanes and reminds us of our loss when we least expect it, when we thought we were "over it." When the last door to a child by birth is closed for them, some couples will immediately begin a plan for adoption. Some are ready and some are not. The two distinct threads need to separate: the thread of loss and grief over the child that will never be born and the thread of an adoptive child coming to the family. Weave them together only after the work of grieving is undertaken. The temptation to link them prematurely is ever-present. Often we don't want to be reminded of painful times, not when we can commit our energies to having a child come home to us. Still, when a couple pursues adoption before they are emotionally ready, they are not escaping from their painful emotions. Those emotions will surface at some later point in time, a point when the couple may be less able to deal with them in a healthy way.

Each couple needs to examine their goals of family-building. Being honest with yourself about your goals, as well as allowing time to heal from the physical and emotional challenges of infertility, will help guide your vision of family and how you build it.

> **thoughts from an expert**
>
> # vision of family
>
> I think what parents have to do is to evaluate their vision of family-building. The parents for whom a child is a child have a much easier transition to becoming adoptive parents. But those who yearn for a birth connection and then elect to adopt have moved yet another step away from their dream. So we get back to a widening gap between hopes and reality because adoption is their last choice. And not all families approach adoption that way. But I do think it's much more difficult for the families who yearned for and made tremendous efforts to have a child by birth.
>
> *Barbara Rila, Ph.D.,*
> *private practitioner*

Maintain ties with the adoption community as your family life evolves. We often think of the adoption community as a pre-placement institution. But as a child grows, obviously what she needs from her parents changes. She grows less physically dependent and more emotionally and socially dependent upon her environment. Peers and their perceptions influence her. Her own questions will begin, usually around age 8 or 9. Yet, adoption issues are never "resolved" for some children and their families. The issues resurface as the answers we give our 3-year-old ("We adopted you because you are special") do not meet the growing needs of our children. The 14-year-old wonders if adoption means "someone was given away." At every stage, you'll need resources to help you understand these questions and how to address them. These answers can be found in the adoption community. There are tremendously helpful ways to maintain ties to the community. For a detailed list of sources and organizations, see page 232.

Learn from all types of families. In tandem with your family's changing needs, adoptive parents tend to differentiate their path from other paths to adoption. You may identify with the type of adoption you chose—international, domestic, kinship—and feel that the experiences of others are not applicable to your family. This is an assumption that should be tested. For example, a seminar for post-Korean adoptive parents may deal with similar issues as other international adoptions. Unless the seminar is culture specific, helpful information may be gained.

Likewise, the kinship parent who attends counseling with a child to deal with the loss of birthparents has much in common with a public adoptive family whose child is struggling with similar issues of loss and abandonment. Whatever your path to adoption, we advise you to embrace your identity as an adoptive parent and an adoptive family. The kinship parent will experience issues similar to those experienced by any other parents raising adoptive children. The child's issues of loss, grief, anger, identity, and acceptance will all need to be addressed, and you may find much-needed information and support within the adoption community. Don't distance yourself from the adoption community based solely on your path to adoption.

Subscribe to adoption magazines. Information on new laws affecting citizenship and adoptive parent rights are important to keep up with. Articles on coping, information on support groups, and personal stories are available through these magazines.

Join adoption organizations. Organizations exist primarily on local, regional, and national levels. National organizations usually hold annual conferences to which families can bring their children (babysitting is often available) and learn about issues they are facing, from attachment and bonding to practical issues of adoptive parenting. When you join, ask about services for families and the emphasis they place on helping existing adoptive families.

Read books. There is an ever-growing body of literature on adoption, attachment, and developmental issues. Reading what it's like from an adult adoptee's perspective may help you understand the dynamics facing your family.

Learn about support groups. In general, two types of support groups exist. One is the person-to-person group that may have been formed around a church, an adoption agency, or a therapist. These groups usually meet once a month and may have open boundaries, welcoming anyone whose life has been affected by adoption. Others may be more selective, open only to adoptive parents. When approaching a group, understand the composition of their membership, the purpose of the group, and the group's history. One group that meets in a small town in Indiana was formed by parents who felt that they needed to share what their adoptive experiences had been; it's open to "people whose lives have been touched by adoption." Another group, in Texas, provides an outlet for adoptive parents who are struggling with issues of attachment and bonding, special needs, and their children's developmental needs.

One caveat about support groups is that you need to be aware that some parents may not have weathered their crises successfully. They may come with their own agendas and needs. You need to

---

thoughts from an expert

support people

When we talk about support personnel to families, we emphasize that it's very important that a stressed parent surround themselves with people who are supportive. They care. They're compassionate. They provide assistance. And above all, they believe in you. Too many parents who are in the midst of depression are enveloped by people who have negative voices. It's terribly important not to surround yourself with negative attitudes and messages, such as "Give up" or "Bad kid," things that really rob your mind of your commitment to that child.

Barbara Rila, Ph.D.

decide for yourself whether a support group is supportive and benefi-cial or deconstructive and critical. If the negativity voiced from a parent is affecting you, then you need to evaluate your situation inde-pendently from theirs.

The second type of group is the online support group. These groups have proliferated in recent years, and the Internet has changed the way adoptive parents can seek support. Many of these groups are open to the general public, and everyone is free to post or e-mail a comment. Likewise, you need to be aware that anyone can read your post. Adoptive parents reported that they had received responses after posting e-mails describing their post-adoption struggles. While some of these were supportive, other responding individuals were quite neg-ative about such admissions. Be sure to explore the rules of etiquette regarding posts for any site you decide to participate in.

Other online support groups are monitored carefully and designed for specific adoption populations. For example, the Eastern European Adoption Coalition (EEAC) has different forums designed to answer questions pre- and post-adoption. The information shared on these fo-rums can be quite valuable and represents the needs of many members.

Finally, adoption agencies often create forums for parents who have adopted from the same country, or even the same orphanage. By re-maining on these lists even after your adoption is complete, you may be able to pick up some tips and helpful advice from others, as well as pass along your own experiences.

Keep your adoption agency up to date with your contact information. Many agencies will sponsor workshops and seminars or notify clients of upcoming speakers. These events are great ways to meet other parents and families.

chapter 2

the world's best parents

As parents, we want the best for our children. We want to make wise decisions, to make them in an appropriate emotional context, and to be right each time. As adoptive parents, we go through such a unique process that the pressure to achieve the impossible is real and overt. Our expectations create lofty goals that lead to disappointment when we take our first misstep. We cannot live up to these expectations of perfection.

your expectations of your parenting abilities

"We have to be The World's Best Parents."

As adoptive parents, we are tough on ourselves, and this self-critique can be unforgiving. Why? Because we've publicly proclaimed to the world that we will be great parents. This proclamation was forced upon us. In order to receive a child, we feel we have to convince many parties that we are going to be The World's Best Parents.

Of course, it's easier said than done. When the child is home and reality rears its head, this unrealistic expectation can lead to a big fall.

Sara, a mother of three and a pediatric healthcare provider, and her husband, Steve, have three children: a son who was adopted through a private attorney 16 years ago; a son by birth 7 years ago; and a daughter, Tanya, adopted from Eastern Europe 2½ years ago. Sara spoke with us about her journey with Tanya and her struggle with post–adoption depression:

> *I felt pressure not to confess what was happening. You work so hard for those first few months to get through to the social worker doing the home study, trying to communicate your beliefs: This is my plan on how we'll raise this child. And these are my two beautiful children that I have now. See how very well adjusted they are. We have a beautiful home. We have a dog. We have a cat. We have two vehicles. We are financially stable.*
>
> *And you try so hard for people to see that because that's what they're expecting, and then when it's all said and done . . . okay, now I still need to be this wonderful mother. I can't feel like I'm pulling my hair out because that would not be acceptable.*

In essence, Sara described a two-pronged issue: First, she had higher expectations for herself because she was parenting through adoption, and second, because of the public process of adoption, she felt she could not express her real feelings. People who adopt are often on the defensive regarding their parenting choices. Somehow, they feel held to a higher standard of parenting. Because of this higher standard, when anything but perfection plays out, we begin to hide our secrets, our mistakes.

Withholding feelings often leads to greater isolation and more inner conflict. Emotions become cyclical and self-perpetuating. No one, after all, is perfect. And certainly there are no perfect parents. Our children need to see us as human beings, and when we voice apologies, our children learn that it's okay to make mistakes.

"I will feel legitimacy as a parent."

When you suddenly realize that you're not The World's Best Parent, you begin to feel a lack of legitimacy. This feeling is extremely common in adoptive parents, particularly mothers, when they realize they aren't as good as their home study says they are. The dissonance between what the paper says and how you're actually parenting brings about stress from an unrealized and unrealistic standard of parenting. As a fallible human being and parent, thoughts creep in: Am I the best parent for this child? Do I have a right to this child? Would this child be better in a black/Asian/minority family? I've taken her away from her birth family. Will she hate me when she grows up? How am I going to deal with all of her questions?

We feel that we cannot possibly live up to the hype we have been compelled to create, and therefore we are not entitled to this child. For parents who adopt from another country, the feeling of being a "rich American" compounds the lack of entitlement. Shocked by the sounds and sights of Third World countries, we return home thinking that we have taken something that isn't rightfully ours, and we have taken it because our socioeconomic status enabled us to.

Louise, a grandmother of a child by adoption and an adoption escort, described her thoughts as she viewed an orphanage in Kolkatta, India, for the first time:

> thoughts from an expert
>
> ## unspoken feelings
>
> I often pick up on the emotions of parents who may not be able to verbalize their feelings. We get a lot of flat affects and psychomotor retardation, or we get agitation, especially with the moms. Irritability is one of the big, big markers that indicate low frustration tolerance. The irritability also looks like kind of an antsy, anxious, critical focus. Many times, that presentation signals parental depression.
>
> *Barbara Rila, Ph.D.,*
> *private practitioner*

I am humbled at my surroundings; people are living in hovels on the street. People cook, eat, bathe, and live on the street. We actually saw a man squatting on the street in the pouring rain getting a shave! At one intersection, a very frail woman holding a baby comes up and pounds on the car windows begging for money.

Devki, the orphanage director, comes in the afternoon to our hotel, and we go to the orphanage to get updates on the babies and take pictures and video. Then Ruth tells me I can take pictures with my camera. When I see the babies for the first time, I think how hot it is. They have these big fans going, but it is still so hot. We are supposed to be there about 3½ to 4 hours, but I don't think I can stay in here for a half an hour. It's just too much. Everything is so primitive. The way they do the water for the babies. The way they do the bottles. They have a water filter system that's right there in the room, and they make the bottles one at a time. They boil the water to make sure the germs are killed.

There was no air. I was just overwhelmed by the babies. There are three rooms there. They have the babies separated according to ages. It is just so stark and crude. They have one room where they have big colorful blankets where the babies can get down and crawl and move. The workers are wonderful with the babies; you can tell they are very attached to them.

I tell the babies about their mommies and waiting families, and feel blessed to be so close, yet so far. I look at them and try to remember each of their mommies' names; there are so many, and it is so overwhelming to know that I am touching the babies of the women I feel so much connection with. I am deeply affected by this place. It will always be with me. . . .

A mother who adopts through an open adoption arrangement—regardless of the preadoption agreement—may also feel this sense of taking a child that isn't rightfully hers. This feeling of a lack of entitlement is especially true during that fragile and exquisite time immediately after birth. Claiming parentage while the birthmother is holding her child in a hospital bed and grieving her loss can be difficult, to say the least.

The adoptive mother feels torn between the intense bond that has formed between herself and the birthmother. They have talked, shared, become family, and now the adoptive mother is faced with a choice: In this vulnerable time after the child is born, with whom should her loyalties lie?

Carmen, an adoptive mother, related what it felt like to see her newborn son for the first time:

I was very torn because there I was holding the birthmother's hand and comforting her through the delivery. She'd been through so much. I wanted to be there for her, but then I wanted to run and see my son. I was very torn, and I kind of stayed with her until she said, "Go. Go see your son." It was a very awkward situation because I wanted to hug him, kiss him, and hold him and say, "My son." But the situation was so awkward, having the birthmother's mother and my son's grandmother there. I felt like I was being judged.

For kinship parents, the legitimacy aspect of parenting depends on generational family dynamics. The birthmother is your daughter or stepdaughter who drops the child off "at grandma's house" for days, weeks, or months, and then returns to pick her up without notice. Or the birthfather is your son or stepson, who is perhaps too young to parent. You have witnessed what the child or children have experienced—uncertainty, inconsistency, trauma, perhaps even abuse or neglect. Or you have been cut off from the family and now a crisis has formed without your knowledge, a crisis that you are expected to deal with. Perhaps you are grieving your own losses, the death of an adult child who leaves behind dependents who need care. When do you become Mom and Dad and stop being Grandma and Grandpa? And what does the name "Mommy" mean to the children?

Bonnie, a 52-year-old grandmother, related her experiences after assuming the care of her two active grandsons, Charlie and Nathan, ages 7 and 4. After the death of her son, Bonnie parented these children for 2 years. Their mother has been an inconsistent figure in their lives:

> *I felt like a parent in the beginning of all this. It seemed to be going okay until their mom tried to get them back. But now it has become a tug of war. I'm telling them one thing they can't do and she's saying it's okay. They call me "Grammie." I don't feel like their grandparent as much as I did before. I have six other grandkids. I don't feel like I am Charlie and Nathan's grandparent as much as I feel like I'm their security.*
>
> *I really think in the boys' minds that "Mommy" is a name. It's not a person. It's not the person that does for them, cares for them, and gives to them. Mommy is like their Aunt Sylvia, just another name. Where to me, my mom was my mom. She wasn't just a woman. She wasn't a lady. She was my mom.*
>
> *This morning, Charlie actually referred to me as a parent. I found that quite amazing. He actually is feeling that I am his parent instead of his grandmother.*

Bonnie's role confusion stems from her own experience of maternity and parentage. Legal entanglements can also undermine the role of parent. But the children know. They may not articulate the words "mom and dad," but they understand quite clearly what a mother and father do for them. The people who love them and take care of them are the people they view as their parents.

"I will feel like a real parent."

The fall from grace of not being The World's Best Parent comes hard for those of us supercharged folks who strive for excellence in our lives. Mediocre has never been good enough and never will be.

Fran, a leadership consultant and mother of two adult adoptees, spoke about feelings that surfaced decades after the children became part of her family. She and her husband adopted their two infant children 25 years ago. During their adolescence, the children began acting out. It was a time Fran reflected upon:

> *I was extremely anxious; it was fear. Total fear. In hindsight, the word "fraud" comes to mind. I felt like a fraud in many aspects of my life, both personal and professional. I didn't want everyone to find out I wasn't a good parent. It manifested itself as a crisis of confidence for both my husband and myself. When I started journaling and I got some help for myself, I thought, "Okay, how are you going to handle this so that you can be the best support for them?"*
>
> *After I got over the feelings of being a fraud, then the fear was, "My gosh, how are we going to be able to save these kids from themselves?"*

Although Fran admitted she wasn't sure how much of the behavior was due to her children's adolescence and how much was due to being adopted, we contend that the adoptive parent tries to live up to a very high standard of parenting until the child reaches emancipation and then some. Many of the parents we spoke with were tremendously self-reflective and circumspect about how they parented.

Single parents and same-sex parents create families that differ from the cultural representations faced daily on television, which is generally a two-parent household with multiple children by birth. These parents may wonder if they have a right to their children based on these violations of patterns. One single mother we spoke with stated that when she adopted her niece, she received little attention from her friends. It registered as no more than a hiccup in their social calendar.

When you lack a feeling of empowerment, you feel unworthy. This unworthiness translates into an inability to fully embrace that child, your family, and your role.

"I will be able to keep every promise I have ever made to my child and her birthparents."

Adoptive parents do everything they can to keep their word. They make promises to birthparents and their children in an honorable, genuine way. This commitment stems from striving to be The World's Best Parent and putting in print for the world to see that your home will be the best home for that child. But circumstances may betray you through divorce, loss of employment, or a special needs child whose requirements exceed your financial and emotional resources.

Nancy unexpectedly became a single parent when her husband decided he wanted to separate and ultimately divorce. A full-time professional, Nancy talked about what it was like to single parent an 8-month-old child by birth and a 2½-year-old son by adoption:

> My son, who was a toddler, was opening up with some wonderful gifts and also beginning to show some difficulties. Things that I didn't know about. Having to do this alone, there were some real challenges there. I'm not sure if it was because I was a single parent or because I was single. I kept thinking, "Am I doing it right? Am I doing enough?"
>
> The feelings were exacerbated because my son was adopted. I wanted to make sure I had everything that I had promised to him, the promises you make when you bring a child home. I had made the same promises to a birth child. There are promises you make in your heart and you plan to keep those. I felt I was letting them down. There were some financial difficulties that I had not planned for. When I brought this baby boy home, we had a beautiful home. We were going to build a play set in the backyard. All those things were gone. I felt like I was letting him down.
>
> I felt like if I ever met his birthmother, I would have to admit that I couldn't give to him what I had promised her. I couldn't give her what she thought she had chosen in me.

Nancy's words point to how we not only promise to be a perfect parent to our children and the world, but we promise the birthparents, as well. Look in any newspaper at the ads placed by would-be adoptive parents; the promises are there for all to read. We feel indebted to the people who gave life to our child, and it's a debt that somehow can never be repaid.

coping strategies

When combating the perception of perfection, how we internally frame ourselves is critical. Here are some ways to make your parenting experience more grounded.

Reset your internal voice. There are no perfect parents. Being The World's Best Parent is not possible. Mistakes are made and mistakes are to be learned from. Your status as an adoptive parent isn't equivalent to a "master parent" license. By taking a step back and gaining objectivity at your parenting patterns, you can move forward. Ask questions such as: How can I change my behavior the next time this situation arises? How does my child best learn? What motivates her? How are my actions creating reactions in my child?

Put-downs and inner voices that berate your sense of self are not going to help you become a more effective parent. Nor will these voices help you regain your self-esteem. You will make mistakes. There are events and occurrences that cannot be predicted, and if you made errors in judgment, accept that fact and seize every opportunity to take responsibility for it.

Reframe the promises you've made to the birthparents and the child. Ask yourself what is most important to a child, material gifts or gifts of love? Nancy spoke to us about how she realized her humanness and sorted through her guilt over the unmet material promises by reflecting on the heart of the decision made to the birthmother:

> *My son's birthmother was in very different circumstances where she truly gave him the gift of a future [by giving him up]. I appreciate her and the gift of life she gave to me, her courage. . . . I honor her. I believe in the decision she made. Feeling this gratitude has offered me peace and allowed me to take parentage of this son. Handing this gift from one to another.*
>
> *Confidence in my relationship with my son, with my daughter, with all my kids, confidence with him in particular, allows me not to worry about where he's going to be 5 years from now, 8 years from now, 10 years from now, in relation to a birthparent or to our family. We all accept in our lives people who are not related by blood. Each*

child has been a gift, but also a passage. We help them grow up to be the person that they are. We are the home, the parents, and the caretakers. They move through our lives to ultimately be their own people.

You are this child's parent, not her "owner;" what we "own" is how we choose to parent. Understanding this is extremely important in order to legitimize our roles. Veronica related how she consciously took on the role of mother to her infant son:

As I took on the parenting role with the baby, I felt the guilt ease off. I felt the [decrease in] guilt and the increase in my role were related. Once I was able to own the mothering, the guilt eased up.

Write it down in a journal. Some mothers find that keeping a journal is a safe way to express their feelings. The secrets you carry inside are less frightening when you put them on paper because of the private nature of a journal. Going back and reading your journal entries will allow you to see patterns of behavior and cycles of emotions. It can also allow you to see progress toward resolution.

As you begin to write, you may initially feel self-conscious. Here's what to do to overcome that feeling:

- Keep writing. Let the ideas and emotions flow.
- Remind yourself that this is a private journal, not a public document.
- Keep at it for at least 5 to 10 minutes, and the hesitancy will melt away as your inhibitions dissolve. This time can be the most productive in terms of getting to the core of your issues.
- Don't judge what you write. You may surprise yourself and uncover issues that you hadn't allowed yourself to think about. This is your space and time. Use it to increase your self-awareness and then to problem solve.

Take care of yourself and your health. In order to nurture and care for another, you have to take care of yourself first. Mothers are not culturally prepared to do this. They put the needs of others first, believing that being second or last is part of the job description. But when the mother struggles, the entire family is affected.

In addition to taking care of yourself through eating healthfully (don't wait until you're famished to eat), exercising, and getting enough sleep (easier said than done, we know), you also need to step back and realize that right now, you're not going to be able to do it all. The house may not be neat and tidy, the meals may not be home-cooked, and the clothes may not be folded and put away. Your child won't remember those things. She'll remember if you smiled and had time to play with her.

Sara gained weight while struggling with depression and shared this with us:

> *I did my share of crying. I actually gained weight. I gained a lot of weight. In the first year I gained close to 30 pounds, which added to my depression. I ate because of stress and to have the extra energy of food. I was saying, "Here I am, almost a 40-year-old woman, and I'm chasing after a 3-year-old." So that was part of it as well.*
>
> *I think the turning point was her third birthday. I thought that I needed to take myself out of this. I knew I couldn't continue because it wasn't healthy for me.*
>
> *One thing that helped me emotionally was taking a kickboxing class. It really gave me the energy I needed. Since I started the class, I have lost 37 pounds. I think I was angry with myself.*

Your stress, panic, or depression can affect how your child will respond to you and how you respond to your child. Your child will sense a fatigued, withdrawn mother who doesn't like how she looks and feels. Yet there are times when you'll have to focus on your needs before you can truly focus on hers. Sleep deprivation and poor eating habits can have dramatic effects on your behavior. For this reason, you owe it to your entire family to live healthier and more in balance. Rather than feeling selfish about taking care of yourself, accept that the better you feel, the better your family will be able to deal with the stressors it encounters. As one mother put it, "When mama don't dance, nobody dances." Indeed, the ability of a mother to cope with stress and her emotions significantly influences her family in many ways.

chapter 3

attachment to your child

Books, articles, seminars, and theses have been written addressing attachment theories and behaviors from a child-to-parent perspective. Far less has been documented about how we as parents attach to our children. The attachment of parent to child is considered a natural occurrence. An emotional transference is *supposed* to take place immediately, spontaneously, and intensely. When the attachment doesn't form right away, needs some nurturing, or takes time to intensify, we panic and wonder if the bond will ever form. Many of the parents we spoke with said that they were extremely stressed over the attachment issues they faced. In this chapter, we discuss parent-to-child attachment and how we can help this bond to form.

your expectations about **attachment**

"I will immediately feel that this is my child."

Society and all its armies—the media, the healthcare system, and history—dictate that maternal and paternal love are natural, instantaneous, and assumed. But bonding and attachment may not happen instantly. The parent-to-child bond often takes time to develop. Or in some cases, a deep-rooted love may come early and be tested later by the child's behaviors and needs. There may be a feeling of loving the child, but not really liking him.

When a maternal bond is lacking, a close assessment is called for. The mother may not feel protective and nurturing. The child may even be in danger of neglect or abuse. Simply put, without that maternal love, the child may become more of an object than a person.

Falling in love with a child that smells different, looks different, and behaves differently than you expected can be difficult. In some cases, immediate and visceral feelings of rejection of the child ensue. Then overwhelming panic grabs you as you realize that you have no idea what you need to do to change the situation. It seems you cannot fix this. What you thought you knew about yourself and your value system is questioned at a deep level. The guilt over what you're thinking ensnares you in a vicious circle. Before you know it, you feel you can't break free of these recurring thoughts that are driving you toward emotional crisis.

While you may feel great temptation to judge yourself harshly, it isn't productive to do so. Immediate intervention is critical, and we'll discuss ways to help you regain a sense of control over yourself and your world.

Sophie, an educated professional, and her husband, David, decided to adopt later in life. When they began the adoption process, they were in their mid-40s and had traveled the globe and nurtured their successful careers. Because of their age, they knew they wanted an older child, perhaps a 3- or 4-year-old girl. To their surprise, after a 2½-year wait, they were given an 11-month-old infant from China, whom they named Jill. Sophie reflected on her feelings after receiving her baby from the orphanage caregivers:

> That moment was awful for me. I thought I had ruined my life, that I had made this huge mistake. The guilt chases that. What kind of a monster was I to feel this way? I thought about leaving her there in China. I thought about saying, "I'm not the right person for this child. This is not fair to her. It's not fair to me. It's not fair to my marriage. I can't believe I didn't think about these things." I didn't sleep.

I was horrified that I was thinking these things. But she didn't feel like my baby, and I didn't feel like her mother. This poor little squirt.

No one talked to me about the bonding process prior to placement. I think I'm a relatively smart person who usually thinks things through. I couldn't believe that I was sitting in this hotel room thinking this. I would have thrown up all over the place, but I didn't eat anything, so there wasn't anything to throw up. I couldn't believe I had made such a stupid mistake. And such a big one with somebody else's life.

I didn't realize how I had been behaving toward her. I showed up in the restaurant of the hotel the third or fourth day after placement— and we met, as we usually did, other couples for breakfast. And one of the other moms, Audrey, said to me, "That's the first time I've seen you hold her." I gasped and said, "Oh my God, you're right." I put her in the stroller. I took her out of the stroller. But I didn't hold her. I couldn't believe I had done that, and I didn't notice that I had done that.

Things got worse before they improved. Immediately upon their return home, Sophie's husband had a 3-day business trip, which meant the care of the baby was totally Sophie's responsibility.

We got home on Easter Sunday, and we spent Monday trying to get on the same time schedule, which the baby did very well. My husband and I did not. Then Tuesday, my husband went on a business trip. I took her upstairs to the bathroom with me because I had to go to the bathroom, and I hadn't thought that through—that I couldn't go to the bathroom by myself. I had just fed her a jar of pears. She simply rolled over on her belly and threw up the pears. She wasn't uncomfortable. She just threw them up because she had put pressure on her belly. Then she slapped her hand in it and I went, "Oh great. This is good." So I cleaned that up and she had a really dirty diaper and I cleaned that up and I came down the stairs and the cat threw up a hairball and I thought, "I've died and gone to hell. I think I've died and gone to hell."

For the next 6 weeks, Sophie lost her way in life. She fell into a depression and her self-esteem plummeted. Referring to herself as The World's Biggest Jerk and mentally kicking herself for not thinking through the decision to adopt, her anxiety over whether or not to disrupt the adoption grew to a paralyzing level.

In retrospect, Sophie realized that she had been totally caught up in the process of the adoption and its paperwork. The energy expended in that process had robbed her of the precious time that's necessary to think of the real child who is coming. She and her husband had carefully considered the decision to adopt a child. What she hadn't thought through was the reality of a child and that the attachment to her child may not be immediate. And because no one had mentioned to her that bonding might not be instantaneous, Sophie believed it would never happen.

"I will like this child."

Many adoptive parents believe that not only will they attach and bond immediately, they will also immediately like their child. (We will talk about matching parent and child in chapter 6.) Temperaments, personalities, and skills learned in institutional settings can throw off your ability to like your child—at least initially. Experts agree that they hear "I love him, but I don't like him," quite frequently.

Sara struggled with liking her daughter, now a toddler. The bond was immediate in this case—Sara felt that this was "her child" after meeting her for the first time at the orphanage—but because of Tanya's preference for her father and her angry outbursts, Sara felt confused as to what her long-term relationship would be with her daughter:

> thoughts from an expert
>
> # liking your child
>
> I see parents who say, "The child is fine. I don't like this kid. It's me. It's not the kid. The child is well attached." Then they feel guilty. I always try to put it in perspective in a humorous way: "Yeah, aren't you waiting for their parents to come and get her?" It's like when your child has a friend over, and you can't wait until the friend goes home. But this kid never goes home.
>
> *Debbie Joy, M.S.,*
> *private practitioner*

I was depressed. I had returned to work after 3 months off, and I would tell everyone how great things were. That she was doing great. Then I'd go home and I'd have to fight with these feelings of the Lord pushing me just a little too far.

I feel close to my boys. The emotions, the touching, the love, and all that came very naturally. For example, one of the things that both my husband and I enjoyed with our babies was bath time at night. We would put them in the bathtub, and afterwards we gave them baby massages. I went through the whole infant massage class, and it was such a special time for the boys and me when they were babies.

Tanya hated it. She did not like to be touched. She would get frustrated easily, hit her head on the floor, and scream at the top of her lungs. She didn't like to be touched. She was so oppositional.

"If I maintain some emotional distance, I won't get hurt."

The child may have lived with you for months or years, perhaps since infancy. Now, the decision to adopt or become a full-time parent has been made. You're making the transition from being a foster parent or grandparent to being a mother or father. The stakes are high. This step means that the child will live with you forever. And yet there may be lag time, created by the birthparents' fight to regain custody or being indecisive over whether or not to relinquish parental rights. Questions arise within you: When will I really be this child's parent? Can I keep going emotionally in this limbo state? Fatigue from the court appearances sets in. The financial costs may increase and leave more concerns. But the overriding question becomes: Will I ever be this child's legal parent?

Because of that uncertainty, you may find yourself unconsciously trying to protect your feelings by erecting an emotional wall between you and the child. Mary and her husband, Mark, who are in their early 30s, are 10-year veterans of the foster care system. Four small children placed into their care are now finally eligible for adoption. Mary speaks to the 18 months of time between when they received the children and when they knew they were going to be their mother and father:

The parents were not doing their service plan, what the court had ordered them to do to regain parental rights. They were getting arrested. The time was very stressful, especially the holidays, because we never knew where the kids were going to be. As time passed, we fell more and more in love with these children. You try to put up a wall at first. My husband and I tried to keep in the backs of our minds that to properly care for the kids, you're going to get attached. Now, when I speak with other foster parents and they say, "We just have to put up the wall," I tell them, "No, you have to get attached or else you're not really doing your job. The children need that." If the wall is up, the home becomes more an institution and less a home. But it leaves you vulnerable to more hurt.

The laws, which vary from state to state, can also leave an adoptive parent with a sense of guardedness. Will the birthmother change her mind? Is this baby really mine? After so many disappointments and after such a long wait, can I trust that this is really happening?

The presence of a birthparent can also contribute to a sense of hesitation. Birthmothers have a right and need to see, speak to, and touch their child, particularly after the labor and delivery that has left them so full of emotions and grief. Yet this critical period, so charged with life-affecting decisions, often leaves the adoptive mother incapable of embracing her role as a full-fledged parent. One mother, Veronica, who had arranged an open adoption, spoke about these feelings immediately after her son was born:

In the preadoption counseling, our counselor said, "Be prepared to walk out of that hospital alone. Be prepared for that." But after he was born, I was almost able to say he was my son—yes and no. I never, ever was told during our preadoption counseling that I might experience some guilt. I saw what the birthmother was going through. The guilt was a barrier to owning the parenting role. It was a big barrier.

Once we got home, a lot of the guard came down. There was more relaxation. I lost most of my guard that first night, but when the birthmother came to the house the next day, all that guardedness came back. There was also a little bit of fear. Would she change her mind? I probably had a little bit of guardedness until the rights were completely terminated. The waiting period in this state is about 45 days.

Kinship parents may be confused over the relationship they have with the child, especially prior to a legal arrangement being decided. They ask themselves, "Am I Grandma or Mom?" When you aren't fully embracing the parenting role, either because of uncertainty or fear of being hurt, you cannot fully monitor the child's behavior. Virginia, a 40-year-old step-grandparent and newly adoptive mother to three small girls, commented on what happened when she and her husband hesitated:

> *When we first got the children 3 years ago, I was still giving them lots of leeway. I would look at them and think, "Oh, you poor babies. Your mom and dad aren't doing what they need to do. Let me hold you, hug you, make you better." I also was faced with the daily possibility that these parents could come in at any time and take these kids.*
>
> *But I wasn't setting enough limits. Now that they're adopted, I have three little terrors on my hands. Looking back, I would have made sure I had the legal issue settled a lot sooner than 4 years.*

"I will handle the changes in lifestyle that parenting brings."

Children are children: dependent, raw, impulse-driven small beings who need direction, time, and discipline. They are not little adults. They are not born with an innate sense of right and wrong. They are exhausting, lovable little creatures that make you nearly forget what life was like before they came to you. The decision to become a parent cannot be a rational one. We believe it can be legitimized through rationalization: We have the means to support a child. We can offer a child a good home. We have this warm comfortable house, and there are so many children needing a good home.

For all our rationalizing, parenting comes down to something less quantifiable. Inescapable sensations reside in us that guide us to parentage: the sheer desire to be a mother and father; to share our lives with a child; to explore the world, with all its wonders and challenges; to teach; and ultimately, to learn about ourselves through our children.

Day-to-day reality arrives. Sleep deprivation, the inability to take paid leave, and the responsibility of a child 24 hours a day, 7 days a week fatigue you. Getting a daily shower is a new personal goal. You may not have anticipated all that a child will involve. In this hurried, hectic life, children can add a lot of stress.

These lifestyle changes are particularly evident to the childless couple and to kinship parents, both of whom may have believed that planning for retirement would be their next life stage. Caring for children seems synonymous with that four-letter word: w-o-r-k.

Bonnie, a 52-year-old grandmother of two active young boys, had this to say about her new life:

One of the harder things for me was the adjustment to small children again. For a period of time, I came home to the solitude of a quiet home. If I wanted to work late in the evening, I could do that. Now there are times I have to bring work home. Because of interruptions, I really can't be on the computer and start working until they're down for bed. Before the kids, people would call and I could yak all night long. Now if the phone rings, the boys torment me to get off the phone.

Physically, it's harder. It's hard to get the little one in the car seat. I even pulled a back muscle. I'm tired. Then there's the extra laundry. I was used to doing laundry once a week. Now it's at least every other day. I was always a fanatic about washing, drying, folding, and then putting the clothes away. I would get the dryer cleaned out and the washer cleaned off. Now I'm doing well if I can get the load out of the dryer. My daughter said, "Mom, I can't believe you've still got clothes in your washer."

coping strategies

Although rarely discussed, disharmony in the parent-to-child bond is devastating. Here are some ways to nurture this relationship.

Understand that time can be your friend, but know when to seek outside help. How do you know when you should be sensing that things might get better? How do you know when it's time to seek help? While many mothers admit that time was the key to resolving some of their feelings, recognize that feelings of being continually overwhelmed, a pervasive sadness, or feeling paralyzed and panicked all require intervention by outside resources. *If you have thoughts of doing harm to yourself or to your child, seek help immediately.*

But for those parents whose negative thinking hasn't progressed to levels that threaten their safety or the safety of their child, time has a healing quality. Janice, a 45-year-old mother, adopted a boy from Russia. She commented on the effect of time and her bond with him:

I didn't feel what I knew that I was supposed to feel for weeks . . . literally weeks. He was cute, and he was amusing to watch and all the rest of that. But I didn't feel the closeness at all. It started, finally. One day, he walked down the street by himself for the first time. Up to this point, he had been wrapping his arms around my leg, sort of dragging himself around. So he walked down the street for the first time, and I felt this pang. I was worried. And I thought, "Ah, ha! This is it!"

I was relieved. Not what you would call happy, but I knew that there were going to be feelings strong enough to get us through the hard times.

Time also allows your child an opportunity to begin responding to you, her parent. Many parents admitted that once they saw their child seeking them out, calling them "Mom or Dad," they were able to begin the attachment process themselves.

Separate issues of personal identity from issues with parenting. You know by now that super-women and super-parents don't exist. Not in real life, anyway. At the other extreme, television and movies portray dysfunctional mothers who somehow come through the parenting years as successes. Between these two extremes, find balance in your role as a parent. First and foremost, take the blame away. Your decision to adopt was made in good faith with good intentions. In other words, forgive yourself.

Prioritize your life in the present time. The push and pull of everyday life can blur your perceptions at times. Add a new child, and your internal equilibrium can be quite tilted. So take a step back. Wait. Take a few deep breaths in and out. Ask yourself a few questions: What are my priorities? Do I really "own" these priorities? Am I committed to achieving them? Are they realistic? What adjustments could be made to these priorities?

when parents seek help

Parents often call too early or too late. International adoptive parents typically call us on Monday and say, "We got home from China on Saturday and she's not attached." We'll say, "Of course she's not. She just met you." Or some of them will call when the child is 12. We'll ask, "How long have they been acting like this?" They'll reply, "Since they were 2 years old." Where have they been for 10 years? But it's getting better.

We see kids as young as 2 and as old as 18. Most of the parents who come here want help and want a happy family. They're very motivated.

Regina Kupecky, L.S.W., coauthor of Adopting the Hurt Child *and* Parenting the Hurt Child

What resources are necessary to make these adjustments? What choices do I make every day that lock me into these priorities?

Provide respite care for yourself. Many professionals encourage a new adoptive parent to make sure that they are the primary caregiver to that child. The caregiver is the individual who feeds the child, changes the child, and for the most part, holds the child. In this way, the child will form an attachment to that parent. But if you are having difficulty bonding with your child, this advice can exacerbate your feelings and intensify the cycle of guilt and anger. It also may not be in the child's best interests at that time.

Taking a respite through quality childcare or babysitters can lessen the feelings of panic and resentment. Sophie, the mother who was struggling with bonding with her infant girl, expressed what a break from parenting meant to her:

> *The doctor at the international adoption clinic suggested I take some time for myself and put her in daycare. I said the most horrifying thing to him, "I can't even stand to look at her. It is such a big mistake, and I messed her up. I don't even want to look at her." He said, "Put her in daycare. Put her in daycare right now. She's used to being in an orphanage. Just put her in daycare," which I did. That helped a great deal because it gave me time to calm down within the house. I just sat there and thought for days. And I don't know what to say, it just worked itself out.*
>
> *The doctor told me, "Go do what you used to do. Go back to work. That's what you're used to doing." I thought that I had messed her life up, but I don't think that I thought that she had messed my life up. I went halfway around the world and pulled out this kid that I'm sure would have gotten a better home there than I could give her. Look at what I did for me. I did it for me.*
>
> *It's like an arranged marriage, but it's much more intense. I don't know how you could know this: how it feels to have somebody so dependent on you at that level 24 hours a day, 7 days a week, 365 days a year, to the point that you can't breathe. It's almost like I was suffocating. Like I had someone physically attached to me, and I didn't like that. The thing that I felt awful for was that this poor little thing had this monster for a mother who wanted to shake her off her leg like she's a dog or something. Jill would wrap her arms around my leg and I'm like, "No! Oh my God!" shaking my leg. "Get off of me."*

After seeing a disastrous counselor, I found a good one. I knew that whatever decision I needed to make, I needed to make it very quickly. Of course, I thought I had made a decision. But everyone else knew I really hadn't. They thought that I was going to come to the conclusion that there was no way I was going to give this child back. But I honestly thought that I might not complete the adoption. I honestly thought that the adoption might not happen, and everyone else who had any experience, the doctor, even the adoption agency, kept saying, "Give it time, it will go away." Everybody else was just biding their time, waiting for this to go away. Which it did! They were absolutely right. But I didn't know that then.

At a deep level, I knew there was an attachment. It wasn't that long afterward that I was staring at Jill while she was eating—and you know when you're thinking something and you're thinking this isn't rational, but I don't care? I honestly thought that there was no child on this planet that was prettier. This is the prettiest baby that ever lived. I knew that wasn't accurate. It's like falling in love. I fell in love with Jill.

We want to stress that you can't just wait and hope for the best. We believe it is imperative that your emotions be addressed. Why? Your feelings may get stuck and not evolve if you take a "wait and see" approach, and while you're waiting, you lose valuable time. Remember, your whole family is affected when you are stressed or depressed. Have confidence that attachment will come, but also have the courage to seek help as that attachment evolves.

Seek professional help through counseling. Numerous parents told us that a coping strategy they employed was to seek professional therapy. And many times, this strategy has proven very helpful. We strongly urge a parent who wishes to seek counseling to be diligent in finding a therapist who understands and "gets" adoption. To be effective, the counselor needs to understand the dynamics of adoption in order

trusting another

Once a parent is struggling, the first avenue is not necessarily to pathologize the struggle by making a diagnosis—and I know that sounds strange coming from a mental health professional. The first thing to do is to talk to the spouse or whoever is co-parenting. Most people have that resource or they have a best friend. Single parents probably have one identified person who is not a partner, but is a close friend. So the first place to go is to the person who knows you best.

Barbara Rila, Ph.D.,
private practitioner

to separate the symptoms (behaviors) from the underlying issues. A therapist who is effective will appreciate loss, grief, and separation issues.

One family confided in us that their counselor told them that their child's behavior was entirely based on genetics; the child's acting out behaviors were due to the gene pool she had come from. What was even more damaging was that the sibling was told this and believed it. Another mother, after a 1-hour session with a new therapist (who happened to be an adoptive parent herself), was advised to disrupt the adoption, as the child would "ruin the marriage."

If a crisis has descended upon you, you may feel a well-founded ur-

---

Putting the Pieces Together

Sophie and Jill

Let's hear the rest of Sophie's story.

Soon after arriving home from China with Jill, Sophie realized the extent of her difficulties, which included impaired bonding, feeling that she was suffocating emotionally from the intense responsibility, feeling disoriented, and berating herself for not having "thought all this through." David took over the bulk of the parenting during the "worst of it"—about 2 months. Sophie's anxiety skyrocketed. She was thinking of not continuing with the adoption, saying: "Jill didn't feel like my baby."

Fortunately, Sophie realized she needed to take action in order to cope, and she reached out to others for help. After seeing a psychologist who didn't understand adoption, Sophie called her adoption agency. A social worker referred her to a new, more enlightened counselor. This therapist told Sophie that what she was feeling was normal and not uncommon. She listened in a nonjudgmental way to Sophie, and offered her support and guidance.

At about the same time, Sophie took Jill to an international adoption clinic for an evaluation. The medical director, who sensed Sophie's mental anguish, encouraged her to have Jill attend daycare. Sophie returned to her job, an enjoyable, important part of her life. With Jill in daycare, Sophie had time to think, regroup, and reflect. Sophie also confided in a close friend whom she could call any time, day or night. The friend babysat Jill so that Sophie and David could discuss Sophie's feel-

gency to get help quickly. Yet an incompetent therapist can prolong and exacerbate the crisis. Don't give up after one therapist. When calling around, ask what therapeutic interventions are used, what the therapist's background in adoption is, their philosophy of adoption, and what contact with adoption they have had personally and professionally. Look for a therapist who individualizes counseling techniques and adapts them to the needs of her clients.

Begin to trust in those who know you best, and those who love you. By seeking out a spouse, a significant other, or a friend, you will find comfort and acceptance.

ings. About 3 months passed. Sophie's anxiety slowly began to dissipate. She looked at Jill's clothes and discarded those that reminded her of her "dark time." Sophie began to forgive herself and stopped punishing herself for emotions she didn't understand.

With the help of the counselor, she was able to name what she was experiencing: post-adoption depression. She realized that she shouldn't—and couldn't—have known how to process what she was feeling. That the problem had a name also meant that she didn't cause these feelings, and most important, that she wasn't alone in this struggle. Other parents felt like she did.

Sophie wished desperately that someone had told her about post-adoption depression: "It wouldn't have changed anything in terms of our decision to adopt. But if I had heard about it and then experienced it, I would have thought, 'Okay. I understand what's going on.'"

Another important coping strategy was to realize that time was helping. Sophie told us: "I remember knowing I was in love with her. She started to call me 'Mom' and I thought, 'Well, I guess I am.'" Although still haunted by guilt over her early feelings toward Jill, Sophie's life has returned to her in a fuller manner than before her daughter came home. During our interview, Sophie related how much she enjoyed spending time with Jill, who has a very strong sense of family. Sophie and Jill share a deep attachment to one another—an attachment that Sophie has no doubt will last a lifetime.

Sharing the secrets in your heart, takes away the secrets' power. The shame, guilt, and anger that have been kept under your close guard are finally disclosed. The feelings are there for your confidante to see. Yet what a risk! How difficult to trust those whom you desperately want to trust. What will they think of you? Will they judge you as you've judged yourself? What if they don't understand?

We understand these feelings from our own experience. Karen slowly began trusting in John as she disclosed her difficulty attaching to Annie. The lack of bonding mystified Karen. She couldn't explain it to herself, let alone another person. Yet when she disclosed her emotions, John validated them as real, and most importantly, he didn't judge them. She even confided her worst fear: that her emotional bond with Annie would never come. Again, John's listening and patient understanding eased Karen's pain.

While you cannot guarantee what the reactions of others will be, chances are that their love for you will show in their supportive words and gestures. They will see how this is affecting you. You will feel relief. By speaking the unspeakable, you can regain some perspective and start to get the help you need.

Seek strength in spiritual renewal. Parents we met with reminded us again and again how important their spirituality was to them. This sense of spirituality translated into many aspects of their lives, from making sense of their decision to have a child by adoption, to instilling hope for the future, to making peace with the present.

Veronica described her faith in this way:

I coped by the use of faith. I know I had depression. I felt lonely, and the work that my husband was doing at the time was very stressful for him. I was tired all the time. Not just the normal, "I'm tired from not sleeping enough."

But I had a voice that kept popping up that I attribute to faith. It kept saying, "Just give. Just keep giving, and I'm going to take care of the rest. It is going to work out. Everything is going to work out."

Spirituality took many forms with different parents, from private meditation to organized religious services. Whatever form it took, their spirituality renewed the parents and helped them with their daily lives.

part II

your **expectations** of your child

the well-being of your child

As powerful as the expectations that you hold for yourself are, even more powerful are the expectations that you hold for your child. You long for information about your child preplacement: What kind of care did she receive? What happened during those years in foster care? Or, for kinship parents, How did my son and daughter-in-law parent her before I took over caring for this child? Unfortunately, many questions will never be answered.

With any child, a parent takes a leap of faith, developing a sense that whatever they are faced with, they'll be able to handle. In adoption, there can be unexpected challenges, unknown information that wasn't disclosed, and a mismatch of temperaments between parent and child. You may feel that your every move is being judged by your children, who are trying to determine how equally you love, and the extent of your love within the household. You may have felt prepared, only to be startled by the realization that the reality you face now had never crossed your mind.

Three major themes emerged from our research. Our discussion will be structured around these three sets of expectations, starting with this chapter's look at your child's well-being. The next two chapters will focus on the the emotional needs of your child and integrating your child into your family.

your expectations
of your child's **well-being**

"My child will be okay."

No matter what your child's life was like before you were united with him, you want to believe he'll be okay. As parents, we were faced with a child by birth who experienced severe delays, and we can attest to the overwhelming nature of the situation, the years of chronic fatigue and stress, and the peaks and valleys of therapy. Yet we expected a healthy child. Even when you know things are very rosy at the moment, the reality is that the child's needs may overtake the family system in the future, and there's no way to foresee that possibility.

Cynthia, a teacher in her early thirties, confessed her feelings about the two children that she and her husband had adopted from an Eastern European country. Her eyes searched for answers and her heart searched for hope as she related the crisis she was experiencing:

> I have these two feral children who hate to be touched. The 3-year-old can't even talk. The 4-year-old isn't attached to me at all. I don't know if they're going to be okay. I don't know what to do. I'm a teacher, and I thought I could handle their needs. I had no idea this would be so overwhelming. We weren't told.
>
> My students are bonded to me. Why can't these children bond?

Many adoptive parents enter two cultures simultaneously: the culture of special needs children and the culture of adoption. Each culture has its own political correctness, mores, and values, including terminology and accepted vocabulary. For example, the term "birthparent" is preferred over "biological parent," "international adoption" is preferred over "foreign adoption," and "learning differences" is more acceptable than "learning disabilities."

Eventually you'll learn the lingo, but how can you learn to address your child's needs? New technology has exploded in the private sector of special needs. Computer programs, sensory integration therapies, and modified listening programs are designed to manage diagnoses such as attention deficit disorder, auditory processing disorder, and sensory integration disorder. (For more on these disorders, see the Glossary on page 226.)

What's important is to focus on the distinction between the emotional needs, neurological needs, and environmental regulatory needs of your child. Is the child's difficulty rooted in her emotional development, one of grief, sadness, or bonding difficulties? Or are her problems related to inadequate neurological development that makes it difficult for her to take in the information available to her? Can her skin tolerate tags in her clothing? Can her ears tolerate loud sounds? Can her mouth and tongue swallow certain textured foods? Can her eyes track a line of print along the page? Maybe her struggles lie along both emotional and neurological lines. We'll talk about how to begin to understand these needs in the next chapter, as well as how easy it is to misinterpret the feedback from the love you offer.

Other times, parents believe that a child who is adopted at a young age or as an infant—because they have come to you so early in life—will be okay. But many of you have come to realize that developmental needs may arise years later, when the child is a toddler or school-aged. Developmental milestones may not be reached. Schoolwork may become difficult or impossible. You feel you've been asleep, gliding along, and now you're facing a challenge that overwhelms you.

In many instances, we need to give up our vision of the "dream child:" the child you have fantasized about; the child who is happy, healthy, can ride the bus to school and perform well; the child who should have been born to you; or the child who you hoped you would have adopted. You feel an instant sense of guilt. You love your child . . . the one sitting on the sofa, the one who has softened your heart with love and made it ache at the same time. You didn't know you could feel this much caring for another being. But it's so hard at times.

Sometimes, a crisis swoops in and takes over your life. Annette, a 41-year-old woman who works in finance, adopted a child from Russia 2 years ago. The child was 7 years old at the time. Annette and her husband knew they wanted an older child and discovered a program that brought children to the United States for 6 weeks during the summer. During this long visit, the parents and children could spend time with each other and assess the match. Annette and her husband fell in love with Catherine, and she fell in love with them. Annette had prepared herself by reading about issues regarding adoption of an older child, but

the child you received

Humor can be very effective. We tease the parents a lot. You know, adoption is not like Burger King. You don't get what you ordered. We're sorry you wanted this kind of kid, but you got this kind instead. But now you have to parent him. It's not your fault. You didn't create this kid, but it's your problem to fix him. You can do it. We'll help you. We'll be there with you. I think that's the biggest thing. The parents don't feel blamed. They don't feel criticized. But that doesn't mean we don't help them make changes. Usually, bottom line, we say, "Why would you know how to parent this child? No one taught you. You were getting ready for a child with no problems. You have a child with a problem. You have a child with cystic fibrosis, and you need to learn how to pound on his chest. You have a kid with cerebral palsy, and you need to learn about leg braces. You have a child with emotional issues, and you need to learn to parent him."

Regina Kupecky, L.S.W.,
coauthor of Adopting the Hurt Child *and* Parenting the Hurt Child

she wasn't prepared for the crisis that fell upon the family. The private school that Catherine has been attending informed Annette and her husband that they could no longer meet Catherine's needs:

> *I knew there was a family history of alcoholism. Catherine has no features of fetal alcohol syndrome, but what I didn't know about were the fetal alcohol effects that can come into play later in life. She's not aggressive. She has a huge heart. After talking with the doctor in Moscow, I knew there might be some learning issues. I was aware.*
>
> *The feeling that I feel closest to right now is guilt. Horrible guilt over the fact that we don't have the financial resources to do what we should be doing to help her. She needs a specific program to learn to read, but where are we going to come up with the $20,000 to do it? Where do you go? We've been told she has poor short-term and working memory. But I know there are services out there that could help her.*
>
> *If you ask Catherine, "Which life is easier?" she will tell you that her life in Russia was much easier than her life in America. There were no expectations there. They didn't school the kids.*
>
> *She has shown a lot more anger. Catherine was very quick to react*

to things and she reacted very severely. She would just shut herself in the bathroom and lock the door. One night she said, "I just want to die."

Sometimes you feel exhausted from the chronic nature of the problems. Years have passed, and you're still struggling alongside this child. One mother, her voice almost a whisper said:

My child is now 9 years old. We adopted him when he was 3. I never realized the long-term chronic nature of his problems. He won't talk to us. I've tried to talk to him, and he turns away. He's having trouble in school. I get so tired.

You've come to realize that your child has delays, deficits, and/or behaviors that require professional intervention. The period of time prior to evaluation and diagnosis can fill you with a mixture of anticipation, dread, and even terror.

Then the tests are performed; the evaluations completed and the reports arrive. Questions tumble from your lips and there may be no professional there to answer them. Isolation creeps into your life as you begin to see yourself different (again) from others around you. You process the information and try to frame the plan of treatment— what to do next to meet your child's medical and emotional needs.

But why? Why did this happen to you, your child, and your family? The family you traveled with received a healthy child. Your friend's caseworker disclosed all the suspected difficulties that were possible with her child. Why weren't you told about your child's history? Why me? Why my child? Why my family?

Making sense of life events is natural and part of our journey through life. We long to understand and even pinpoint why something happened. In many of our situations, there simply won't be answers. This void will have to be processed and accepted. Grief over the loss of our fantasy child, the child who can socialize with ease, take the bus to school with safety, learn to read and do math computations with her peers will have to be admitted. Grieving over these losses doesn't mean you don't love your child.

Time takes on a new meaning. Your long-range thinking of where your child will be in 5, 10, 15 years leaves you wondering if she'll be able to live a happy and independent life. The world's expectations have changed so much. It seems a generation or two ago, a child with a deficit could make it in society, positioning herself in a niche that reflected her strengths and provide for her economic security. Now the world we live in doesn't seem so tolerant. The standardized tests, the public schools whose resources are limited, the private schools whose academic standards are daunting, and the forced labeling do little to instill our hope for our child's future.

Your child's needs may tax the family's resources: emotional, spiritual, and financial. These needs seem to dominate the family with the child getting more attention, more resources, and even directing the family's future course-when and if vacations are taken, the family's daily schedule, and whether or not you can or should return to work. Your family's identity changes, and you find yourself looking at the world with new, tired eyes.

However, for all these challenges, we believe a child with needs develops a special compassion in us. In our family's situation, we believe our lives are forever changed—for the better—because of our son's delays. The challenge forced us to reevaluate our priorities, give thanks for gifts we might have overlooked, and understand what we value in the world and society. John believes he has become a more astute and skilled clinician, picking up on patient diagnoses and needs that he might have missed prior to having his son. He has helped many children because of this extra knowledge gleaned from helping his son. We believe hope and advocacy for your child are the keys; hope that life will get easier and hope that your child will benefit from the help that you have advocated for him.

"My child's needs will be disclosed."

Complete and full disclosure of the child's background information is legally mandated by the majority of states. Indeed, adoptive parents have filed "wrongful adoption" suits at the state level. These cases have been tried based on fraud (deliberately providing inaccurate or deliberately withholding information) or negligence (carelessly providing inaccurate information or failing to provide information). The adoption agency is required to provide you with the background information available to them, and they must make reasonable efforts to obtain this information. However, you need to understand that some information may not be available to them and therefore, unavailable to you.

Incomplete information about your child makes uncovering her needs that much more difficult. You, the parent, the most important person who needed this information, was left out of the loop. Elaine, birthmother to five children and adoptive mother to 12 more, complained about the information she received from her public caseworker:

> One assumes that a single caseworker has all the information. This isn't reality. Some of these children have had multiple placements, multiple schools, and endless healthcare providers. Their files are tall and getting taller. I had one child, a 5-year-old girl, who we needed to hospitalize. And we found an 8-year-old boy's health record interspersed with hers.

Other parents echo this difficulty. One couple described how they were told that for every year of abuse suffered by their child preplacement, one month of counseling would "fix it." The father stated, "I figured that she had probably been abused for 6 years or so. Well, I did the math and thought that 6 months wasn't such a long time." The couple described the years of therapy and turmoil the family had experienced post-adoption. Then they eagerly shared the photographs of their grandchildren with us.

In disclosing information about the child who is adopted internationally, agencies often can guarantee only to disclose the information they possess. Translation errors, cultural differences, and medical terminology variations provide gaps and inaccuracies in what you will know about your child. You may be asked to sign a waiver that states you have been supplied with the information that was available, not that the information is accurate or correct.

The true nature of the child's background is often revealed over time. For example, kinship parents may become aware of their child's layers of needs as trust grows, testing of parental limits ensues, and every day life unfolds.

common reactions to unmet expectations

By the time you're evaluating your expectations, you've realized that you are responsible for a wonderful, active, and challenging child. Let's talk about how you may have reacted to the child, behaviorally and emotionally, in ways that may not be helpful to you or the child.

Just as we react to defend ourselves emotionally when we don't meet our expectations of ourselves, we defend our emotions similarly when our child doesn't meet our own expectations. We use these defense mechanisms in reaction to stress and depression—many times in the moment and without prior thought.

anger

Your child is not what you expected. Her behavior is disruptive, too much for you to handle. You feel angry, but you aren't sure who to be angry with. There's lots of it to go around: yourself, your spouse, your family, and your child.

sadness

Instead of the joy you expected, you experience a heavy sadness. Your anger has dissipated into melancholy. Obsessive questions run around in your head: What will the future bring to me and to my family? Will my child ever grow to love me, to live an independent life? What will happen to us?

panic

You truly aren't sure whether to fight or flee. The situation is overwhelming. There is so much to learn all at once and no one to ask. Unlike the pregnant woman who has ties to the healthcare community through prenatal visits, the resources you have are new or unknown. Panic runs hand-in-hand with anxiety. You're never able to relax. You find yourself eating more and pacing the room. It's hard to sit still. Sleep, when it comes, is restless and unsatisfying.

sublimation

You devote your energies to constructive activities (or work) outside your family. You do this because—in your mind—it's in the interest of your family; yet the challenges facing the home are ignored. Marital conflicts arise because communication is breaking down. Your spouse complains about your absence or your inattention to the family. No one seems to appreciate what you are doing to help.

denial

You deny that the child needs help. You believe that time and love will remedy the situation. You and your spouse bicker over what your child needs. Still, when you find yourself alone, you may accidentally visit that frightened place inside you, only to return to the safety of denial.

avoidance

You aren't denying there is a problem, but you either consciously or unconsciously engage in activities that allow you to avoid the situation. You procrastinate, use excuses to not engage, or change the subject in an effort to avoid the real issues.

coping strategies

Once you have received your child, take the time to look at how your family is operating. Read through the questions in "Evaluating Your Situation" on page 62.

evaluating your situation (post-placement)

Family Strengths

- What makes your family unique? How would you describe your family? How would you tell the story of your family?
- What strengths do you and your significant other possess? Do you feel balance and support in this relationship?
- How can you adapt these strengths to meet the new challenges?
- What about the family as a whole? Do you employ humor? Do you hold family meetings to discuss "business and decisions"?

Family Resources

- What are your resources—spiritually, financially, socially, emotionally, and physically? List their strengths and weaknesses.
- How can you use these resources to build successful relationships within the family?
- What new resources are available? (Use the Internet for information and ideas, and the local telephone directory and the daily newspaper for community events and ideas.)

Individual Emotional Assessment

- Where are you emotionally right now?
- Have you had an emotionally exhausting and physically draining journey trying to have a child by birth? Have you suffered through terrible loss in miscarriages, or even the tragic loss of a child? What issues have been resolved? What issues have yet to be clarified? Do you feel healed?
- Do you have a history of depression? What treatment, if any, did you seek to get your depression into remission? What warning signs do you know to look for?
- Do you over- or under-eat? Do you have difficulty sleeping? Do you feel anxious or irritable? Feel that you have to pace the floor or be doing something? Or do you feel tired most of the time and even small exertions wear you out?

Once you've reviewed your answers to the evaluation, you may better understand your family's situation and your reaction to it. You may also realize that there are others who can help (and finding new ways to reach them).

Dolly is a 55-year-old grandmother who has been raising her 13-year-old grandson, Justin, since he was 18 months old. Justin has been diagnosed with multiple mental illnesses, including obsessive-compulsive disorder, bipolar disorder, attention deficit/hyperactivity disorder, and severe depression with psychotic tendencies. Dolly is a veteran of navigating the system and finding resources:

I was an anticomputer person. A "you can't teach an old dog new tricks" sort of person. But my husband has some abilities with computers and so we got one. I finally got coaxed into trying it, and I haven't gotten off it since. It's a whole world out there. It is a smorgasbord of help and support.

I would advise others to network. In other words, you may have to get the yellow pages and look under "social services." Sit down and start calling and tell them your circumstances. I also found information through reading the newspaper. I received a stipend to go to a grandparent conference that was held at the state level. Even though I have been through the welfare mess and the intrusion of government, I was determined to get this child the help that he needed. I knew enough and had enough courage to strike out and start learning.

Set aside the child's chronological age. Appreciate the developmental age of the child and realize that short-term medical needs can influence behaviors. The difficulties your child is experiencing might be resolved once the medical issues have been addressed.

Adopted children may experience developmental delays. Consider how long the child has been in an institutional setting or in various placements. Think about the environment that the child was exposed to, and whether he suffered neglect or abuse.

Our daughter, Annie, had a very underdeveloped ability to drink from a bottle. and she was suffering from anemia when we received her at 5 months of age. She was tiny by American standards and delayed in how she could move her body. Two months before we received Annie, we'd seen a 10-second video from the Kolkatta orphanage, the *ayahs* (nurses) speaking rapid Bengali in the background. We saw Annie slowly wake up, begin to cry, and pacify herself by putting a trembling thumb in her mouth. We wondered how many times there simply weren't enough ayahs to soothe the babies. We wondered how many times Annie's cries to communicate her needs had gone unheard. When looking at development, months—even years—can be deducted from the chronological age of a child. Sara spoke to her assessment of 17-month-old Tanya in the Eastern European orphanage:

I felt she was at least 6 months behind, developmentally. She was not walking. She was not talking. She was scooting around on her butt. I immediately saw her stubbornness. I was trying to get her to stack blocks. I wanted to see how her fine and gross motor skills were. She didn't want to stack blocks. When I would stack a block, I would say, "Mama stack block." I would try to get her to stack a block. She would throw it across the room. So I'd go and get the block and say, "Mama stack block."

She threw it across the room again. (Chuckles.)

When a child's developmental delays are understood, your expectations of behaviors are likely to be more realistic. And keep in mind that immediate impressions can be misleading. Some children, because of short-term medical illnesses (such as ear infections), the effects of malnutrition (such as anemia), jetlag, and the shock of the new placement, may behave very differently during the first hours and days than after these issues have been addressed. Sophie vividly recalled first meeting her baby girl in China:

We got her on a Monday, and she slept almost 100 percent of the time and would not look at us. She would not sit up unsupported. I thought we had a retarded child. Her head was floppy. Food fell out of her mouth. I thought, "Oh my God, we have an 11-month-old baby who cannot sit up."

By Friday, it was clear that she could almost walk, and that she liked us. By Friday, she had decided that we were okay.

I think she had been in total shock. I think she was absolutely horrified. She had been taken from the only home she knew. She had regressed. She didn't understand it. We looked different. We smelled different. Knowing we couldn't explain anything to her, she was hor-

thoughts from an expert

what to do first

Based on our studies here, while there are kids with significant attachment disorders, the vast majority seem to make that transition of attachment and bonding. What I see impairing that attachment are kids with, for instance, sensory processing problems where everything is a noxious stimulus. They are trying to attach to their parent, but they don't like to touch. The tag on the back of their shirt is noxious. Life is full of noxious stimuli, and until you address some of the senses that permit you to attach and bond and react positively to it, I think you may be in trouble.

The same holds true for kids who are visually or hearing impaired. If you don't address those issues, it's harder for the kids to make that attachment and bond. And it's very difficult for parents to interpret their behaviors.

I see where, when one aspect of the child is addressed, other areas begin to improve. Where you start looking at attachment issues, you start looking at sensory processing issues, and suddenly, the child's speech starts getting better. It's hard, even after all these years, to know exactly what to do first. We have a saying here for some of the kids who come into the clinic: "It's time to take them to the shop." That saying came from my early years when we would have a TV repairman come to the house and say, "It's time to take the TV to the shop." The child presents with so many problems, you just can't take care of them in one visit. Some kids really need to go to the shop.

The child needs to have a lot of different evaluations—sometimes, including a cognitive evaluation. I think knowing as much information in as many areas as you can will help the parent be effective.

Dana Johnson, M.D., Ph.D.
professor of pediatrics, director of the Neonatalogy Division,
and director of the International Adoption Clinic, University of Minnesota

rified. Everything was different—the language. Everything. It must have been just awful for her. Sometime around Friday, I was holding her in my lap and I heard this very funny noise and couldn't figure out what it was. I turned her around and realized she was laughing. That's when she decided we were okay.

Obtain as much information as you can about the child's history and current needs. You've passed the home study and now you're in the waiting phase. You feel that you have an invisible child out there who is waiting for you to be her parent. Then the next step happens. You have referred child. This is the time of the matching, a critical time.

If you are in the pre-placement phase or pre-finalization phase, make sure you aggressively take steps to get as much information about the child as possible. For public domestic adoptions, call a case conference or staffing, a meeting where the various professionals who have dealt with a child will be present. Don't feel rushed. Take your time. Read the information carefully. Ask about discrepancies in the files. Ask which person has spent the most time with the child, speak with this person. Try to get to know as much as you can about the daily life of this child and what strengths and weaknesses the child has. Ask about historical periods when little information was available. Track the child's life, if possible. Slow the process down, if need be.

Ask for copies of the child's files for your own records. Ask questions. Take copious notes and demand answers in writing. Refer to this information as the child matures and issues arise. This information will not only help you parent more effectively, it will also help future service providers as they work with your child. So much is happening at this stage that writing information down and receiving written information will help in future years, when memories fade.

Material should include case notes (chronological information) as well as medical and mental health files. Ask for reports from educational, medical, and mental health testing, if applicable. Ask for school records, pictures, social security cards, and birth certificates. The caseworker may have these documents, or the previous or current caretakers (foster parents) may have them. If the relationship with the birthparent or family still exists, some early family history may also be available to you. Keep contact information current in case you discover gaps in the post-adoption period.

To protect yourself, it's a good idea to sign for receipt of written disclosure information—actual reports whenever possible rather than summarization—and your signature should be witnessed by agency personnel. You should be retained one copy of these documents; one copy should be retained by the adoption agency; and one copy should be retained in the court file.

Be sure to take advantage of the early intervention program in your state. These programs are free and will give you excellent assessments of your child's needs. The baseline first assessment will also allow you to follow your child's progress.

In international adoptions, request medical histories through your agency, and arrange to speak with the physicians abroad. If you have a videotape of the child or other records, contact international clinics here for input from medical professionals.

Also, take into consideration the normal growth patterns of children in the country of birth. Annie was a very tiny infant by American standards, but fairly normal sized by Indian growth charts. Most

listen to the risks

After the initial counseling, you get into a situation of an actual referred child. After the referral, when we talk about the individual risk factors of a child, the parent will listen to you more. Now sometimes, they'll look at the picture and decide that she's the cutest thing they've ever seen in their lives. They can't imagine living without her. They don't want to hear my concerns about the risks I see. They'll say, "Well, we can handle that." Well, no.

Then it's time to be a little more forceful with one's opinion. So I make sure they understand what they may be getting themselves into. I think there is some validity to considering the age of the child. I think that even though the child's risk factors might be lower, there are still risks. There are biological risk factors. There are environmental risk factors. The child may have been exposed to alcohol. She may have been premature. She may have been growth-retarded. All those things are going to put a child at risk. No child is at zero risk.

This happened twice yesterday. I looked at the medical history of a child and it said, "Mother drank during pregnancy." So I said, "Sometimes a kid looks great. They are growing fine. They have no facial features that indicate problems." But I'll add, "You know there is a possibility that there might be some impairment."

Other times, kids are small, and I'm really concerned. I will say, "Do not adopt this child unless you feel you can parent a child with fetal alcohol syndrome." The child might be fine—but again, it's setting the expectations so that they're reasonable.

I think parents need to prepare for the worst—hope for the best, but prepare for the worst. Most of the time, they're not going to have to worry about the worst-case scenario.

Dana Johnson, M.D., Ph.D.

thoughts from an expert

securing a pediatrician

After a child was referred to a family, I would advise them to find a doctor. Then take the child's information to their first visit. For families that didn't do this, the first visit with the pediatrician was with the child. That change—the parents meeting the doctor before the child came home—made a big difference because the parents knew the physician [and could decide whether they liked the pediatrician before introducing the child]. Being able to meet and talk about the potential needs of the child without the child being present is very helpful.

*Karin Price, B.S.W.,
regional coordinator of
Dillon International, Inc.*

agencies and international medical clinics have growth charts to share with you, so be sure to compare your child's size with what is most appropriate.

The cultural practices of infant- and childcare should also be taken into account when assessing the child. For example, at one time in Korea most babies were carried on the backs of foster and birthparents. Therefore, Korean babies who were adopted tended to be a little more delayed with gross motor skills because they hadn't been placed on the floor or in a playpen to crawl.

Take your self-inventory and see if your strengths and weaknesses match what you know about this child. See chapter 14 on page 212. The "Pre-adoption (and post-referral) Support" questions as well as the "Family Survey" will help you to better access the available information about your child as well as assess your family's ability to assume the care of this child.

Educate yourself on the potential and real emotional, medical, and developmental challenges facing your child. Unlike a couple that is expecting a child through pregnancy, the adoptive couple's ties to the healthcare community are not ready-made. Indeed, there are (usually) no baby classes taken at the local hospital and no postpartum visits to make. You are, in many respects, on your own in terms of post-placement healthcare. So it's up to you to act preemptively to understand health issues you may face and to find the right pediatrician.

The American Academy of Pediatrics recommends a roster of screening tests for infectious diseases for internationally adopted children. In addition to a thorough medical exam, the physician will also perform developmental screenings, vaccination titers (or repeat vaccinations), and other laboratory tests on your child. The pediatrician also has another important role in this day of managed care: referring you and your child to specialists. (See chapter 14 on page 212 for more information.)

Prepare yourself. Read about these topics: adoption; attachment and bonding; post-institutionalization and its effects; normal growth and development; grief and loss (to address both yourself and your child's needs); and special needs literature.

New words may be presented to you by professionals. Try not to be intimidated by them. Your healthcare professional is responsible for explaining medical terminology as well as test results so that you may become an informed parent (see the glossary on page 226) or the resources section on page 232.

Empower yourself through a team of professionals. If you begin to suspect that your child has special medical, emotional, or developmental needs, begin to assemble a team of professionals. This team can include teachers, daycare workers, a pediatrician, a child psychiatrist, a therapist, a social worker, a physical therapist, an occupational therapist, an audiologist, and an optometrist—whoever is needed. There are some important points to remember as you gather this team and work with them.

First, make sure you, the parent, are the person leading this team. Each professional has a special role in helping to meet your child's needs, but they need to respect that you are the parent of this child and therefore you have the most complete information about him. We don't see loving a child as having a bias; we see it as completing the child's history to the world.

The second point to remember when working with a team of professionals is that each one has been educated, and is experienced with a certain set of diagnoses. The university they attended may have

thoughts from an expert

empowering you as the parent

The concept of professional support requires that the professionals honor the parents as the experts on their child and that they are the ones in the driver's seat. They have the greatest responsibility. They have the greatest understanding of that child, the greatest source of information. The rest of us are there in support roles to help them as the parents of the child. Empowering the parent is terribly important in our interventions with adoption to make sure the parents experience the sensation of being the parent. Anything that is empowering like that is really an antidote to depression.

Barbara Rila, Ph.D.,
private practitioner

instilled within them philosophies about growth and development that will also influence which diagnoses they are more apt to assess in your child. For example, a speech–language pathologist may diagnose expressive and receptive language disorder, while a developmental pediatrician may conclude that the child has autism. Or a child may be diagnosed with attention deficit/hyperactivity disorder, when in fact they are sensory seeking, and will respond to interventions such as a weighted vest that will help them become more aware of their body movement in space.

We want to again emphasize how important it is to find therapists who understand adoption. The assessment of your family's needs will be much more accurate if the therapists understand loss, separation, and grief, as well as how those emotions translate into developmental needs.

Who sees the child as a whole being? You, the parent, must form a partnership with an experienced clinician who can piece the needs of your child back together, taking care of her as a whole person. Having to tease out what may be attachment issues and what may be other neurological or processing disorders further compounds your task. Yet the correct evaluation done by a competent and caring professional can save you and your child time, heartache, and frustration.

chapter 5

the emotional needs of your child

Ask any professional in the adoption community about adoption issues and they will tell you how much we currently know about how adoption affects the child—and what we continue to discover. What is talked about less is how adoption impacts the entire family. Your child is experiencing the world through his own unique eyes. By understanding your child's needs—needs that may include difficulty attaching and bonding, an "anniversary response," grief, loss, and stress—you will gain an understanding of how the experience of adoption has influenced your child, and thus, your family.

We emphasize the importance of the *process* of helping your child make sense of her adoptive experience. A process is not a frozen moment of epiphany. It includes many moments of insight, occasional setbacks, and movement through time toward your goals. This process evolves through triggers—rites of passage, cognitive and emotional needs, and the intimate conversations mom, dad, sister, and brother have about adoption. This chapter is devoted to making you more aware of how your child—the child who has come to your home through adoption—sees her world.

your expectations about the emotional needs of your child

"My child will like me, attach to me, and learn to love me."

There are many books that address the dynamics of the child's attachment and bonding, but few have explored how the lack of a child's attachment and bonding create feelings in the parents. These feelings can manifest themselves as confusion, anger, rejection, and deep sadness. Many parents believe that if they love enough, their child will reciprocate that love. Many times the child learns to respond, but there are also times when intervention is necessary. Your child comes to you with months, perhaps years, of learning how *not* to trust in others. Logically, you understand this; but if attachment is delayed, it can be nearly impossible for you to depersonalize this lack of attachment.

Esther confided to her support group how it felt to feel rejected after years of living with her daughter, Linda. She and her husband had adopted the child 4 years before, when Linda was 3. Now Esther lives with her anger, which has created a power struggle between her and her daughter:

> It hurts. She turned to me and said, "You're not my mother anymore. I don't like you." I had just had it with her. I told her, "Fine. You will give us our name back. You will not be a part of the family. If you reject me, you reject the family."
>
> Then she tested that on my husband, whom I hadn't said a word to. She announced at the dinner table that she didn't want me as her mother anymore. He echoed everything I had said to her: she would give up the last name and not live here.
>
> We never heard another word about it. But she constantly tells me, "I don't trust you." I answer her, "I don't trust you either. You haven't earned my trust."

At times, children will attach to one parent more than the other. This preference for your partner can be painful. You're torn between the relief that your child has been able to bond to another and feelings of being alone and confused because that person wasn't you.

"My child will be as happy as I am."

You've waited months, years for this child. The anticipation of finally welcoming your child home is filled with joy. Her room awaits her. You have painted, wallpapered, purchased furniture, and changed your life to make everything ready for this child. But wait. She looks so sad. She's crying. She's confused. This holiday was supposed to be so happy for the family. Why is your child sullen and unhappy at Halloween/ Thanksgiving/Christmas/her birthday?

Perhaps you thought things were going well. Your child had adjusted and her behavior had improved dramatically. Now, suddenly, she is exploding again, acting inappropriately in public, and crying for no reason. You're lost and wondering what is going on.

Anniversary responses to placement or other traumas can trigger unexpressed sadness in your child. She probably doesn't understand it herself and acts out the way children do—through behavior. In some cases, she may have been placed so many times that she has lost track of those specific events and focuses on birthdays and holidays, traditional family times, to express how she feels through her behavior.

Your child may also come into your home with some chronic levels of stress and depression, feelings that are rooted in years of struggle. Responding to her past environments, the child has coped by using skills that were appropriate to that setting; yet behavioral changes (responses to perceived threats) could not alter her stress, depression, and anxiety (generalized fear).

If your child is older, she comes with a past that is one of the most

---

thoughts from an expert

anniversary reaction/response

On the first anniversary of the placement, the child may reexperience the trauma of placement. And that can happen for many years after placement. They sense that anniversary. I think the anniversary can be felt forever. If they act out with bad behavior, that decreases as they get older because they learn how to deal with it. But for lots of children, the feeling goes on for the rest of their lives.

I explain it to parents in this way: It's almost like when there is a death in the family and the particular date is forgotten. But the next year, that month comes around and that feeling of melancholy comes up and you don't know why. Then suddenly you realize, "Oh my gosh. That's when my dad died." But you don't consciously acknowledge the reason at first. You subconsciously know it.

When this mystery is solved, parents feel much better. The child's behavior is understandable.

Debbie Joy, M.S.,
private practitioner

significant influences on her present ability to feel and enjoy happiness. The joy of childhood may have been, at best, interrupted; at worst, that joy never existed. All human beings have basic needs in order to sustain life: oxygen, water, and food top the list. But there is also the need to feel safe. A chronic lack of feeling safe may be at the root of your childs inability to live a happy life in her new family.

---

thoughts from an expert

levels of stress in the adopted child

We've been collecting data on cortisol, a stress hormone, and the data are preliminary and complicated in some sense. But both our data and data that other people have collected show that many kids who are adopted have a chronically high level of cortisol in their systems. This indicates that they're stressed, depressed, afraid, and so on—after they've been adopted.

What we've observed, at least in 1 year of our camp (Camp Hope), is that during second week, those levels dropped off dramatically. You also consistently see the change behaviorally that second week. Two years ago, we had a really nice, clear picture—very dramatic. It's just like there is a switch. Parents will literally say, "I can't believe this is my child."

Sometimes kids who haven't been speaking will start to speak. Kids who haven't been looking at their parents—we work a lot on eye contact—start looking at their parents. Kids who haven't been hugging their parents start to hug. It's really mind-boggling. We don't tolerate nonsense, but the central, core feature of the camp is to create an environment of felt safety.

Parents think they have a safe home because intruders can't come in, there is plenty of food, and so on. But it's not safe because it's not comfortable. The children are afraid. And they're afraid because they don't understand the rules of the game, and usually they are at odds with their parents. And they sense their parents' fear, too.

The breakthrough can be permanent if the parents know how to sustain it. We have tried to bring education and service along with the research so that we can help the parents learn. And that's been one of the biggest changes in our program: trying to find ways to help. We're not a clinic. It's primarily a research project. We only have so much time and resources, so we have to find efficient ways to try to help.

David Cross, Ph.D., associate professor of psychology,
director of the Developmental Research Laboratory,
and director of Camp Hope at Texas Christian University

"My child's needs will be the same as those of other children."

There are a multitude of parenting books that teach us about development and the "normal" milestones of children. As we've discussed, with time you will understand what needs your child may have. Multiple placements and damaging caregivers can leave a child with multiple and complex behaviors—behaviors that overwhelm you, frighten you, and fill you with a sense of hopelessness.

But what about the tea parties? What about throwing the ball in the backyard? As with any child, adoptees need to be kids. Their play is their work. That's what they need to do, despite other needs that may exist or develop.

The evaluations by experts, the hours of therapy and tutoring, on top of just keeping a household running, can make us forget that playing is important to the child and to you. When you play, the child begins to know you. You are reminded of why you wanted to parent and of the joy parenting can bring.

Yet there may have been so many disappointments, so many celebrations gone wrong. Perhaps your child has accused you of horrible acts. Your resentment builds upon your anger. The child takes on the persona of a saboteur. A cycle forms. You become defensive when planning special events, anticipating that your child may act out. All of your strategies have failed up to this point. And on top of the anger, you feel helpless to change your behavior or your child's.

At times, you don't think of your child as a child. You forget that underneath the hurt and detachment, there is a young soul. You can't get past your anger to try again. You feel a stalemate has been reached. Yet the status quo doesn't seem to make anyone very happy. You wonder where is the happy family you envisioned.

You know your child needs something, but you aren't sure anymore what those needs are, or where to find help to meet those needs. You know your needs as a parent aren't being met, either. Where has the laughter, the light-heartedness, and the solidarity of the family gone?

"My child's story is our family's story."

Photograph albums now include a new face . . . a new child . . . your child. She is part of you now and is making family history along with

what the child and parents need

What keeps us going as parents are smiles and hugs and fun interactions, playing games and so on. If you have a child who is unattached, who seems to be defiant, or who is poorly regulated, you're not getting any of the good stuff that keeps you going, basically. As parents, we have very strong needs. In normal situations, we take those needs for granted.

If you talk to parents, there are certain things that they expect that they're going to get. They don't really think of it until they're asked. But one of the things is that they'll get some joy from parenting. The other thing is that their kids will do what they ask them to do. Those are not always expectations that are met.

David Cross, Ph.D.

other family members. But her history is different. She will need to make sense of it. Her peers and the public she is exposed to will ask questions of her and she will need answers for them.

As we discussed in the first chapter, points of vulnerability exist throughout the child's life, periods when physical and mental growth spark new interest in the question "Where did I come from and how did I get here?" When the child becomes sexually aware, they begin to think of their own creation and their birthparents.

Lee Anne spoke eloquently about her daughter, Erika, now 11 years old, who was adopted from Haiti at 8½ months old. Lee Anne and her husband are Caucasian and have a child by birth, a son who is 18 years old. Lee Anne related an experience that enlightened her as to the impact of Erika's personal history:

Erika's birthmother was very ill when she had her. Even though we never could get a death certificate, there is documentation that after she signed the relinquishment papers, she probably passed away. In some ways, knowing that information has been good. There is closure. But in some ways, it's really hard. Erika doesn't know for certain, and she wonders about her mother. So we have those issues.

For example, my father passed away when Erika was 5. It was difficult because we were living in China at the time, and we weren't going to be able to come back to the States as a family. Only I was going to be able to come back. The day he passed away, we were talking about it and crying. My son, who was about 12 at the time, said, "I'm really going to miss playing Monopoly with Grandpa." It was a game they always played together.

Erika said, "Do you think he's met my birthmom yet?"

I thought, "For us, this was our first loss." My husband's parents are still living. But for her, this was her second loss. This loss immediately made her think of her birthmom and whether Grandpa had met her. We couldn't have known about Dad for 30 minutes.

I answered her, "You know, Erika, you were so precious to him, I'm sure he has met her."

coping strategies

There are layers to understanding the dynamics of your child's attachment to you. One layer is an appreciation of the dynamics of how adoption has affected your child. Educating yourself is critical, and here's how to begin the process.

Empathize with your child and her view of the world. Susanne, a 57-year-old mental health professional, and her husband, Larry, adopted two children 25 years ago. Suzanne and Larry were self-professed products of the idealism of the 1960s and influenced by the egalitarian philosophy of the Quaker faith. Susanne shared her thoughts on how her family life had developed with her children. She told us how, in hindsight, she understood a bit more about how Emily's placement into their family might have affected her:

We received Emily at 9 months, and we had this huge house with hardwood floors and 10-foot ceilings. We were in a neighborhood where kids were in and out, and it was very open. Our older kids were running around, and we had a big porch. Emily wasn't walking yet, but I would put her in

---

thoughts from an expert

questions surface

When children first start school, they figure out that not everyone is adopted, or that most parents look like their kids in terms of physical characteristics. I receive a lot of calls on kids who are 9 because [children's] thinking changes into abstract thinking between 8 and 9. So the story the child believed about how they came to be in the home doesn't wash anymore. She's saying, "That girl is 16 and she's raising her baby." Or he's saying, "There are poor people in this city, and they're raising their kids. How come I was adopted?"

The beginning of the teenage years, around 14, is also a very challenging time. Again, they're questioning their place in the home. Early adulthood, that emancipation age—18 or 19—when they're trying to separate from their parents and leave home is also stressful.

Debbie Joy, M.S.

the middle of the living room, and she would sit there and not move. She was just an adorable child, and she's a very attractive woman now.

But she would sit there and look around. She was very, very quiet. And as we lived with her and tried to incorporate her into our family, she became more and more quiet. She emerged from that, and my theory is at that point in time, she was going through all this awareness that she no longer had the family she had bonded with. She decided at that point—I think it was about the time she was a year old—that this world was not a good world to be in, and she was going to fight it every inch of the way. And boy, did she ever.

Children who have spent time in institutions or have experienced multiple placements have challenges from a young age that are difficult to appreciate at times. Yet learning about those early environments, and how the child's needs were met there, is critical to understanding your child's behaviors. Imagine for a moment that a hungry, crying baby is left for hours. Picture multiple hands—loving hands—holding the child, each caregiver smelling different, sounding different, and feeling different.

Try to think of all the times a mother and father pick up their infant and toddler to soothe, to scold, to direct, to play, and to love. Now contrast this with a child in a place without that consistent nurturing. Imagine silence, coldness, and fear. Feel the rejection as foster parents are changed time and time again. Hear the taunting of peers because they realize you're different, mock how you dress, and wonder why you have no parents at school functions.

Children who have attachment issues or have been diagnosed with reactive attachment disorder view people and things differently than their parents and the people in their new world. The child's early life circumstances can force a perverted hierarchy of emotional investment.

Look for signs of depression in your child. Because of all they have experienced, depression in adoptive children is not uncommon. Keep in mind that depression in children manifests itself differently than in adults. Normal activities that were once enjoyable now leave the child flat. When depressed, children often function below their level of potential. This subpar level is evidenced from preschool through high school.

In younger children, the child may also regress developmentally

attaching to people

A ttachment is a core issue and within that, a deeper core issue is making people salient.

For unattached kids, things are more important than people. If you think about infancy, infants don't care about objects. They care about their mother. They care about their primary caretaker. That's who they like to look at. That's who they like to listen to. In a sense, you're duplicating what's happening in infancy. So one core strategy is that you replace a world of objects or a world in which objects are the most important things with a world in which people are the most important things. There are a lot of families in which objects are more important than people.

You have to be very careful with behavior modification since the rewards are *things*. You don't use rewards or tokens until you've established the importance of people. Sometimes, you don't have a choice, particularly in the case of a single-parent family where the parent cannot take off work for any length of time. Sometimes, you have to make compromises. But the ideal situation is, somehow, you want to make people the most important thing.

The other important issue is that everything is explicit. There are no secrets. You talk about exactly what you're doing and why you're doing it, all the time. One of the deficits that our kids have is that they don't connect their mental world of words with their mental world of actions. We know what to expect with normally developing kids by the time they're in third, fourth, and fifth grade. You can say "it's now time to do X, Y, and Z," and they go off and do it. Or "I expect you to do this," and they do it. There is a natural connection between words and actions.

You very often see that those connections aren't there with children who are adopted and have these atypical developmental pathways. Lots of times, their behavior is interpreted to mean that they did not want to do something, but it's simply that they were not able to. This connection emerges out of healthy parent/child interactions. As kids develop in infancy and toddlerhood and so on, there is a parallel between what is being said and what is being done; a mother or a father is talking about what is being done at the same time that they're doing it. And so the connection is developed naturally, but that connection hasn't developed with some of these children.

David Cross, Ph.D.

when distressed or depressed. For example, when a new sibling is introduced into the home, the child may have to relearn previously mastered skills, such as toilet training. Again, for these children, the parents' actions are more important than their words. For example, the more you play with your child, the smoother the transition for her. The young child communicates through play.

If this is your first child, it may be difficult for you to know how to play with her. The bottom line is: Spend time with the child. You don't have to be an expert in play. Take your cues from the child and follow her lead in how she plays. A room full of newly purchased toys may not immediately interest your child. She may select a play item that surprises you. Something that seems old or uninteresting to you, she may find absolutely terrific. For example, one child ignored the toys in his room and found mud a delightful, sensory, tactile substance. The mother, who tended to be very fastidious, was dismayed at the mess, but compromised by buying clay for her son.

The child may feel anxiety, in addition to depression. To an untrained clinician this may appear to be attention or hyperactivity problems. The child may be jittery or have trouble sitting still. Some children become more obsessive in response to anxiety. They may become more "clingy" and hard to separate (if there is a bond between parent and child). Often, these behaviors trigger annoyance in the adults around them. When depression is assessed, the parent is usually more empathetic.

In structured settings when anxiety is present, the child will show more difficulty concentrating on tasks at hand, such as schoolwork. Sleep may be disrupted to some degree, and the child may appear to be tired. She may be unaware of the sleep disturbance (she may wake and return to sleep repeatedly through the night), and therefore she doesn't tell the parent about the problem. Disruption of dietary habits and the introduction of new foods can also trigger stress in your child. Consider what type of diet the child has been used to eating to help decide if this could be a factor in the anxiety.

The child may be angry and unable to verbalize how she feels. You may see her as oppositional, yet inside she may be a very sad child. Avoid making assumptions and drawing conclusions based on difficult behavior until you've ruled out depression in your child. By doing this, you'll be saving you and your child a lot of pain.

The earlier these behaviors are assessed, the more effectively they can be addressed. Be proactive; be aware that the immediate changes in the environment will be very stressful for your child. Expect anxiety and some depression, and openly communicate with your child.

De-personalize your child's reaction to you. Immediately after placement, you and the environment are new to your child. She may react to you with a variety of emotions: shyness, sullenness, anger, eagerness, or joy. Your child may also reject you—at least for a time. She is reacting to the change, not necessarily to you.

That being said, it is natural for a mother or father to feel a sense of personal rejection when their child repeatedly ignores or fails to reciprocate their love. Certainly, a parent's first reaction to this rejection is an emotional one. But you have to understand that the foundation of life has been different for your child. It's important for you to find ways to protect yourself and your child from some of your reactions when you've been pushed away again and again and again.

- Don't withdraw from your child, but detach enough to think clearly, behave responsibly, and act effectively toward your child. You are also emotionally protecting yourself; you're not putting your emotional self out there for your child to reject in times of escalating behaviors. Set your expectations early and consistently, but don't stop loving, and don't let yourself lose control.
- If you feel yourself losing control or having repeated thoughts of striking or hurting the child, *seek professional help immediately*.
- Time-outs can be as much for the benefit of the parent as for the child, at times. The physical break and separation from your child will allow you time to regain your composure and to think about what triggered the time-out. Time-outs are a great learning opportunity for parents and children. The aftermath of the time-out is also a wonderful opportunity to nurture, teach, and soothe. Beyond the occasional time-out for discipline, you may find you need time away from your children for your own sake. Using babysitters to provide you a respite can be a very important part of your approach to parenting.

Help create the child's history. The child has a history that needs to be processed, made sense of, celebrated, and grieved. Particularly with closed and international adoptions, the gaps in history can overwhelm a child. Processing the experience of adoption is an ongoing,

therapeutic quasi-detachment

A parent who is very emotionally connected will usually be less effective than a parent who can be emotionally detached when faced with the emotions of their child. The reason for that is that these kids will push your emotional buttons. They'll make you angry. They'll frustrate you. They'll make you despair.

And you've got to continue to love and you've got to continue to be a parent, but you have to pull back emotionally. You have to become a therapist, really. It's to protect the parent; it's to protect everybody.

What we've seen in a few cases with this downward spiral is an escalation of violence. Unfortunately, we've had to report a couple of families. One of the things we learned right away is never to blame the parents. It is a very, very difficult challenge. Never blame. But sometimes, the parents get pushed right to the edge.

So you, the parent, may be more effective and able to provide a safer environment if you can become quasi-detached. You really have to continue to care, but you have to make it so that you are not reacting emotionally. It is counter-intuitive: People seem to act as if you need to influence the way that people deal emotionally by being emotional. But that's not the way to do it. Again, how we interact with infants is a great model.

Think about an infant. What happens probably thousands of times during infancy is that the infant is upset: they're hungry, tired, cranky, or hot. They get upset; they might cry and then they are soothed. But how do we soothe them? Well, we talk to them, but the words really have no meaning. It's a voice. It's the soothing nature of our voice. It's the hold and it's the comfort, the rocking or whatever it might be. So we soothe them through our actions and we soothe them by staying detached. If they get upset, we don't get upset.

So it's the same thing with these kids. Obviously, we don't do exactly the same thing. But in general, the principles are the same. Through our actions. Through our words. But it's not the content of the words that is going to do it. It's the tone of voice and what we do. We teach parents to have a very simple and consistently applied set of rules for emotional circumstances. We're working with a single mom right now whose little boy is pretty aggressive. He's really sweet and he really loves his mom, but he acts aggressively a lot. We tell her this is a zero-tolerance thing. Every time this happens you do X, Y, Z. Be consistent about it. Don't get upset. This is just what you do. Time-out. If he can't do time-out by himself, then he has assisted time-out where she stays with him. If he can't go to time-out, then he goes to a restraining hold.

David Cross, Ph.D.

lifetime experience for many. Some are desperate to fill the voids. Effective ways of doing this are through family discussions, grief counseling, heritage camps and ethnic resources, and tools such as lifebooks.

Lee Anne and Erika, who came from Haiti to live with her adoptive family, share open and frank discussions about their losses and love:

> *Erika said to me the other day, "You know, if God is such a good God, why couldn't he have kept my birthparents alive and doing well, and I could be with them?"*
>
> *How do you argue with that? I don't know.*
>
> *But one thing that has been helpful is a lifebook. I started it before Erika even came home. When she was about 4 or 5 years old, that book helped a lot. There was information in there at her level. It was a story, her story. We would read it at night. It begins when my husband and I got married, how each child joined our family. Then it talks about me going to Haiti and making that decision to bring Erika home. It also has copies of her adoption paperwork. It's in a three-ring binder.*
>
> *It's more like a scrapbook now with decorations. Erika can take out personal pages when her friends come over. So if she has a new friend, she can say, "Well, let me show you my book." Then she'll go and read the book to them. Sometimes, she'll take out the stuff about her birthmother. Sometime, she leaves it in if she's showing it to someone she really knows.*

The lifebook allowed Erika to begin making sense of her adoption. First, the book was tangible—you could feel it, touch it. Second, the binder format allowed her to determine the boundaries of her trust in those around her, giving her control in an area that is so very public at times. A lifebook can be as involved or as simple as you and your child need it to be. As they grow older, the authorship can be transferred from the parent to the child.

Other parents take advantage of their trips abroad to bring home future keepsakes of the child's original homeland. Sara, adoptive mother to Tanya and a son (domestic adoption), knew each of her children would have questions about their birth families.

> *I knew my son's chances of finding his birthmother were probably greater than Tanya's, so I tried to learn as much as I could about her country and its culture and history, prior to going to get her. One of*

the things we tried to do was to experience her culture and experience her country. My friend suggested that we buy things from her country to give to her at different times of her life, and we did.

We brought home a toddler costume that we had bought from the area Tanya was born in. For her seventh birthday, we have a doll in a costume. For her sixteenth birthday, she has a ring made of Russian gold. For her wedding, we have a tea set. And for her first child, we have an embroidered outfit from the town where she was born. That's so important to me. I feel that everyone has to have a beginning. I'm sure one day we'll visit this country with her.

Elaine is the birthmother to 5 children and adoptive mother to 12 more. She was matched with a 5-year-old boy of Native American descent and shares this story of how her son came to accept his home, and begin creating his own history with her and her other children, his brothers and sisters:

This child had really pushed me. I mean I didn't know if I would survive this kid. But let me back up a minute. His birthfather had kept his brother Robbie, a full sibling. (Elaine rolled her eyes.) Don't ask me why.

Well, it was time for the adoption to be finalized. You know how the kid can rename himself once he's adopted? Well, he couldn't come up with a name.

Finally, one day, he came up to me and said, "I know what I want my name to be."

I said, "What?"

He said, "Robbie. Cause 'Robbie' is a name for kids you don't give away."

[Elaine began to cry.]

For the kinship parent, the family's history has been altered, somehow skipped. Even when a birth parent remains present in the family, questions surface; confusion is expressed more as the child becomes aware of the dual role of the mother and father. This isn't necessarily role confusion—the child seems to be one of the first people who understand who her mother and father are. She is processing the family structure.

This leaves the kinship parent to sort through the questions, to decide what to tell the child and when, and to try to explain how their own birthchild or a step-child experienced life in such a way that they could no longer parent effectively. Candice deals with the questions her 7-year-old daughter (birth grandchild) puts forward:

In all actuality, Mallory has been a joy to us. But learning how to deal with a little child in these days, in these times, and trying to explain it all to her can be difficult. She's at an age now where she asks questions and doesn't understand that great-grandmother is my mother and then she'll ask, "Why am I your daughter?" Mallory doesn't understand the concepts.

We went to see a counselor, and she advised me to talk to Mallory about my sadness because sometimes, I would just start to cry because I didn't have any relationship with Amber [Candice's daughter and Mallory's birthmother] and because things had changed so much. The counselor said, "Tell her. Tell her why you're crying. Tell her why you're sad and what makes you sad. Work with her."

So we have a pillow that we beat on when we get angry. For example, if Amber cancels a visit, I would cry because it hurt Mallory. And I tell Mallory, "Mommy is just very upset because Amber was supposed to come and visit you."

Now Mallory is starting to understand more. Before, she would want to cry or get angry, but she would try to hold it in. But now she's able to let me know, "I'm throwing a fit and screaming and hollering because I can't believe Amber didn't come again and it hurts."

holding therapy and restraining holds

Holding therapy covers a wide range of activities (including touching, holding, and massaging the child) and a wide range of techniques and settings. The goals of these types of interventions are to promote bonding and attachment; allow the child to express pent-up fear, anger, or grief; show a positive model of touch; and stimulate development. One therapist may see holding therapy as anything from parent/child cuddle time with a child sucking on candy (or otherwise orally stimulated) to therapist-assisted holding of a child during a counseling session. Much of the intensity of the holding is dependent upon the needs and history of the child. Again, a professional can inform you about the techniques and contexts of holding therapy.

Therapeutic holds, sometimes referred to as restraining holds, can be used when the child has lost control and needs to be physically restrained for her own or her parent's protection. You need to be trained by a clinician to safely do this type of hold.

Find an adoption buddy. Many experts agree that finding an adoption buddy—another parent that you can create a support system with—is invaluable. Some parents communicate through e-mail, which has the advantage of privacy. However, Internet relationships lack the intimacy of face-to-face contact. Another important consideration: Your adoption circumstances do not necessarily have to be identical to your buddy's (international, wait time, and so on). The validation of feelings, sharing strategies toward positive outcomes, and having a caring listener are what will provide you with the support you need, no matter what your unique paths to adoption.

In fact, even if you do share some similarities with your adoption buddy, remember that each adoption experience is different. What was an easy step for your buddy may cause a lot of frustration for you. A buddy can provide a frame of reference, but not a crystal ball of what your experience will be.

Ideally, one buddy should be a little farther along in the process so that she can share her experiences and advise you on what she may have found to be successful. Primarily, an adoption buddy releases you from the secrecy and isolation that you may be experiencing. It builds on your motivation to make things better. This person is safe. Make sure, however, that your adoption buddy will embrace your efforts to build your family in a positive way.

Buddies can be matched by adoption agencies, social workers, or by adoptive parents themselves. Online discussion groups often make it possible for members to continue discussions privately. Post-adoption support groups can also offer opportunities to meet others in your situation. Good adoption buddies are not quite family, but they are more than friends. They are confidantes joined by common experiences and feelings; with them you will create a relationship that is hard to replicate with other people. Because shared territory already exists, time and energy is conserved, especially in crisis situations. The buddy understands what it's like to be part of a family grown through adoption. As one mother said, "My daughter was 15 months old before I reached out to another adoptive mom. And she immediately validated me: 'Yeah! I felt like that.'"

Vigilantly support your child's need to process her adoption. As we've discussed, anniversary reactions or responses may come at times that are confusing to us, especially when they are responses to placements that we may not even be aware of. But they can also be anticipated and discussed, as in the cases of birthdays and holidays. The child may be grieving losses while the family celebrates a holiday.

Another assumption in our culture is that when you make sense of an event, there is a moment of epiphany or acceptance. That particular time represents a peak of understanding that is followed by a leveling off of additional insights and finally, inner peace or acceptance. We believe the road for an adopted child is not a once-in-a-lifetime experience, but more of a process. David Cross, Ph.D., associate professor of psychology, director of the Developmental Research Laboratory, and director of Camp Hope at Texas Christian University, and an adult adoptee, articulated the ongoing nature of this process:

I'm adopted. I actually spent some time in a county home in California. This has really come full circle for me. One of the things I'm very sensitive to and have experienced in my own life—but I've seen it in the kids we work with, too—is that you come to terms with that whole business of being adopted over and over and over and over again. When I first really became clued into it was when my sister-in-law married a black man. They couldn't conceive at first. So they looked into adoption.

This couple was kind of a prized adoptive couple. They adopted a black kid who had been terribly abused. He still has scars on his body. Things went reasonably well until he was 12 or 13 and the wheels came off. We started looking into that, and it's almost universal.

So I started thinking about the reasons for it and so on, and what I came up with is that it is a function of developmental events. First, the big thing with adolescence is that there are all the hormones; and second, you actually truly understand what happened for the first time. Cognitively you can understand it. That there was some kind of moral code that was violated. And I don't think kids can really understand that until adolescence. Understanding about procreation is one of the

thoughts from an expert

being vigilant

If a parent assesses an anniversary response, I advise them to go home and write this date down on their calendar because this may happen next year and they won't remember it. So while we don't want to predict the behavior, we want to be aware of it. Next year, look for the child to demonstrate sad behaviors for a week or two around this day. It may be the official "Gotcha Day" or another day of some placement.

If the parent sees stressed, sad, or angry behaviors, then the parent might say, "You know, you might be feeling kind of anxious because this is the time of year that you came home. Sometimes kids feel sad. How did it make you feel when you left X place and came to a new family? Some kids might feel nervous. Some kids might feel sad."

And then they can just talk about it. I can set my watch by my kids. It's unbelievable.

Debbie Joy, M.S.

things that biological kids and adopted kids think about early on. Something happens at the 8- or 9-year-old level; they understand [pro-creation] at some level. But I think it's the kind of sense of obligation and the sense that there are codes and all of that stuff, that is something that you think about first as an adolescent.

But for me, working with the kids at Camp Hope has been a rite

Sara and Tanya

The past 2 years have pushed Sara to her mental limit many times. She became depressed after Tanya was adopted from an Eastern European country at 18 months of age. Her self-perception changed from a desire to be the perfect parent to feeling "like some kind of monster." Sara and her husband, Steve, already had two older boys, one by birth and one by domestic adoption.

Although Sara realized that Tanya had about a 6-month developmental delay when interacting with her in the orphanage, the full extent of Tanya's behavioral and emotional difficulties didn't surface until after the family returned to the United States.

Being a private person, Sara hid how she felt about the situation and didn't feel that seeing a counselor was the right choice for her. She returned to work about 6 weeks after Tanya arrived home. Sara felt extreme emotional pressure, asking herself questions like, "Did I bite off more than I could chew? Will I have the same relationship with Tanya that I have with my boys?" In response to her stress and depression, Sara overate and gained 30 pounds.

A few months later, the family took a vacation to Florida, and Sara related how Tanya was again rejecting her by screaming and kicking as they walked along the beach. "Tears are running down my face, and I'm just saying, 'Lord, why are you doing this to me? What do I need to do to get over this? I can't stand it anymore.' I think that was a breaking point for me."

Then the answer came to her: "Sara, there will come a time when she turns to you and wants you. Right now, she needs her daddy." Sara finally "let go" and realized her time with her daughter would come.

Things at home slowly improved. After about 18 months at home, Tanya began to outgrow the "terrible twos." She also began to acquire the necessary language to express her needs. The family no longer had to play a "guessing game" that often ended with a screaming toddler.

of passage. And then having my own kids has been another rite of passage. So there can be all kinds of developmental events that people have to continually keep dealing with as they process the issues surrounding being adopted.

In some sense, it doesn't seem like people in America have a sense of process. Everything is a quick fix.

After this event, Sara began actively utilizing strategies to help her cope. Sara began confiding in a few close friends, taking the risk of sharing her struggles with them. She took a kickboxing class and lost the weight she had gained. Her sons and grandmother gave her positive feedback on her handling of her daughter, telling her how patient she was with Tanya. Hearing from others that she was doing a good job allowed Sara to reevaluate her parenting skills, skills she thought were lacking. She used time-outs successfully to allow herself and the child to regroup. Steve supported his wife and was able to complement Sara's parenting when he saw she was fatigued. She sought strength through prayer and faith. Sara also confessed to letting go of the anger she felt toward herself, and part of that anger stemmed from the expectations she'd held prior to receiving Tanya.

Sara's aunt, who had adopted three children from Eastern Europe and also had three children by birth, became Sara's adoption buddy. Talking with another adoptive parent helped Sara feel less isolated and frustrated. At work, Sara became an adoption buddy with a prospective mother who was considering adopting a child from China. Sara shared what she had been through with Tanya. Initially, the coworker felt hesitant, unsure what to do with the information. A short time later, she expressed her appreciation to Sara for having disclosed her personal journey. Finally, Sara uses humor when she can, chuckling at how she and Tanya have an understanding.

By accepting support from her family and friends, realigning her expectations (rather than repeatedly thinking "This was supposed to be a joyous time"), gaining inner strength through spiritual renewal, and taking care of her physical needs, Sara began to heal. Sara now talks about baking Christmas cookies and playing dress-up with Tanya. She says her darkest hours are behind her. And Tanya loves to be cuddled, but in her own time. According to her mom, Tanya takes a while to warm up.

chapter 6

integration into your family

How do we form our families? As we add children to our family, the family's personality changes a bit; its essence is altered by the new member's contributions. We complement one another with our unique characteristics. We dance a little differently, sing higher and lower musical notes, and keep rhythm to a new beat with each child.

This chapter will discuss our research into the factors that affect a child's integration into the family. The family is a system; one change affects the other members, and other members effect change in return. This beautiful social unit called the family is precious to our society, and we believe our future as a society lies in its preservation.

your expectations about making your child part of the family

"My child will be a good match for this family."

The way a child is matched to a family varies with different adoption paths. Clearly, in kinship adoption, the match was made biologically. A daughter, son, daughter-in-law, or son-in-law has relinquished care to you, the grandmother, grandfather, aunt, or uncle. Typically, international adoption has fewer opportunities to match, although it varies by country. Infant adoption matches are made based on the matching of birthparents with adoptive parents more often than they are based on any conscious choices about the child.

Public adoption has the greatest opportunity to match child and parent. Agencies assess the strengths and weaknesses of the child and attempt to pair these with an adoptive family's strengths and weaknesses (as well as an assessment of the community). Adoptive parents usually suggest the matching criteria because they have thought about the gender and age of the child they would like to adopt, but other characteristics are just as important to consider. For a good match, you have to think about the child's temperament; the emotional and physical needs of the child; and the history of the child. The public adoption system is recognizing that gender, age, and even location shouldn't drive the match. Much progress has been made toward erasing geographic lines (regional and state boundaries) that may have previously hindered a parent/child match. Sometimes matching is not given the attention it deserves because the availability of a child may sway you toward a decision that may not be what is best for you or the child. Keep in mind that just because a child of the gender and age you were looking for is suddenly available does not mean that this child is necessarily right for your family, or that another child who doesn't meet those criteria is not. We encourage you to look at the "bigger picture" of your family and not be steered only by the child's demographic traits. Rather, open yourself to the uniqueness of the child and how she could become a part of your family.

Elaine, a mother who adopted 12 children through the public system, commented about one of her children who was matched based on ethnic characteristics:

I have some Native American blood in me and this 5-year-old kid did, too. So they thought we'd make a good match. [Elaine rolls her eyes.] This kid, Robbie, almost outdid me. He put soap in the aquarium. He stopped up the toilet. He did everything he could to make me go crazy. This was before I had officially adopted him.

I finally took him outside the house and pointed upward. I said, "Do you see a sign up there that says 'Hotel' on it? Cause if you do,

*you need to start paying me rent—or you need to realize that there is
no sign and start acting like this is a home."*

Matching is about more than age and gender. It's about the child.

"My child will behave in a consistent manner."

Many children who have been in institutional care have acquired a significant number of skills. They have developed these skills in order to
achieve some sense of control over their lives; in order to manipulate
others to meet their needs; and to survive in a parentless, private world.

This also means that when the child comes home, these skills will
be intact and the child will consider them as useful in her new environment as she did in her old. She needs to learn different skills, but
first she needs to learn that the old skills will not work in her new
home, and that ultimately they will not be useful tools for her in her
daily life.

---

thoughts from an expert

matching

Matching is about getting to know the child much more thoroughly than
we often do. Matching has little to do with sex and race and age and
more to do with personality. I don't think we help parents to think about that.
For example, a 2-year-old child may be a mean and difficult little girl and
need vast amounts of intervention. And a 6-year-old boy may be quite fine.
People tend not to get it. They assume that if they get a younger child, then
everything will be okay.

In the foster care system, we need to spend more time with the kid. Or
speak with the person who knows the child. A foster care worker who knows
the child really ought to be involved in the matching. It is the adoption worker's
responsibility to find a home for the child, but they ought to be spending a lot
of time with the child. But that means we need more workers, more people,
and more money. And we're back to budget.

But I believe that ultimately, everybody ends up where they're supposed
to be.

Regina Kupecky, L.S.W.,
coauthor of Adopting the Hurt Child *and* Parenting the Hurt Child

One old skill the child may employ is splitting the parents. While in the institution, there were few adults. Now, your child is the total focus of the family. She may feel that "dividing and conquering" may get some attention and focus off of her, and thus, some of the pressure off as well. It may work: The parents are busy trying to figure out who's right and who's wrong, and the child is no longer receiving such intense attention.

Or her behavior may be chameleonlike and change based on who is in her environment. She may act one way in the presence of one parent and an entirely different way in the presence of the other. Therapists, teachers, and other tangential people may also be charmed and awed by what a good child this is. They may think, "What is this parent's problem?"

Elaine, the adoptive mother of 12, told us about a therapy session with Robbie before he was adopted:

> *So I took him to a therapist. And we were sitting there and he decided to sit close to me, kind of cuddling. He was charming, articulate, and answered all her questions. She kept asking me, "And your issues are . . . ?"*
>
> *She obviously didn't believe there were any issues. She thought that it was me! Then Robbie, sensing that he was impressing her, puts his arm around me and calls me "Mom." [Elaine shakes her head and chuckles.] He was a pro.*

"My child will respond to my parenting style."

Our two sons, Ben and Pete, usually responded to our parenting style, which included time-outs and verbal redirection. Annie needed a different style; with her, we picked which battles were worth fighting and we were careful not to create a power struggle. We found that it was often effective to ignore her behavior and to offer her choices. But we had to learn a different approach to discipline with Annie, which was something we hadn't prepared ourselves for.

Many parents believe, as we did, that their past parenting style has served them well. Previous children in the home have been reared on a successful path to adulthood. Martha, adoptive mother to Collin, spoke about the changes she and her husband had to make in order to effectively parent Collin. Their older daughter, Melanie, was now 16 years old and on the brink of independence.

There is this sort of fantasy of a child. And since we already had a child who was really smart and talented and did what she was supposed to do, our expectations were that children were like that. Even my sister-in-law said, "You know, not everybody is like Melanie." We were patting ourselves on the back about what good parents we were and we thought negatively about people who couldn't control their kids. We would say to each other, "They need to set limits."

I am embarrassed. Melanie was so easy that that was sort of our attitude. With her, the effort as a parent was helping her practice piano and taking her to ballet lessons.

The differences in parenting Collin and Melanie definitely caused some stress for me. I think we had to really shorten our view. With a child with special needs—Collin has AD/HD and some oppositional tendencies—you can't look toward adulthood. You can't think about "When he gets into college," or "When he gets married," because it's hard to see how they're going to be successful doing those things. My husband knows he's going to be successful and that's good. But Collin's college experience may be in a different way. It's really hard to look that far in advance and see how he's going to be or what's going to happen to him.

You say you want a "happy and productive adult life" for your child. But you may still put your own spin on what "happy and productive" are. It's kind of a low-level, ongoing stress. You're not always proud of the things you say, but you're human.

Many kinship parents feel they've been given a second chance, a chance to improve their parenting and rectify any past mistakes with new parenting behavior. Joy, a 50-year-old grandmother, is raising and has legal custody of two baby boys, 1 and 2 years old. They are the children of her birth son and daughter-in-law. She has been a widow for 2 years.

I love parenting this time around. I have more patience. I've learned from past experiences what not to do. Back then, my husband was an abusive man, so I know how important the environment is. These two little boys are living in a home filled with love. I love being a single parent. I'm having so much fun. I get down on the floor and play with them. I don't allow loud voices in my house. The parents will come over for visitation, and if the two of them get into an argument, I tell them that if they're going to raise their voices, to get out. You're not allowed to yell in my home. No fighting.

But sometimes I wish I could go on vacation. The younger boy has appointments that are about 2 hours away, and I have doctor's appointments, too.

"My child will be integrated into our family."

In couples, the relationship of the parents, which is either formalized by marriage or is an informal agreement, is the foundation of the family. Ties are often strengthened when a couple begins parenting a child. But other dynamics can surface.

Some couples find, to their surprise, that after a long journey into parenting, this child isn't the solution to their problems or yearnings. Perhaps the grief of infertility or the temperament of the new child overrides the stable family functioning.

The father may not understand why his partner is suddenly so despondent. She may not be able to communicate why she has changed, why she has become such a strict disciplinarian, or why she feels so tired all the time. The father feels her style is too heavy-handed and compensates by allowing the child privileges that counter the mother's authority.

Resources are usually channeled toward the child with the most intense, acute needs, which is often the child who has been adopted. The parents are in crisis and the siblings often suffer from benign neglect. Some children withdraw into a quiet world to weather the storm, only to surface with a loud burst when a lull in the crisis is perceived. In their confusion, a child may seem uncaring or detached from the problems facing their new brother or sister. Depending on their age, they may be unable or unwilling to care. Others act out in order to receive their share of attention. The ripples of stress

thoughts from an expert

sanctity of the union

In adoption, I tend to see more divisive interactions between partners when stress and depression occur. The child has an opportunity to do the "divide and conquer" deal. What that does is to immediately stir up trouble in the marriage and undermine the sanctity of the union that put the family together in the first place. Then all of a sudden, this union is shaking on its foundation.

Barbara Rila, Ph.D., private practitioner

reach outward as old patterns have been suddenly and vigorously changed due to the new member's presence and needs.

Nancy, a 45-year-old mother, describes the dynamics between her 11-year-old daughter by birth and her 13-year-old son by adoption who had recently been diagnosed with sensory integration dysfunction, attention deficit disorder, anxiety issues, and impulsivity problems:

At times, Jennifer's life has been more stressful because of Vincent. There are times when she says very honestly, "I wish my brother were different. I wish my brother didn't have such and such. I wish my brother were like me." She is implying genetic influence because she's seen some very different behavioral and academic challenges.

But at other times, she is very proud because she can help her brother in some things. She's 2 years younger, but in other ways, she's 2 years older. So there's a real complement between the two of them and their strengths and weaknesses.

Even when she was younger, she would ask, "Why did we have to adopt him?" and I answered, "Because I wanted a baby boy."

For kinship parents, the situation may be generational. The new family takes on an identity of its own. Roles shift from grandparent to mother and father. In many cases, the child brings the role of mother and father into the family consciousness. Still, you may be put in the position of choosing between your daughter or son and the grandchild who is now your child. Candice, a 45-year-old grandmother raising Mallory, her 7-year-old granddaughter, related how it felt to make the difficult choice that evolved.

Candice's daughter, Amber, had neglected Mallory during her infancy, and Candice and her husband took over the care of Mallory when she was 18 months old. They have full custody and are fighting to adopt the little girl. According to Candice, Amber has a long history of sexual acting-out behavior. At 15 she became pregnant and when the adoption plans fell through, Candice and her husband took the baby and Amber into their home with the understanding that Amber would parent the child:

Despite all of Amber's actions, despite all the absolute hell that we had been through in trying to get help for her, raise her, despite the things she did, all the lies, I felt sorry for Amber and for the choices that she made. Even though she was given the opportunity to do better, it all boiled down to her choices. I don't know if she was molested as a child or the full extent of it; all I know is that she has shown some abnormal sexual behavior. But we had her in counseling for years.

We kept thinking, "Something has got to give here." We fought for her before Mallory ever came along. We fought for her every step of the way. We fought for her even after Mallory came along. She just didn't accept it.

I did have to make a choice. First, I had to go with the child who was the most helpless. Second, the older child had the ability to make choices. From that point, when Mallory was 18 months old, Amber made the decision to walk out the door, to be with a 28-year-old man rather than make the life that she was supposed to make. Here we were supporting her. She had her own room, her own bed, and her own clothes. Everything.

Still, she tells people I love Mallory more than I love her.

coping strategies

Keeping in mind that your family is a system, here are some ways to harmonize family members and appraise their functioning with open, honest eyes.

Acknowledge your feelings toward the child's behaviors. It's okay to feel anger, and it's okay to feel hurt. Would you be human and, given the circumstances, *not* feel these feelings? It's not your fault.

Martha, mom to 8-year-old Collin, shared with us how it felt to be the least-preferred parent and receive the brunt of her son's oppositional side:

Collin is very negative toward me: "Shut up!" "Get out of here!" "Leave me alone!" "I don't want to work." We had counseling for a year about a year ago. The counselor worked a lot on my relationship with Collin because Collin just loves his dad.

Even as a baby, he cried a lot. And he was kind of an angry child. I think that's toned down a lot because we've really worked hard with him in terms of setting limits and just accepting him for who he is.

If I had to do it over again, I would. But sometimes, I think of the path that our lives would have taken if we hadn't adopted. I think it would have been easier and more stress free, but it's a hard question. My days are not always enjoyable. But I don't know if that's how you judge success in life: if all your days are enjoyable. My days would be a whole lot better. I would be doing a lot more self-fulfilling things. I love to garden and read and do volunteer work. They might be more satisfying than dealing with a child who tells me he hates me and to go away.

However, I think if I take the longer view and believe that we are going to be successful in raising and producing a loving person who will be a successful person in society, that it will be worth it. I do think that adoption is a good thing to do and it was right. It's just that there would have been an easier path.

Admitting that parenting this child is hard can release some of that sadness. The gentler you are with yourself, the gentler you will be with your child. While there are no "easy" kids to raise, there are children who are more challenging than others.

Forgive the child and forgive yourself. Forgiving oneself can be very difficult. After expressing her feelings about raising Collin, Martha called herself "weak" and "wrong to think that way." But there comes a point in time when you have to let go to begin again. And you can't let go before you feel what it is you need to feel. Examine what is a barrier to you and this child. What past behaviors have influenced how you feel toward this child today? Has a special event or events been continually ruined by acting-out behavior? Have you been accused of being too strict or too harsh by others who see only your child's most charming and appropriate behavior? Has your anger surfaced at times, to the point of being inappropriate? Do you resent this child for how your life has changed?

Susanne, a 57-year-old mental health professional, is married to Larry, a 61-year-old writer. Twenty-five years ago they adopted two children who were biracial and younger than their two children by birth. The boy Larry and Susanne adopted committed suicide at age 18 and their adopted daughter, Emily, had difficult teenage years, becoming pregnant when she was 17. Her adolescence and adulthood have been marked by conflict with and anger toward her parents. The couple went to therapy, arranged for Emily to be admitted to an inpatient psychiatric unit for a short stay, and later, when Emily was an adult, bought her a home to live in. Larry talked about the effect this experience had on him:

I think I have probably changed as a person. I'm more accepting of people being the way they are and not being able to do much. With someone who dies, we've heard people say that things do get better over time. Life doesn't stay the same. It doesn't necessarily stay bad. I would encourage people to find ways to keep communicating with their kids even though it can be so awful. One of my colleagues gave me that advice and I thought, "You don't know what you're talking about." But I think he was right.

I think it did make me a better person to go through this. It kind of gave me a set of experiences that have made my life a lot richer. There has been something in it for me. I am more patient. I am more sensitive to the needs of others. I think we did give the children something they wouldn't have gotten elsewhere. I did give them something.

Much of our self-worth comes from how successful we are as parents. Yet our children are "on loan" to us. During this short period of time when they are "ours," we try our best to shape our children for an independent and happy life. We have to focus on the process of parenting because no matter what we do, part of the outcome is out of our control. Larry's child ultimately made the decision to end his life. In the final analysis, Larry had no control over that act.

Think in terms of reality parenting and adapt your parenting style to the needs of the child. Despite all you have been through—despite all the suffering, the waiting, the longing, and despite the love—you need to make sure you're thinking realistically. As we've discussed, we all hold the fantasy notion of the "dream child." Now we have to readjust our notion of how to parent this real child.

When Annie came to our home, we believed ourselves to be fairly competent parents. With John's background in child psychiatry, Karen's work exploring the world of special needs children, and having experience raising two birth children, we believed we were ready to parent again. We were wrong. The pitiful wailing of Annie as we drove home from the airport in the darkness of night sounded like no human utterance we had ever heard. At that moment, we realized that this was going to be different. And this difference was reinforced as we grew to understand Annie's temperament, her grief, and her needs.

reality-based parenting

We expect we're going to be so bonded to our children and that we're never going to hate them and want to throw them away. When the truth of the matter is, no matter how you come to parenting, you end up having those feelings. That is the part of parenting that we don't talk about much, which is "I could throw this kid in the trash can right now and walk away."

We'd be back in 5 seconds, though. Let's do reality. Let's not falsely sell adoption. That sale plays directly into the false expectations that drive the machinery of depression.

Barbara Rila, Ph.D.

We had to openly acknowledge that what we did before as parents was not working with this child. We had to acknowledge our own feelings toward Annie, step back, understand her behaviors in context, and move forward. Patience was often more important than love.

Play with your child and search for common interests. One of the joys of parenting is spending time with your child—playing, singing, acting silly, getting on the floor and jumping like a rabbit, giggling at funny faces, and cooking with batter-covered fingers. Sometimes, you have to dig deep inside yourself and the child to uncover those needs, put aside the past, and forget your hectic schedules. As grown-ups, it's not always easy to see the purpose in playing, but it's as important for us as it is for our children.

"You can have it all" is a fallacy, one that needs to be examined very closely as we look at family goals. You can't have it all—at least not all the time.

Sara explains what happened after her adoptive daughter, Tanya, had been home about a year (Tanya was about 3).

I think of little things that Tanya and I share now—things that I cherish. At Christmastime, I was making cookies, and I was at the counter. She pushed her little stool up next to me and said, "Watcha doing, Mommy?" I answered, "I'm making cookies." Then the phone rang and I had to answer it.

My sister was calling, and I sat down and pushed Tanya's little stool up to the table. She said, "Watcha doing, Mommy?" I said, "Mommy is talking on the phone." So she climbed up and sat on my lap.

When I was done, I went back to making the cookies. She pushed her little stool back up and said, "I make cookies?" I said yes and let her help me. It's those kind of interactions that finally made me think we were bonding.

Play teaches the child and play teaches us about the child. When playing with your child, follow a few rules:

- Let the child chose the play activity (but you have veto power if the activity is inappropriate).
- Select appropriate toys, both by age and development level and by issue (if your child is aggressive, choose nonviolent toys—meaning no guns, knives, and so on).
- Model appropriate behavior. For example, if playing with a dollhouse, model rules and behavior that reflect what you want to teach your child.
- If the child's behavior escalates, redirect them to another activity. Avoid saying, "No! Stop that." Instead, say, "Let's color now. Let me show you this picture I wanted to color."
- Learn about your child. Watch for clues about what the child has been exposed to. For example, aggressive behavior usually means they've been subjected to or have observed aggression.
- Remember, you are in charge. You can be in charge by being firm, clear, and consistent. Being in charge also means providing nurturing structure and a predictable environment. It means conveying a feeling of comfort and safety.
- Be consistent in your play times. Don't go weeks without playing with your child.
- Have fun. Enjoy it. Don't be distracted by other things you think you need to be doing. Don't worry about how to do it "right." Just enjoy your child.

Remember the emotional needs of the siblings. Children who are already in the home need to understand who this new sibling is, how she is affecting the family, and that their parents will still be there to meet their needs. They need to understand that they're not being replaced. As we've discussed, children may withdraw, act out, or become pseudo-parents. They may grab hold of authority in the home if the parent becomes unable to fulfill that role. Or they may regress to an earlier developmental stage and need retraining on formerly acquired skills.

There may also be unspoken fears, misconceptions, and confusion. Lee Anne, mom to Erika, described what her birth son, Steven, said a few weeks after Erika had come home from Haiti:

sibling perceptions

Be sure to pay attention to how your other children perceive the changes in their family.

Perceptions of Equity/Parental Love: Is the sibling feeling an inequity of love and material gifts from the parents? Is this voiced to the parent? Are you being overly vigilant in making sure all is absolutely equal between the children? Is this putting extra stress on you? Have you been able to tell your children that in the end, all will be equal even if every trip to the store may not end that way?

Perceptions of the Child: How does the sibling view her new brother or sister? Does the sibling realize this new arrangement is forever? Does the child understand what adoption is and is not? Does the sibling feel free to voice her feelings about the newly adopted brother or sister?

Perceptions of Self: Has the sibling regressed? Is she unable to do self-tasks that were once mastered? Is she more clingy and sullen? Is she louder and attention-seeking? Or has the sibling taken on a more adultlike role that is not appropriate for her age level? Why was this role taken on?

Steven was about 7 at the time. He said, "I decided I want to learn Creole." I was surprised, but thought, "This is great. He's interested in his sister's ethnicity." I told him we'd try to line something up. At that time, there weren't any Haitians in our community. But I thought I'd try to get some tapes.

I said, "I'm just curious. Why do you want to learn Creole?"

He said, "I was thinking today that if something happened to you or dad, they would probably send Erika back, and I decided I would go with her."

I thought, "We need to let him know about the will and the arrangements."

The adoption hadn't been finalized, but that was something I hadn't even thought about. So we sat down and talked about it and the arrangements. I guess you don't know what your kids are thinking.

Like any new child, your adopted child will take up more of your time and energy, especially in the short run, than your other child or children. Spend time with the existing child; emphasize how much you care and that love is an infinite resource. Tell your child that the additional love you show to the new child isn't taken from the love you hold for her. Ask the child how she views her new brother or sister.

One adult sibling of two sisters who were adopted from Korea said that the experience made him feel special. But there was also guilt about how fortunate he was to have been born to his parents and in this country. His mother would awaken him with a slide show of Korea upon her return home with each sister. And guilt spilled over into his teenage years when, for example, the high school counselor wondered if one of his sisters, who had been adopted at age 3, could speak English.

Be sure to include the children already in the home in conversations about what is happening with the adoption. If possible, prepare them for questions from others in society. The sibling should feel safe enough with the adoption to be able to answer questions encountered at school and from friends.

The sibling role in the family should not be underestimated. They face the outside world just as parents do. Our son, Peter, came home one day to ask what city Annie had come from and whether she was going to stay forever. One of his friends at school had asked. On that day, his 5-year-old face reflected a lot of confusion. Family dynamics and functioning are dependent upon the siblings and how well they process the new child into the family.

Don't compare one child with another. Comparisons are easy to do, even when intended innocently. But children's lives are cyclical, fluid, and evolving. A child that was "easy" one year may be exasperating the next. The "terrible twos" and teenage years are examples of how a child will test you during different developmental stages. We have found that direct comparisons between children diminish their acceptance of personalities, gifts, and unique traits.

---

thoughts from an expert

preparing siblings

My contention is that there still needs to be much more [preparation] for the siblings who are home. When I work with families who have children, I realize that those children are going through everything the parent is. It's not uncommon for children to be asked by others, "How much did your sister cost?" I think we have stumbled in terms of meeting the existing children's needs.

Whatever is done in the home study with the parents, in terms of adoption issues and race issues or whatever, should be addressed with the child. There should be more family heritage camps that welcome siblings, whether they are born or adopted into the family.

Karin Price, B.S.W.,
regional coordinator of Dillon
International, Inc.

expectations
of **others**

expectations of family and friends

P art of the wholeness of family lies beyond the primary family unit, reaching to extended family and close friends. The joy that we feel as parents is often contagious and includes the exquisite anticipation of sharing the fact that a child will be added to the family. But adoptive parents may be surprised and ill-prepared for their families' and friends' reactions. Kinship parents may be equally surprised at the reactions of extended family members, who may view them as the "bad guys" for demanding boundaries or legal rights with the birthparents.

When you acknowledge that you can no longer rely on the support of your family and friends in the way you anticipated, the hurt can run deep, exacerbating the vulnerability that you may already be feeling. It's easy to feel a need to withdraw and hide the emotional wounds that have been inflicted. Based on your family's reaction, you may feel uncertainty and question your decision to adopt. Instead of confiding how very frightened you are at times, you find yourself vigorously defend your decision.

And it's easy to feel anger at the "second-class" reception you've been given. You've witnessed and participated in the baby showers, watched the growing tummies, heard "Oh, he looks just like Grandpa" so many times. Their reluctance not only makes you sad, it makes you resentful.

When you put aside the doubts and fears, you understand in your heart, mind, and soul that adoption is the right decision for you. But you wanted so very badly to be able to share it with those you need now more than ever. Your family's and friends' reactions nag at you, linger in your mind as you contemplate that perhaps you will never have both their blessings *and* your child. If you have to make the choice, you know you will choose your child.

your expectations of
family and friends

"Our child will be welcomed into the family."

Adoption isn't for everyone, just as parenting isn't for everyone. There are people who could not adopt another person's child and open their hearts to her completely and willingly. We honor those choices, just as we would like others to honor our choices.

Vanessa, a 38-year-old adoptive mother, and her husband, Joe, had struggled with infertility, including a miscarriage. They had made the decision to adopt, and Vanessa described what happened when she and Joe told their families about their plans to adopt internationally:

> So we started taking the adoption classes that are required in this state. We were not going to tell any family members until we actually had a referral. We were taking the classes, and we had some name tags on the night we went over to my sister and brother-in-law's house. We didn't remember to take the tags off. They asked something like, "Why do you have those name tags on?" They had the name of the agency on them. So we just kind of looked at each other and grinned and said, "Okay, we'll tell them."
>
> So we told them. My sister was just so thrilled. She couldn't be happier. We didn't think the rest of the family would have any reservations at all. But we didn't want everybody constantly asking, "When is it going to happen?" We just didn't want to deal with that.
>
> But my sister talked us into telling the rest of the family. I have

two brothers who live out of state, but they happened to be in town. And we kind of made it a point to get everybody together at my parent's house about a week later. We were all sitting around and talking. I come from a big family so there were a lot of us in the room. We said, "Well, we have an announcement to make." Of course, everybody thinks, "Oh, you're pregnant."

We said, "No. We're in the process of adopting an infant boy from Vietnam." And it was just incredible support and excitement from every single person. It was just so exciting. My parents are in their 70s, and they were so excited. There was not a single bad thing. It was very memorable.

The very next night we had a party for my husband's side of the family because it was his mom's birthday. So we went over to their house expecting the same reaction. His parents were sitting at a table eating cake, not too far away, but it's on the other side of the room. Everyone was within hearing distance. We said the same things. We have an announcement to make, and told them about the adoption plans. You could have heard a pin drop. My sister-in-law was the only one who said, "Congratulations." She was interested and excited, but everybody else just sat there. His parents never got up from the table, never came over.

We always joke about his side of the family as the "Smith Enthusiasm" because the family has never been the type to get overly excited about anything. I guess I just compared it to if somebody said they were pregnant. Or when my sisters-in-law said that they were pregnant, then it was exciting.

There could be some prejudice. My father-in-law fought in World War II and was stationed in the Pacific. We never asked them why they had the reaction they did. To this day, they don't know how hurt my husband was about it all. But we just kind of looked at each other and got into the car to leave that night and said, "That's certainly not the reaction we expected."

I went home and cried the whole night. It's definitely a rejection. Because if we had said we were pregnant, there would have been some excitement. They have changed now, since my son is home. But I can tell that my son isn't as close to them as my nieces and nephews on that side of the family. I really don't know if it's a biological thing or if it's because we don't see them as much. Although they live in the same area as my parents and we do see my parents more. My personal *feeling is that I'm still very much hurt by it. And so I'm sure if we'd been welcomed with open arms, we might be closer to them. But I don't know, we've never talked to them about it.*

Kinship parents may find that although the child is clear on family roles, the roles may not be as clear to other family members. Stella raised her niece, Sally, on and off for several years before finally adopting her at age 12. There were many hardships for Stella, a single parent. Because she was single, the family assumed she should be the one to adopt her brother's child. Financial hardships, finding childcare, and dealing with Sally's history of abuse made parentage difficult at times. Stella recalled her extended family's attitude toward her and Sally:

Being single, it was a scary decision to make. I had brothers and sisters and we talked. They said, "You're the single one, you should do it." Financially, it was hard. I felt like the child never has a choice. They always have to go with the flow. My brother, Sally's father, never paid me any child support. I took her out of foster care. We went to court, and he gave up all rights.

Nobody knew anything about adoption. My friends didn't know. They thought, "Oh, Stella has a daughter. She can't run around with us as much." Taking Sally completely changed my lifestyle.

My mother is still alive. My choice was either to move my mother in to live with me or move Sally in with me. That was the biggest decision of my life. My mother has Alzheimer's disease, and she doesn't remember Sally. She remembers her as this little, little girl. When I got Sally, she was just as tall as I was and my mom didn't like her because she thought she was just another lady or neighbor.

Other roles within the family become cloudy at times. Adult birth children may begin to resent their mom or dad for assuming the role of parent to other grandchildren in the family. Bonnie, a 52-year-old parent to Charlie and Nathan, continues to fight to legally adopt the boys, but other members of the family see her as the boys' grandmother. Bonnie has two other adult children by birth whom she feels are sometimes sensitive about the new family arrangement:

The lack of defined role does create stress. It's hard to know what I should and shouldn't say to my son and daughter as to what I did for the boys, what I bought them, and so on. Or talking about them too much. I re-member when I had my kids and my mother was bragging about my brother's kids for something. I remember feeling, "What about my kids?"

I probably wouldn't have a problem clarifying my role if it weren't for my other grandchildren. It's really hard. I'm sure it's hard on Charlie and Nathan, too. As a grandmother, I never had to be the disciplinarian. I'd say to go ask their parents for permission. With Charlie and Nathan, I'll tell them, "No more candy!" I would never do that with my other grandchildren. I don't know that my kids or my grandkids see that part of it. I think they only see that Charlie and Nathan get to stay here all the time and the other grandchildren only get to visit now and then.

Formerly childless couples and individuals or doting grandparents now have a child to care for and thus, they have less time for other members of the family. The special aunt or the couple who have always been willing and able to be the family babysitter now have their own family units. The roles have shifted, and this shift can create resentment.

April, kinship mother to her granddaughter, Cathy, spoke about what adoption had meant to her 7-year-old step-granddaughter:

I have a step-granddaughter and the situation has been very confusing for her. She had me as "granny" for 7 years before Cathy came along. When Cathy was born, she said, "Okay, this is my cousin." Then we adopted Cathy and we said, "Well, now Cathy is your aunt." She just became totally mixed up.

Now she's beginning to understand it, but she still doesn't think it's fair. She is about 11 years old and still doesn't like that Cathy takes time away from her and me. She'll say, "Granny, why does she take so much of your time?" She doesn't understand it yet.

Kinship parents may also be questioned about why they didn't force the birthparent to parent the child. The extended family may be unaware of the abuse, neglect, or abandonment that is often known to, or discovered by, the kinship parent. The kinship parents have to decide whether or not to get the authorities involved and what that would mean to the child. Sometimes kinship parents realize only too well that the choice is either to care for the child or to put her into the foster care system. Sometimes they live in fear of the birth-parent with a history of violence, substance abuse, or incarceration.

April described the questions she fielded when she decided to adopt Cathy:

We've had some family members ask, "Why didn't you make your daughter take care of the child?" I believe you can't make anyone do something like that. The other choice was to relinquish the child to foster care, and family and friends brought that option to us. I told them, "There's just no way I can do that. A foster parent or an adoptive parent would have said to us, 'I'm sorry, but now we're her parents, and we're not going to let you have contact with her.'" And they would have every right to do that. I couldn't handle not knowing where she was and all about her life.

"I'll receive support in the same manner as I would with a birth child."

For birthparents, the period immediately following delivery and homecoming is filled with well-wishers who bring meals, throw baby showers, offer to sit for the other children in the home, and in general, provide emotional and physical support. This may not be true for adoptive and kinship parents. With adoption, friends and family obviously do not witness the mother going through the physical processes of pregnancy, labor, and delivery. Therefore, they conclude that she has no physical needs. The father didn't have to be with the mom in the hospital, so coworkers barely sense a hiccup in the family's routine. Of course, these inaccurate impressions lead to a lack of support.

Later, when a child's needs may become more apparent, we ask friends and family not to stereotype our child's needs as those associated with adoption. However, as we've discussed, the unique emotional needs of the child by adoption cannot be overlooked. As our child's emotional and

> ### thoughts from an expert
>
> ## support
>
> Parents feel misunderstood by friends. The parent might say, "My daughter has temper tantrums." The neighbor says, "Oh, my kid does that, too." The neighbor doesn't understand that there is a difference. Yeah, all kids have temper tantrums, but all kids don't have rage. All kids get mad, but not all kids get into rages. So the adoptive parent feels misunderstood. I think they feel that most people are trying to be helpful, but they don't understand. They don't get it.
>
> *Debbie Joy, M.S.,*
> *private practitioner*

physical needs unfold before us during an incredibly vulnerable time, we need our friends' and families' understanding and support. Again, we must decide how much we are willing to educate those we love so that we can feel support for those we love.

Adoptive parents who are dealing with their child's attachment and emotional issues, special needs, or processing issues may be quite vulnerable at family gatherings. Instead of being met with support and warmth, family members may chose instead to contribute to the adoptive family's sense of difference and lack of acceptance. The respect and integrity of the adoptive family is violated by those who mean the most to them.

"My family and friends will understand that our motivation and need to parent is the same as others' motivation and need to parent."

In contrast to the ambivalence and even coldness that sometimes greet adoptive parents is the "saint" metaphor. Is it a compliment? People mean it to be. They believe the comparison is a favorable one, setting the bar high for others to reach. They imply that others would not and could not do what it is we have committed to doing. Yet each time we admit to our

---

thoughts from an expert

support from families

I think families are less than supportive especially with special needs adoption. They feel the parents are taking on other people's troubles. They may say, "What are you doing? Why are you doing this?"

One little boy had parents with a very integrated extended family. Every holiday was a big family picnic—Memorial Day, Labor Day, Fourth of July, Christmas, everything. The little boy was less than perfect, and the extended family finally said, "You can come to the family functions, but you can't bring him." They said, "But he's our son."

The family answered, "Well, he's not really family."

In another family, the grandmother has a Christmas party for all the grandchildren, but doesn't invite the adopted grandchildren. Because they're not real. This happens with inheritances, as well. The adopted child is left out of the will. There are very real differences sometimes.

Regina Kupecky, L.S.W., coauthor of Adopting the Hurt Child *and* Parenting the Hurt Child

---

shortcomings as parents, we feel a sense of failure a bit more acutely because we've been equated with a saint.

This metaphor offers us no support, for saints did good acts selflessly, in blind obedience, and in the name of God. People we spoke with affirmed that they had been presented with this metaphor, felt uncomfortable with the comparison, and said that it was difficult to respond to it. Kinship parents were confronted less often with this metaphor than other adoptive parents, perhaps because of their genetic ties to the child.

Let's look more closely at the dynamics of this metaphor. Our family and friends tell us, "You are such a saint to adopt this child." Uttered by friends, family, and strangers, this carries unspoken messages that confine and frustrate us. One adoptive mother summed it up by saying:

> *I've heard that I'm a saint. It's not a matter of being a saint. It's a matter of being a parent. When people have a child by birth that has learning difficulties, people are very accepting of that. But I've also heard from people, "Oh, you've adopted him. No wonder you're having so much trouble." That's not it. He's got whatever issues he's got—by birth. Just as my daughter has issues by birth and that's that. It's hard to get society to understand that. It's hard to get your neighbors to understand that. It's hard to get grandmas to understand that.*

And underneath the top layer of the saint metaphor, as this mother implied, is that an adoptive parent has to be a heavenly being to undertake the task of raising a nonbirth child. Birthparents are rarely presented with this metaphor. Instead, others usually remark how challenging parenting can be or what an exciting time it is. By comparing adoptive parents to saints, there is also an underlying assumption that the adopted child is somehow less of a child than a birthchild. They are damaged or challenging or will test the parent, who by the sheer act of parenting this child will be elevated to saint status.

Being a saint implies suffering and a life of devotion to a higher cause through hardship and endurance. It also implies an acceptance of whatever divine intervention has in store for you, making you a willing accomplice and humble conductor of fate. It implies passivity, humility, and all the virtues of "saintliness," a person who makes one conscious decision and then allows that consciousness to be taken over by a higher power. Reality parenting and saintliness would seem to be at odds.

Saints often suffered in silence, too. They prayed to God when things got tough, but didn't go among the people complaining about their persecutions. The implication, then, is that adoptive parents should remain silent about their hardships. The parent support group attendees that we interviewed made it clear that the only place they felt safe enough to voice their feelings was at the group meeting. Why? Because the saint metaphor, even when unvoiced, pervades common thought about adoptive parents. There is culpability to being an adoptive parent. You created this situation by choice. You didn't *have* to adopt. Therefore, you should be stoic, silent, and strong.

There are spin-offs to the saint metaphor, stated in questions or comments by friends, acquaintances, and even strangers. Typical comments include:

"Your child is so lucky to have come to your family."
"What a gift you've given this child."
"I couldn't do what you're doing."

Many parents have been able to skillfully counter these comments by answering, "We're the lucky ones to have her in our family," or "No, she is the gift to us." People kind of look at you funny, but they usually accept these answers.

All the implications wrapped up in the five-letter word "saint" do not reflect the reality of adoptive parenting.

And yet. And yet.

Gosh, haven't we done an extraordinary thing? Haven't we done something for the greater good, for all of humanity, by adopting this child? Yes, our daughter. Yes, our son. But you feel that by this act, you have changed the world, not just your life. You have chosen not to produce another child to add to the world's population. You have exercised your right to parent a child who needed a home, needed a parent. This act should count for something. Shouldn't it?

Yes, it should. It should count toward respecting our need to voice concerns at times, without fear of being judged; it should count toward eliminating the insensitive comments made to us in the middle of department stores. It should count toward being accepted as a family first and foremost and an adoptive family second.

coping strategies

Family and friends—their opinions and feedback mean a lot to you. You share a personal world with them, but sometimes adoption makes you reexamine that world. Is it a choice of one family member over another? Loyalty? Is your adoption viewed as a betrayal to an elderly family member?

Let's talk about ways to preserve the family and keep the integrity of friendships intact. Because while we often don't like to admit it, we need the people we love to support and understand us.

Understand that your views, philosophies, and ideas of being a parent may not match those of your family and friends. Myths, conventional wisdom, and stereotypes are baggage that is tied to the cultural phenomenon of adoption. As part of our American culture we, as a country, pride ourselves not only in being a melting pot, but also in loving those in the stew with us. Friends and family hear stories of tangential people in their lives who have adopted, and these stories influence how they see adoption within the family. While domestic adoption goes much further back historically, international adoption is a relatively new path to adoption, coming into being after the Korean conflict.

Adoptive parents reported that when they were the first in the extended family to adopt, there was more education to do and more hesitation. To you and your partner, adoption is a natural choice and a path to parenthood that is filled with joy. To your family, it may be a huge risk, without logic or merit. The narcissism that comes with birthchildren—who they look like and whose mannerisms they share—isn't present with adoption.

Likewise, adoption means that the patriarch of the family can't announce that his daughter is pregnant with the first grandchild. How important these issues are to a family will impact their reaction to an adopted child.

One adoptive mother explained to us that she knew going into adoption that, although she would have no problem with it, her extended family would never accept a transracial adoption, so she did not pursue it. Part of her decision was based on the fact that she'd struggled with infertility and knew she already felt very tired inside. Another battle to win was something she knew she wasn't up to.

While many adoptive parents reported that friends and family members influenced their decision to adopt in a positive way by being role models, there is a certain level of understanding that is either present or missing in extended families. Either the person "gets" adoption or doesn't. Depersonalize their reaction to you. Is their reaction really about your new family—something they may know very little about—or is it based on what they have heard or seen on TV? You do not have to take responsibility for your family's agendas and biases.

Give people time to adjust to your decision. Decide how much education and information they can handle at the time. Discuss what their fears are and what you have done to approach this path to parenthood. And tell them what you need.

Have they coped with the loss of a child who will not come into the family by birth? Have they resolved or processed the infertility that has affected you?

Let your spouse deal with his family and you deal with your family. That way, it's clear what—or whom—each of you is responsible for, and you won't end up resenting one another because one of you took on the burden of telling everyone.

Finally, surround yourself with people who do "get" adoption, whether it's through adoption support groups or some other avenue. Feeling acceptance and a sense of belonging will help give you strength.

Realize that you can have boundaries that protect you and your children. Even with time and your best efforts, some family members may not choose to accept your child or see you as a legitimate parent. If that happens, you need to decide what boundaries are the healthiest for you and your family. Continual pain and slights perceived over time wear away the integrity of your nuclear family.

Before becoming a parent, Patty, now mother to six children, four of whom are adopted, experienced two miscarriages and a stillbirth. She described what she finally communicated to her mother just before her first adoption:

> *My mother was very nonsupportive. No one in our family had ever adopted, and I'm an only child. I can remember saying to my mother, "I'm not asking you for your opinion. I'm telling you for your information. You have to choose what you want to do with it. But I'm going to be a mother in 2 days. You can be a grandmother or not. It's okay."*
>
> *That was tough because I was an only child. And also it was something so unique to my family. My dad was 1 of 14 and my mother was 1 of 5. People didn't want to tell me when people in the family were pregnant. Cousin Bonnie kept "gaining weight" until she had a baby. Nobody wanted to hurt my feelings and everybody was having babies.*
>
> *My mother really loves my kids now.*

Consciously admit that your life choices diverge from your family's preferences. Yet admit, also, that you want their approval. Feelings of disloyalty, even betrayal, can be countered by strategies such as 1) realizing your life cannot be lived through your extended family; and 2) not allowing your extended family to live their own values and choices through you. Conflict can often be expected if you cannot provide a carbon copy of past generations to your family. Change is difficult for others to accept, especially when your choices diverge from the wishes of your elders.

Old family dynamics echo well into adulthood. How you were parented greatly influences your choices in parenting, and the experience of having a child may bring past childhood issues and memories of inappropriate or hurtful parenting to the forefront. Some experts cite a pattern of adoptive mothers who are overly critical of themselves in part because their own mothers were overly critical of them. If the child isn't what she had hoped for or the challenges feel overwhelming, the adoptive mother taps into those past feelings of inadequacy.

Coming from a high-functioning, intimate family can also have an impact on your ability to parent. When your child cannot duplicate

---

thoughts from an expert

making your needs known

As a social worker, during the home study process, I would prepare parents to communicate their needs to friends and family. For example, in the work setting, I would say to the parents, "If you don't want people asking you questions, tell them, 'When I get a picture, I will let you know. Right now, just keep me in your thoughts and prayers.'"

In a church setting or with friends, I would encourage them to tell people if they wanted a baby shower, and whether they would like to have a meal brought to the house or other support when the baby comes home.

Later, I would prepare the parents by handing them information with the child's picture. I would say, "Here is the picture. Your child is coming home in 2 weeks. Have you done this? Have you told your mother-in-law that when she comes to visit, you want to be the primary caregiver because you want your child to attach to you and not to her?" Those specific things are helpful.

A lot of times, parents don't know what questions to ask and what help to ask for. Then, when the child comes home, they are in the midst of all of it and don't know what to do. Getting the support system in place beforehand is very helpful.

Karin Price, B.S.W.,
regional coordinator of Dillon International, Inc.

the dynamics of this close family unit, you may feel the loss very acutely.

Experts also reported that an adoptive mother who has left a dysfunctional family behind may be more stressed and depressed by a child who destabilizes the family. She sees her history repeating itself, her family growing more and more out of control. The dynamics begin to resemble post-traumatic stress disorder—an intense period is repeating itself in your life. Your response can range from generalized anxiety to a more incapacitating episode of mental breakdown. If you feel this kind of reaction, try to identify the source of the emotions. What past event is triggering this reaction in the present? Explain what you're feeling to your significant other—and why, if you're able—so that they can offer you more support.

Seek out other family members, such as siblings, who can help you process the past. Ministers and other religious professionals can also help make sense of what you are experiencing. These individuals, who are very supportive of adoption, can offer safety and support while helping you look at your past to better understand your future.

If you feel out of control or in crisis, seek counseling for yourself as soon as possible. A separate counselor for you and

> **thoughts from an expert**
>
> # family of origin
>
> Our family of origin is our genetic family. If you have a predisposition and you add a sufficient load to the stress, you're going to get what your family gets: depression.
>
> The difficult adjustments plague women who come from very, very high-functioning, close, intimate, and warm family relationships. They meet a child who is unable to reciprocate at that level. The disappointment is enormous.
>
> Or a woman who has experienced and overcome tremendous tribulations in her family of origin—her birth family—will also not handle a difficult child well. With the onset of stress in her parenting experience, she is flooded with thoughts such as, "Oh my God, here I go again." It is similar to post-traumatic stress disorder. She is panicky and may be unable to cope.
>
> Really, the best adjustment comes with women who have had tribulations along the way and have consciously dealt with the fact that life doesn't always smell so sweet.
>
> *Barbara Rila, Ph.D.,*
> *private practitioner*

the child may be necessary to sort through the agendas that you both have. We have found that there is nothing like the experience of parenting to prompt self-examination and knowledge.

Own your parenting experience without reacting to the saint metaphor. Your comfort level with adoption speaks volumes to others. Do you feel empowered as a parent? Sometimes, your life path can be challenging. Work on decreasing your defensiveness about your

Stella and Sally

Stella, a 44-year-old quiet and reserved woman, adopted her niece, Sally, and has raised her as a single parent for the past 6 years. Family and friends assumed that because Stella was single she had fewer responsibilities and should be the family member to adopt Sally, then a 12-year-old pre-teen with a history of abuse. But Stella's mother, suffering from Alzheimer's disease, also needed intense care. Seeking the counsel of her pastor, Stella took Sally out of the foster care system and began parenting her.

Stella had also taken care of Sally when the child was 5 years old. However, Sally was returned to her birthmother. At that time, Stella says, "She was this happy child, and you could see it in her eyes. When I got her the second time, that was gone because of all the abuse. I had to adjust to her being changed, plus be there for her."

The change in lifestyle tested Stella, who worked evenings and nights in the food management industry. Finding childcare was especially difficult, and money was tight.

But Stella used coping strategies that worked. First, Stella and Sally went to counseling and talked about Stella's household rules: attending church was the number one priority. The counseling also helped Sally transition from the foster home to Stella's home and opened discussions about

choice. Many parents we spoke with felt that they should have known about the challenges they would encounter. Yet much of the adoption process—dealing with the paperwork, the glitches, and the lack of control—can cause the family to experience difficulty staying focused on the "real child" who waits at the end of the process.

Appreciate the difference between owning this parenting experience and feeling that you have to defend and explain it to others. Again, our self-worth is emotionally tied up in how competent we feel as parents. You know you're not a saint, but that doesn't make you a bad parent, either.

Communicate your needs to loved ones. Educating others about adoption and educating others about your needs are two different issues. The former has to do with our society and the latter has to do with you.

Specific, concrete statements that express your needs will help others to understand and support you pre- and post-adoption. The more you

the differences between Stella and her brother, who was Sally's father.

Second, Stella proactively relocated to a smaller community that she felt was safer for Sally, sensing that Sally had too many opportunities to make bad choices when interacting with peers where she currently lived. The move provided them with a fresh start. The community also offered them a larger church with more resources, such as an adoption support group that was "open to anyone whose life had been touched by adoption." The minister and congregation formed a support system for Stella and Sally.

Third, Stella refocused her mental energies by praying and taking it one day at a time. The time spent in prayer gave her a sense of peace and renewal. "When I have God, I have time to myself," she said. Stella empathized with what Sally had gone through—the change in homes, the abuse, and the grief and loss—and believed she needed to be "strong for Sally."

Gradually, Stella and Sally's bonds solidified into a mother and daughter relationship. Sally is now in college, majoring in psychology, and calls her "Mom" more often than she does "Stella." At her high school senior banquet, Sally gave a speech telling the crowd how "wonderful it was that Stella had given her a life" and thanking Stella for encouraging her to attend church. Stella observed, "I thought I'd hear, 'You're not my mom.' But I never did."

own this experience, the more others will be able to meet your needs.

Extended families can grow closer as they reflect on the unconditional love of this child. Carmen, who was in the labor and delivery room with the birthmother, also has an adopted sister. After years of infertility followed by adopting her infant son, Carmen had this to say about her extended family:

I feel a closer bond with my mother since I adopted. We were always very close, but my son has brought us even closer. And my sister—our bond has changed also. I think partly because we're both mothers now. She sees me as an equal instead of as her little sister. But I think the fact that I love my son unconditionally, the way that I love her, kind of touches a soft spot in her. I know she loves all of her nieces and nephews equally, but she definitely has a different bond with my son.

expectations of birthparents

As adoptive parents, we have been trusted with parenting a child that two other people created. This biological connection will never be severed. We have discussed how children and adults continue to process adoption throughout their lives. Similarly, adoptive and kinship parents continually process what the birthparent means to them. One major factor that contributes to our perception of the birthparent is whether or not the birthparent is physically around.

Regardless of whether or not the child is familiar or has contact with her birthparents, as an adoptive parent, you share the parentage of this child with others. Forever. And that can be a beautiful thing.

your expectations of the birthparents

"I will understand the birthmother's decision and circumstances."

As adoptive parents, we compare what decisions we would have made if we were faced with similar circumstances as the birthparent. Then we compare the similarities and differences. We try to empathize, to put ourselves in the other's place. What we are doing is trying to make sense of the birthparent's decision. This sense-making process is not a judgmental one. In fact, we long to understand because we know we will have to help our child understand.

First, let's discuss the situation of a confidential or closed adoption, as is the case with so many international adoptions and past domestic adoptions. You have never met the birthmother. She may be just a signature on a legal document or someone known to a doctor or an orphanage director. But you, the parent, and your child will not know who this person is, what she looks like, or why she relinquished her rights. Questions will haunt the child, and the image of the birthparents, primarily the mother, will haunt you.

How you fill in those gaps will shape how you make sense of your own parenting experience. There is a temptation to idealize the birthmother, to elevate her beyond human status, to a being who did something we could not do. A fantasy person takes form in our minds as we struggle to piece her life together with little or no real information. These images tend to erode our feelings of legitimacy to parenting this child.

Many times, prospective parents choose international adoption because they believe they will not have to deal with contact from birthparents. While at the time of placement the birthparent may only be represented as ink on paper, this may not be the case when the child is 18. For example, many Korean parents are returning to the adoption agencies when the child turns 18, seeking contact with the baby they placed almost 2 decades earlier.

In our case, we received a deed of relinquishment from the courts in Kolkatta. Annie's birthmother, a 24-year-old single woman, was accompanied by her father to the orphanage. We had heard many different rumors about the various circumstances that brought women to the orphanage with their babies. The primary reasons were socioeconomic, the stigma of bearing a child out of wedlock, and the gender of the child (baby girls greatly outnumbered boys). But then Karen started to yearn for a connection with this woman who gave birth to Annie, a connection that existed only in Karen's mind.

Karen wanted to tell her that Anusree, the child we called Annie, was safe and loved. She empathized so intensely with the birthmother that she began to feel sorrow and loss on her behalf. In some ways, these feelings began to make Karen even more hesitant to embrace her role as Annie's mother. Karen placed her feelings of joy and happiness second to the pain and grief that she imagined Annie's birthmother felt.

For mothers who choose to parent a relative's child, the birthmother is usually in the periphery of the child's life, visiting occasionally, communicating through phone calls and letters, or possibly still functioning as a member of the family. The relationship between the kinship parent and the birthparent can be emotionally charged, and it is certainly changed forever from the previous relationship. A new parent–child relationship has been formed.

April, a grandmother raising her 7-year-old granddaughter, Cathy, spoke at length about how she continues to process her anger at her daughter, who left her infant daughter in April's care:

I ask myself when I'm melancholy, "Why in the world did this happen?" I had anger about that. Why did my daughter put us in this situation? Even now, when we would never, ever give up Cathy. But I still think, "Why were we put in this situation? Why did she do this?" I've had more trouble dealing with my anger at my daughter than my husband has. I sort of had a blowup about 6 months ago. One day, I suddenly realized this anger. I thought I was past it. My husband told me, "You've got to get rid of this anger or it's going to eat you up."

My health issues compound my anger. Each back surgery was harder when I went through the recovery time with a small child to care for. When I came home, we had to have a sitter for 6 weeks because I couldn't help at home. It was an adjustment and it wasn't cheap, either.

We had just moved to Alabama and my daughter had called a few times. She'd talk about coming to visit so nonchalantly, like it was no big deal. I never felt she had faced what she had done or asked me to do. It just hit. She was talking about visiting and just hanging out and doing whatever with her boyfriend. I confronted her on the phone and with a letter. She just clammed up and didn't respond.

A few weeks later, I asked her a question through an email. I was trying to understand her side of it. I asked, "Do you feel that I forced you into this adoption and that I stole your child? Do you feel that?" You know, she didn't answer my email. Nothing. I don't think she would have said "Yes." She repeats to this day that she doesn't want kids—ever.

Kinship parents may see firsthand some evidence of abuse or neglect. However sometimes, the kinship parent may be the last to know what the child endured. If the kinship parent was estranged from the family, he or she may not be aware of what has happened to the child.

The kinship parent may also feel fear toward the birthparent and be drawn into legal proceedings in efforts to protect the child. Financial costs can be significant and an added burden. After her son's death, Bonnie fought for the custody rights to her two grandsons due to incidents of neglect—such as letting the younger child wander into the street—which were investigated by the state welfare agency. Conflict with the birthmom escalated into a long legal battle. Bonnie spoke about her ex-daughter-in-law's behavior:

> *What's most stressful to me is the animosity of their mother toward me. She calls me names. The oldest boy is very bright and articulate and nothing gets past him. He tells me what his mother calls me and says that his mommy hates me because I took him away from her.*
>
> *Now, she's pregnant again. I don't know when I'll have a final answer to permanency. I don't know if the court will say to give it another 4 months. This last month has just been torture to the boys. They had started to have better manners and be better behaved. But this last month, their mother has been talking to them about moving in with her, saying, "You're going back with me whether you like it or not." The older boy is counting the days and suddenly, he's out of control.*
>
> *I know in my heart it's about their social security money. I've put it in a trust for them so no one can get it.*

In open adoption situations, the birthmother may select the adoptive parents from hundreds of couples. An intense preparation period culminates in the labor and delivery of the child. Then a period of uncertainty creeps in as the adoptive parents wonder if the birthparent will change her mind about the adoption. After a few hours or a couple of days, the child goes home with the adoptive parents. This is an incredibly vulnerable period for the birthmother, the birthfather, the adoptive parents, and the child. How this period has been planned for will often affect how the openness is preserved.

Carmen reflected on her and her husband's conflict with the birthmother in her open adoption. It is important to note that the adoption was a private adoption arranged through an attorney and therefore did not have the full scope of services that are provided through adoption agencies:

> *Our arrangement has been a less-than-perfect open adoption. It has not always been easy. Information was withheld from us. In filling out her medical history, she did not disclose her mental health status. At the time, she said, "Well, I've been a little bit depressed here and there." We found out that she has bipolar disorder.*
>
> *She contacted us immediately after we came home with the baby and was very upset that we had gone home from the hospital without notifying her. That was scary. I didn't feel like I owed that to her. But she did. Then I thought, Well, am I wrong? Maybe I do owe her this. But do I have to answer to this person about my whereabouts for the rest of my life? Do I have to notify her when I go on vacation or when I go away for the weekend?*
>
> *It has been hard in terms of her expectations. Normally, every Christmas, we go to her state, but we didn't that first year because we had a new baby and other reasons. She became hysterical and threatening. I didn't know how to deal with that. I really felt a sense of debt to her, and I didn't know how to handle that.*
>
> *If we had known about her mental illness, we may not have had such an open agreement. She was taking her meds when we met her and she was a very different person.*

Another adoptive mother, Veronica, also arranged an open adoption with the help of an attorney. She and her husband had gone through weeks of preadoption counseling with both birthparents to work toward an understanding of the relationships. The bond between Cindy (the birthmother), her two children, and Veronica had grown in intensity during the pregnancy with almost daily visits. Veronica would baby-sit the children while Cindy would run errands or nap. With the baby's arrival, the relationship changed:

> *The day after we came home from the hospital, Cindy showed up on our front doorstep. She hadn't even called. I was in shock. I thought she had come to get the baby. That was my first thought. I had bought her materials to make a scrapbook for our son, and I knew eventually*

after the baby is born

There is an absolutely incredible period of vulnerability just after placement. I say to birthparents, "You have given them the privilege of being the parent of this child and so now you also have to give them time to adjust to that big change and responsibility that you've given them." On the other hand, there are certainly adoptive parents that really understand the openness piece and they want to do whatever they need to do to help the birthparent heal.

Open adoptions are harder, of course, because the adoptive parents were there. They saw this child born, and they also saw the tremendous grief and anxiety that the birthparent went through in making this decision. In the olden days, they were handed a baby and sailed off into the sunset. So open adoption is harder.

The legitimacy of the adoptive parents speaks to that whole issue of entitlement, and that's another piece that should be dealt with in the home study. There are many agencies that are gathering a lot of information that the courts want, but they aren't dealing with the real issues of adoption. I'm thinking of entitlement in a positive way, about the adoptive parents really feeling that they have been given this responsibility and privilege of being this child's parents. We don't own our kids, we have them and it is a privilege to raise them.

I'm speaking of a balance. That's another thing that I feel open adoption does. How can you not feel that you are entitled and you are that child's parents if the person or the couple who has produced and given birth to this child are handing this baby to you and saying, "This is the plan we want for this child"?

I have worked in adoption for 32 years and when I worked with adult adoptees, they spoke of the shadow parent in the closet. So the entitlement issues for the unseen parent in the closed adoptions were enormous. The parent and child didn't have that sense of understanding. In a lot of those adoptions, I think, people overcompensated and they over-indulged kids and were afraid to discipline them because they didn't have that sense that they were entitled to be this child's parent.

Dottie Boner, L.I.S.W., A.C.S.W., M.S.W.

we would get together and receive the book. But Cindy had finished it and had written a letter to the baby the night he was born.

Cindy said, "I just need this. I know I have to wean myself off of this. But I need to see him and see him with you guys."

If she had called me on the phone and told me this, I would have said, "Absolutely. If you feel you need to come, come over." But we had such a horrible experience with the hospital nursing staff and finally being able to relax for the first time, it was hard. I was also going into sleep deprivation because I hadn't slept for 3 nights.

I went from planning on no visits from the birthmother to her showing up unannounced for the first 3 months after my son was born. Cindy always came around when my husband was at work. She caught me when I was home alone.

The guilt. It was very stressful. But the guilt was worse. I wouldn't be a mother, I wouldn't have this child if it weren't for this woman. How can I deny her? She acknowledged my role as a mother. Even from the first day in the hospital, she said to her baby, "Go to Mommy."

Even in her visits, she didn't really interact with our son. I think she came to get support from me. Most of the time, we just sat and talked.

Cindy's grief was normal, but in an open adoption, the adoptive parent may witness this grief firsthand. The issues that bring birthparents to place their children do not go away once the child is placed. The issues may be compounded with grief; the adoptive parent will be affected by this grief in an open adoption. Cindy needed to be able to process her grief, and the most appropriate place for that is with a counselor, not with the adoptive family of her son.

common reactions to unmet expectations

Here are some common short-term emotions that surface in response to surprises and challenges we encounter with birthparents.

anger

Depending on the situation, you may feel intense anger at the birthparent for past behavior toward the child and you. You are left to deal with this past, a past that may or may not have been known to you. You may have been forced into parenting the child, leaving you with a different lifestyle than you had imagined. Or the birthparent may have broken promises to the child regarding visitations, vacations, and correspondence. You are left to deal with the child's questions and her anger.

guilt

Thoughts of having "taken" the child away from a birthparent may also enter your mind, especially after witnessing their pain and anxiety firsthand. For this reason, grandparents sometimes hesitate to pursue adoption; they don't want to take legal parentage away from the birthparents.

resentment

You may become resentful of the birthparent's presence—whether they exist only in your mind or physically in your home. Adoption means there were parents before you. If you struggled with infertility, it also means the birthparent did something that you couldn't do.

coping strategies

Clearly, your guiding principle when making decisions as parents is "Do what is in the best interests of the child." But that principle isn't always thought of first. Emotions, even those as powerful as love, can sometimes make us arrive at decisions that we later realize are not in the child's—or our own—best interests in the long run.

Realize and respect the adoption plan that the birthparent made for this child. Recognize that not only was a plan made for this child by the birthparent, but also that you are part of it. Feel and express your emotions, acknowledging the gaps in information, letting go of trying to change what you cannot change, and living in the moment of this precious time with your child. Once Karen accepted that her daughter's path was with her, she could move forward as a mother. Some mothers felt that their child was "destined to be theirs," and simultaneously felt empathy for the birthmother. When there is sparse information, both adoptive and birthparents have little choice but to fill in the gaps.

Ironically, Patty's mother, who wasn't initially very positive about adoption, helped her daughter come to terms with some aspects of her parenting:

> *During my first Christmas with my child, I was just heart-wrenched because I thought the birthmother must be so sad, and that's not necessarily true. I do think you feel some sort of tangential umbilical line to that person. My second child had some health issues and leg braces, and when she finally had her last hip surgery and got out of the leg braces, I told my mother, "I had this overwhelming desire to call her birthmother and tell her that she was okay."*
>
> *My mother said, "She never knew she was sick."*
>
> *But I said, "Surely as a mother, she must have known something."*
>
> *I think you do internalize those kinds of feelings and then feel sadness for the birthmother.*

In some instances, such as public and kinship adoption, adoption plans may not have been decided upon by the birthparent in advance. At times, these plans are forced choices by the child welfare system. They may be the result of poverty, lack of education, illness, inappropriate parenting choices, lack of parenting skills, or problems with the legal system. Birthparents who do not comply with the child welfare system are in effect making a non-verbal adoption plan for their child.

Foster parent adoptions are also open adoptions. The children are often older and have been involved in visits with their families while in foster care. The foster parents have been involved with the birthparents or families at some level. There may be a connection to siblings who may remain with the birth family or who may have been adopted by other foster families. Dependent upon circumstances, the foster family is linked to the birth family by visits or in the recent memory of the children they adopt. However, the adoption agency isn't there to negotiate between the parties.

Communicate honestly with birthparents. The dynamics in open adoption are rich and varied, and as our experts have pointed out, the arrangement can take more effort from all parties. We believe the hard work has multiple benefits, especially for the child. Yet achieving open and honest communication between the adoptive parent and birthparents can be difficult due to assumptions, guilt, feelings of indebtedness, and co-dependency issues.

Veronica and Cindy had established an intense bond prior to the child being born, and Cindy could not break away once her son had been placed with Veronica and her husband. For 3 months after the child was born, she visited Veronica for support and help. Veronica had encouraged Cindy to go to the "after counseling" appointments and establish a support network, but Cindy was hesitant. Finally, Veronica knew she had to have an honest talk with Cindy:

We would have these conversations where Cindy was using me as a counselor. She would say, "I was up all night crying for my baby. I feel that, but I love that you're his parents and I see how happy he is over here. I know I couldn't handle three children right now." She would list the reasons and try to convince herself that she did the right thing.

It came down to priorities. I needed time alone with my son. I knew I needed time to enjoy being his mother without having to be reminded daily of this woman's grief. My father had been diagnosed with cancer and had not seen his grandson. I decided to visit my parents out of state.

I told Cindy that I needed a break and that I understood how hard things were for her. I was glad that she had felt comfortable enough to talk with me and share these feelings with me so I could fully understand what she was going through, but at the same time, it was very hard for me. I told her, "The guilt is making it very hard for me to enjoy being a mom. I can't go pick up my son and enjoy being with him when you're right there telling me it's so very hard."

wipe the eggshells away

I became a mediator to work with families when the arrangement was just not working. People were upset and angry and wanted to pull back. All they had to do was get rid of the eggshells and talk and communicate what their needs were. Once that happens, they have smooth sailing.

When there is conflict and they're walking on eggshells, I think that's when they need some professional intervention. It has nothing to do with being a good parent or a bad parent. It has to do with the changes that occur in their relationship. With adoptive parents, it is like the lightbulb went on. "This is our child. You've given us this responsibility." Open adoption is not co-parenting. But life changes.

Mediation has been successful in every case. One hundred percent. There is no perfect arrangement, though. People have to get over whatever they're angry about—talk about it and get it out—because you can't fix anything unless you do.

We meet in a neutral place. There are certain guidelines in terms of being a neutral party and hearing both sides. And you may need some time-outs where you hear the rest of the story that somebody may not be comfortable hearing all at once. Or they may not be comfortable talking with the other party there. Then the issue is, How can we resolve this? What do you need to come from this? What does the other party need? Where is our common ground? Where are the issues that need to have some compromise? There always have to be some compromises.

All of that makes people anxious. When you're dealing with all those issues, how could you not be anxious?

I think what it really boils down to is people being able to sweep away the eggshells and talk about their needs. We have as many meetings as it takes. I've had cases that it's only taken a couple of sessions to reach compromise. Sometimes I have walked out after one meeting and people are hugging and saying, "Oh gee, I'm so glad we've worked this out."

Dottie Boner, L.I.S.W., A.C.S.W., M.S.W.

Cindy said she understood and that she hadn't wanted me to feel the guilt that I was feeling. She said she never intended for me to feel guilt. I said I knew that and thought that a counselor would be a better person to talk with.

I told her, "I'm probably not the best person in the world to hear everything. I want to understand what you're going through so it can

be relayed to our son, but it isn't an easy confession to hear. I know
you didn't ride off into the sunset after you gave him life."

The visit home was the longest period of time that I had had with
him alone. My husband couldn't go because he was in the military and
on duty. It was just me and my son. I stayed with my parents for
about a week, and afterward, I felt renewed and refreshed.

Cindy seemed to understand, and it was about a month after I got
home that she called and asked if she could come over for a visit. I said,
"Of course."

I want my son to know that I treated his birthmother with honesty
and respect.

Cindy has moved out of state now, and we maintain a comfortable
contact.

Again, Cindy's grief was acute and not being processed. The emotions were too intense for the adoptive parent and birthparent to face alone. Cindy needed a therapist to confide in and share her sadness with.

Don't make commitments that you can't keep. For those who have an open adoption, you may have entered into the initial commitment because:

- You're ecstatic! Of the hundreds (thousands?) of potential adoptive parents, you have been chosen. You've written a heartfelt letter to the birthmother, a message that you agonized over and edited countless times. You've explained why and how you will parent this precious child. Although truthful and sincere, you feel that you have marketed yourself, and that because of how the system is set up, that is what you needed to do. Now you're worried that the birthparent may change her mind. You have established a tenuous, fragile relationship that you want to grow into a strong and solid understanding. But the relationship will change and a third party, the child, will be introduced soon.
- In a kinship adoption, you've been chosen by this birthparent to adopt her child or, you've taken over the physical responsibility of the child from a relative who was incapable of, unwilling to, or malicious in the care of the child.

In this last case, you were faced with an urgent situation that needed to be addressed. The safety and well-being of the child were at stake. The thought of foster care for the child makes you panicky and heartbroken. You take on care of the child, thinking the situation is temporary and will allow your relatives to "get their feet on the ground." But months have passed and what was once thought of as temporary has become permanent.

The child begins to call you "Mom" and "Dad." You realize the situation has changed, and you and the child are vulnerable to these changes.

In any of these scenarios, jumping into an initial, unrealistic arrangement of openness that satisfies the birthparent and alleviates your fears can create conflict, confusion, disappointment, and pain later on. Carmen, an open adoption mother, offered this advice:

> *I would tell any parent considering adoption to realize that they are in control to some extent. I think that was one of my problems. I didn't feel like I had any control. I felt as if I had to just be happy that we were chosen and agree to whatever the birthmother wanted. I just had to go with the flow. I realize now that I did have a say and I could have negotiated. Be more proactive, more assertive, and don't just settle, because it has to be the right situation for everyone for it to work.*

Listen to what is being said by the adoption agency. What level of openness are you able to handle, emotionally? Perhaps you don't know. Give yourself time to think it through. What do visits and face-to-face contact mean to you and your family? What will they mean to your child? What types of children can you parent and what types of adoption are you willing to pursue?

Look at the history of the birthparent. Look at past behaviors as potential indicators of future behaviors. Ask yourself the tough questions: Can you develop a trusting relationship with this person? Have you secured a promise of pre- and post-adoption counseling? Is the birthfather involved? Can you get him involved? Be future-oriented in terms of how you see your relationship with the birthparents evolving over the life of the child.

Be sure in kinship parenting that you legally protect the child. Schools will not recognize you as the custodial parent unless there are legal documents backing you up. Make plans for emergency situations, such as trips to urgent or emergency care centers. If the child changes

a matter of integrity

The system is set up—and I was part of that system—so that the birth-parents and adoptive parents are positioned to be adversaries because of all the secrecy. Indeed, they were never adversaries because they were concerned about these children. Certainly, that's why people adopt, and that's why birthparents choose adoption.

But people need to hear it and need to hear it straightforwardly. I say to them, "You cannot make a promise that you can't keep because it's a matter of integrity. And it's your integrity, and it's my professional reputation, and it's this agency's professional reputation calling to you so that you don't make promises that you can't keep. We will be here to help you if something comes up."

I tell parents, you need to talk about the openness of this adoption. You need to resolve this before I ever present you with a possible child. If you don't feel this is the right arrangement but you agree to it, then you have to live with it. My professional reputation, and certainly the reputation of the agencies I work for, rests on your being a person of your word.

It could be before the child is born or after. But I really believe for adoptive families' sakes, if they have resolved where their parameters are during the home study process, the process works much better.

It's the same with background information. If you don't believe you could accept a child unless you have background on both of the biological parents—and that's where you are—then when there is a possible placement coming your way without that information, it's much easier to realize that this isn't the right scenario for you. If you're not there or you're still struggling with what we can do and what we can't do, then it's very easy to say, "Oh yes, that's fine," and then regret that decision. I don't believe that makes for very solid adoptions.

Dottie Boner, L.I.S.W., A.C.S.W., M.S.W.

residence, you may find that she is now in a different school district. Until you have a legal arrangement worked out with the court, you will have to drive her to the school district of the birthparent's residence. Finally, consider what you would do if the birthparent arrived at your doorstep to claim the child.

Several kinship parents we spoke with were faced with this situation. The birthparent arrived to take her child, and legally there was little that the kinship parent could do. One called her attorney immediately. One invited the police inside the home to see evidence of the child's residence.

For your sake and the sake of the child, make a plan. Be proactive. Gather a support network. If you are filing for custody, you can anticipate a reaction from the birthparent.

Realize that arrangements are fluid and evolving. With the previous discussion in mind, we understand that the immediate period after placement is extremely vulnerable for both adoptive parents and birthparents. Now the child has validated you as the parent, she calls you Mom and Dad. She seeks you out as the loving and lovable people in her environment. So how do you negotiate the agreement between her birthparents and you?

One thing to recognize is that the agreement will change. It is fluid and evolving. People's needs change. The document itself—if there is a document—is not legally binding in all states. And just as all adoptions are unique, so too are the agreements reached. For some families, the more specific a written agreement is, the higher the level of comfort. For others, a verbal agreement works well. Contact information is shared and maintained.

Many birthparents need closure and the knowledge that their child is all right before they can move forward in their lives. Many adoptive parents spoke about what they perceived to be a transition toward closure by the birthmother during the first few weeks and months after her child was born.

If that closure and initial parting aren't processed, there can be prolonged grieving and behaviors that play out in disruptive ways for the adoption triad. Martha described how the birthfather's need for closure transpired during the hospitalization of her son, who was then technically a foster child under her care. Collin was about 10 months old and needed minor surgery. Unknown to Martha and her husband, the birthfather had been contacted by the caseworker, who notified him of the surgery date and time:

> *We took Collin to the hospital for outpatient surgery. He was to go under general anesthesia, and we had to be there at 7:00 A.M. To our surprise, the birthfather and his new girlfriend were there. We had our hearts in our throats because we didn't know what was going to happen. We were shocked that we hadn't been told that he had been*

communicating with birthparents

One of my clients was an adult adoptee who also had adopted a child. About 4 years later, the birthmother contacted the attorney and the attorney contacted the parents because the birthmother wanted a picture. The father went ballistic and had a fit. He didn't just say, no, he said, "Double-hell no." I happen to know this family very well.

I sat down with him and said, "Let's talk a minute. When you take your daughter to school, and she says, 'Good-bye,' what does she call you?"

He said, "Well, she calls me 'Daddy'."

I said, "When you take your daughter to a birthday party, what does she do? She kisses you bye, right? Who tucks her in at night?"

"Well, we do," he said.

"Who takes her to Sunday school? Who held her during her christening?"

"We did. We're her parents."

I said, "Fine. When your daughter is 21, she might want to meet that birthmother, and you are going to be in your 70s. Do you want that birthmother to say, 'All I wanted was a picture. And they chose not to give it to me'?"

I continued, "Not only do you give her a picture, but you write a letter and you save it for your daughter so that she understands throughout her life what you did to make the picture whole."

What's interesting is that he was an adopted child, too. He ended up sending the picture and said several times how much he appreciated that perspective. He didn't want his daughter to look at him when he was 70 years old and crabby and then look at her 42-year-old birthmother and think, "How could they have done that to her?"

June Bond

notified or would be there. I ran to call our attorney to get his advice on the situation. But it was spring break and he was on vacation.

So what we ended up doing was once Collin was in surgery, we said to the birthfather, "We'll meet you in the cafeteria." So they went down to meet us. My husband and I talked about it really quickly and decided we needed to assure this man about our parenting. So the whole time Collin was in surgery, which was a couple of hours, we sat in the cafeteria and chatted with the birthfather and his girlfriend. We tried to let them know the kind of people we were, and we chatted about them, too. They were 18 years old and a kind of normally *self-centered youth. But whatever we did, it must have helped because the birthfather disappeared after that. My guess is that he decided it was okay: "Collin is fine with them."*

Understand the need to honor the birthparent and "step lightly" when speaking. One kinship parent who runs her own on-line parenting group advises others in their communication with family members:

One of the biggest things that I have tried to tell everybody is to "step lightly." One member who had multiple issues with her daughter was beyond furious. It was anger such as I've never seen. She has her daughter's children and a major fight going on. I try to tell her, "Step lightly. Step lightly. Step lightly." She posts so much on the site and there is so much disturbance there.

I finally said point blank to her, "I want you to do something. I want you to go back over your past 2 week's of e-mail posts. Pull them and copy and paste them into a document. I want you to see that anger, and if we're hearing that, what do you think those children are hearing? Because there's no way those children aren't hearing that. If you say they aren't hearing that disturbance, then you're deceiving yourself."

The best interest of the child is at stake. Not only in terms of legal custody or permanent placement, but in terms of how a child forms their own self-concept from how honored they perceive their birthparents to be. If the birthparent isn't honored, how can a child form an identity that they can honor? Remember to honor the birthparent at the child's birthdays and other special occasions. Some families light candles, others form traditions that include the birthparents so that the child can feel a sense of wholeness.

The other issue is that if you don't honor the birthparent, you cannot honor your own parentage, either. Your legitimacy, your claim to this child, your feelings of entitlement will be jeopardized if you don't see the birthparent as worthy of dignity, respect, and understanding. You have to reach that balance: ownership of your parenting role and acceptance of the birthparent as giving life and ultimately choosing love over everything else.

Carmen eloquently described the peace she had sought and finally found with the birthmother:

the role of the birthparent

Of course, 20 years ago, people really debated the nature versus nurture stuff. Today we know about our genetics, and when I really, really understood that was years ago when I started working with adult adoptees who would meet birth families and have had these quirks and mannerisms, things that I call kind of a synchronicity in their personalities. It wasn't just coincidence.

The accusation of role confusion in open adoption is garbage. I think that all comes from adults. Children—if their family is comfortable with it—then they're going to be comfortable with it. Your parents are who "moms" you and who "dads" you. That might be grandma or Aunt Lisa, but that's the roles. So the birthmom is that person that gave you birth.

I think kids are smarter than that. They understand it. I hear these little kids tell people their stories and they are by far the most charming and wonderful, but they've got it under control. Then they get older and get contaminated. I always say to families, "If you are comfortable with this, then your child is going to be comfortable with this." You have a little child here, but you have to work on your feelings about this because it will impact your child.

The birthmother is the one who gave that person life. You know, how you honor the parent depends on the age of the child. I've seen some very precocious kids who understood way before 8 or 9 years old. I think that if you've instilled that self-esteem in your child, then everything else falls into place in their life.

Sometimes, the adoption has happened so fast that people haven't been able to work through every stage: the home study stage, the waiting stage, and the placement stage. Then it's over, and it's like, "Wait a minute." I believe an awful lot of it comes from issues surrounding infertility. I believe that that's where an awful lot of depression comes from. Someone else has been able to do what you have not been able to do, and that's to produce a child for your family.

In addition to the depression, I think there also might be some transference of anger onto the birthmother.

Dottie Boner, L.I.S.W., A.C.S.W., M.S.W.

Now I tend to look at my son and say, "I love him this much." She must love him just as much. That gives me an empathy and patience with her. That's kind of where I'm at now, as opposed to feeling indebted to her. Now it's more compassion. I know how much a mother loves her child. And I hope that she loves him that much and that is why she behaves in the way she does. I know that now she feels some closure. I don't think she felt any of that closure until she saw him for the first time when he was 8 months old. So my feelings have changed.

Seek legal and financial support as well as a mediator, if needed. Privately arranged adoptions that don't go through an agency and adoptions arranged over the Internet are more vulnerable post-placement. When the eggshells need to be swept away and the agreement updated, or when the emotional processing gets stuck, a neutral party can be invaluable.

Bonnie, a kinship parent, actively sought help through the legal system, hiring an attorney and seeking some permanent resolution to the boys' custody. She did this in response to reports of abuse, neglect, and sexual misconduct on the part of the birthmother's boyfriend. She was also fulfilling the promise she'd made to her dying son, to care for and protect the boys.

Bonnie updated us on what had happened since our original interview:

The court ordered that the boys spend 5 weeks of their summer break with their mother. The older boy, now 7, only stayed 1 week and a couple of days here and there. He refused to go anymore, and his mother started cussing and calling him some very profane names. The guardian ad litem witnessed one of the altercations and called an emergency hearing. The judge has ordered a final hearing and stated, "The boys have gone through quite enough." I hope the ruling is in favor of the boys staying with me.

The boys' mom also has a new baby and is trying to raise it alone. It's about 4 months old and the boys say she screams at it. Please keep us in your prayers.

Keep a record or journal that chronicles the actions of the birthparent and the reactions of the child. Because of potential or realized legal involvement, as well as the necessity to prove what is in the best interests of the child, record keeping is a critical step. Mary, the mother of four small children who were adopted through foster care placement, addressed the importance of keeping a journal:

Our daughter came to us as a baby and my husband is very attached to her—he's attached to all four children, but she was the first baby we

homework and help

In an independent adoption, there is no agency. But most communities in the country have some wonderful therapists. I think that adoption issues are very specific and different than a lot of the issues that people usually bring into their ongoing counseling. I would advise adoptive parents to search out somebody who really knows the field and who can help them work through those feelings.

You really have to search for the right people, the right therapist. There are people in this community who say, "Oh yes, I've worked with tons of adoptive families." But they really don't get the issues. They go to the studies that say adoptive children have more problems, and I don't necessarily buy that. I think that is another layer of how children define themselves that is not often recognized. Years of practice and seeing children struggle with that extra layer, I believe that the struggle can be minimized.

States are being asked for more and more data and less and less preparation. We owe it to adoptive families to prepare them for the issues they may face and help them work through those issues if they surface. We certainly owe it to children. Attorneys can't do the preparation. They should give that up to others who are trained. So they need to have somebody really good to refer the families to.

Do your homework and be careful. The Internet is the highest-risk place to seek placement. The information about adoption is fine, but I think the risk to vulnerable adoptive parents is absolutely tremendous. I believe that agency adoptions are superior because the support and education from the agencies is better overall.

It's a very vulnerable time. You just want somebody to help you. You may have people at work or in your family telling you these horror stories. But I really believe you need to do your homework, go on a fact-finding mission, and do some exploring. If you don't like the way you're treated under that circumstance, then some other agency might work for you.

Dottie Boner, L.I.S.W., A.C.S.W., M.S.W.

ever had and the most beautiful baby we had ever seen. Of course, we're probably biased. [Chuckles]

Our daughter was required to visit her birthfather. To see this little 3-year-old girl have to visit her father in prison—which is a scary place for a child—was very hard on my husband. After the visit, she would wake up two or three times a night, screaming with nightmares. As foster parents, you're not supposed to let kids sleep in your bed, so I would be up half the night rocking her in the chair and sleeping in the recliner. Then we would rotate and my husband would do it. There were many, many times that he would say, "I don't know if I can do this. I can't see her go through this." But we decided we loved her and had no choice.

One of the things my first caseworker told me to do was to start a journal and track the parental visitations and the kids' behaviors. It sounds kind of negative, but that was the only control I had. The court later used that journal.

Be as factual as you can when you document. For example, instead of writing, "Sam was angry when he got home from visiting his mom," say, "An hour after coming home, Sam threw the ball at the wall of the house for 20 minutes and slammed the door when he came inside. He started to cry when I asked him what was wrong, and he said, 'I don't want to talk about it,' when I asked what was bothering him."

Include as many details as you can, and be as objective as you can. Write in the style of a newspaper reporter, but use your knowledge of what is normal behavior for the child to guide your documentation. Be consistent in the use of the journal, and directly quote what the child says to you.

Understand where loss has occurred, and find the love. Despite the joy of parenting a child, there is a lot of loss surrounding adoption: Loss of raising a child for the birthparent, loss of giving life to a child, lost time in the child's life for the adoptive parent, and loss of the birthparent for the child. While what is lost cannot always be replaced, we believe that steps can be taken toward dealing with those losses. To begin, take a step back and inventory where your sadness lives. Does the loss surround lifestyle changes, the freedom to live life without the 24/7 responsibility of a child? Is it the loss of not having given birth?

Perhaps it's the loss of control over the situation. If you feel like you're not living your life based upon decisions that you have made, but rather based upon the decisions of others, you may experience feelings of futility and anger.

In the same way you have inventoried loss, now inventory where your heart lies. What keeps you grounded with perspective? How does refocusing on the loves in your life make you feel? What are you grateful for? What hidden blessings have come through this child? Has this new love crept up on you, grown into your heart without your conscious knowledge? What activities do you do that require love? How to they make you feel? How does taking care of this child make you feel?

April, the kinship parent to Cathy, struggled with her anger toward her daughter, who is Cathy's birthmother. Her own words describe her emotional breakthrough:

> *Finally, I decided that my daughter is the one who lost all this and I gained. Once I came to grips with that fact, my anger ended. Once I looked at Cathy in more balance, and knew my husband and I were far more responsible and financially stable, I could deal with the anger. I refocused on Cathy and the family that had been created.*

Another kinship parent, Doris, is in her late 40s and is raising her 4-year-old granddaughter, Paige. Doris' daughter (Paige's birthmother) Candy, lives in a nearby town with her new husband and daughter. Doris struggles financially to make ends meet and also with chronic health problems. According to Doris, Paige is "very hyper" and is challenged in preschool. Yet Doris reflected on how parenting Paige had acted like an antidote to her depression:

> *I'll probably die asking this question of my daughter: Why? How could you give up this precious little girl? I'll never understand it. Candy was raised with love and attention, maybe too much. I have asked Candy if she wants her and she says, "No. She should never have been born."*
>
> *Candy said that to me recently one too many times and I said, "Listen. I don't ever want you to say that to me again. Ever." It was painful. It rips me apart. I wanted to smack her.*
>
> *Last Christmas, I felt depressed. Financially, things weren't so good. Candy could have helped me, but she didn't. The birthfather, God love him, sends checks every month.*
>
> *But Paige—this little girl—helped me through the depression. I took care of her. She is my joy. She is my blessing. Since she has been born, I have never failed to thank God for her at least 20 times a day. I would encourage anyone in a situation like mine to do it, and do it with your heart. Just do it. The rewards are a blessing. Today, Paige came home from preschool with a backpack full of stuff she made for me. That is just a big thrill.*

Nancy and Vincent

Nancy is an articulate and insightful 45-year-old mother of two: Vincent, age 13, and Erin, age 10. Vincent came home when he was 1 day old; Erin is a child by birth. Throughout the years, the presence of Vincent's birthmother, a "shadow parent" in a confidential adoption, has influenced Nancy's perception of her own parenting.

Vincent's birthmother, Sammy, a 13-year-old girl, maintained contact through letters for the first few months and requested a photo of Vincent when he was 3 months old. Although anxious about this request, Nancy came to realize that this photo was important. It would allow Sammy to see that her son was thriving and to understand that the newborn babe was now a chubby, smiling infant. Through later correspondences, Sammy let Nancy know that she had finished high school and had moved on with her life, a signal to Nancy that her family could, as well.

When Vincent was a toddler, Nancy and her husband divorced. Because of the downturn in finances, Nancy felt she hadn't kept the promises she had made to Sammy during the adoption process. She struggled with feelings of inadequacy, asking herself, "Could I do it right for him?"

Now Vincent is a preteen and in the process of being assessed for "mass disabilities," including sensory integration dysfunction, attention deficit hyperactivity disorder, anxiety issues, and impulsivity problems. Vincent is now the same age as Sammy was when she gave birth to him, and he's asking Nancy lots of questions, questions he is angry about: "Why did my mom give me up? Why couldn't she keep me? Didn't she love me? Didn't she want me?"

Although Nancy framed herself as a parent first, she was also cognizant that she was an adoptive mother and part of an adoptive family. And Nancy was proactive. Being an information gatherer and educator, Nancy had read the adoption literature extensively. Now she

Be honest with your child. As we've pointed out, the needs of the child and her perceptions of her birthparents will change as she grows up. How she perceives her birthparents will change based upon her developmental tasks, what she needs to accomplish. For example,

was able to use this information as she coped with this new stage in Vincent's life. She interpreted Vincent's questions as both developmental in nature and as part of his resolution of loss. Nancy felt it was time to tell him pieces of his background that she had withheld earlier because she didn't feel he was developmentally ready to process the information.

Nancy started by explaining, "Your birthmom was so young. She couldn't drive a car. She couldn't get her first job. She couldn't buy you the cool toys you wanted and all that. She was only 13. You're not loved by just one mom, but by two." As mother and son talked, Nancy and Vincent cried together and celebrated together. Vincent became convinced that his birthmother did love him and this knowledge "changed everything for the better for him."

As Nancy began to explain the circumstances of his adoption to her son, she was also able to make sense of her own feelings toward Sammy, who gave a "gift of life." In feeling this gratitude, Nancy has been able to find peace, a peace that has allowed her to process what being a parent meant to her: "There was such a different feeling between bringing my adoptive son home and bringing my birth daughter home, equally so phenomenal. One was a gift of life handed to me, 'Here. Help this child become who he is.' The other, the gift of birth, going through 9 months, taking care of that baby inside, and then being handed that person to meet for the first time, was just a whole different gift of life. But when it comes right down to it, both of them were given to me, to be raised the best that I could, and to grow up and do what they're going to do with their lives."

Only by successful negotiation of the information that had been entrusted to her—by sharing it at the right time and in the right context— was Nancy able to help Vincent process his adoption experience and at the same time, achieve a feeling of entitlement as a parent.

she will negotiate the pull and push of parental dependence and peer acceptance as she becomes a preteen and teenager. Your response to her questions—and sometimes, her silence—is critical, but it needs to be honest and based on the child's level of understanding.

Sara and her husband, Steve, have three children: Keith, who was adopted domestically as a 2–day–old infant; Connor, a birthchild; and Tanya, adopted internationally. As Keith became an adolescent, he voiced more questions about why his birthmother "gave him up." And although Sara met his birthmother and was there during the labor and delivery, face-to-face contact had not been maintained. Sara shared this exchange she had with Keith, now 15 years old:

Keith had a boy in his class from a single-parent situation, and his parents had been in and out of several relationships. This boy's mother had had this child when she was about 15 years old. This boy had seen a lot of things in his life. His behavior was very strange to those around him. There were concerns about depression. This was the first time that Keith had seen a situation like this. One day we were in the car and he asked, "Why does Mark act like that?"

I answered, "Well, honey, we don't understand what kind of life Mark has had. You have to remember that Mark's mom was very young when she had him. She was only 15. Mark hasn't had a steady father figure in his life. Right now, there's no one in his life to be a father figure to help him grow and help him go through these challenging parts of life like you have with your dad. It's very hard for a young parent to help a child through some of these things in their lives." We went on to talk more about this.

Then Keith became very quiet. I let him sit there until it became a little uncomfortable and I said, "Keith, what are you thinking about?" He said, "Mom, I never thought about it that way. But I am so thankful my birthmom gave me up. She very well may not have been ready to raise me and be the parent that I needed."

I hadn't even thought of connecting it to his situation, and I was like, "Wow!"

chapter 9

how society sees you

As we've described, adoption is a very American practice. But when an adoptive family is formed—even in America—they encounter comments, curiosity, and even loss of privacy. One of our friends who had also adopted from India commented, "I was going to go out today to do some shopping, but I just wasn't up to the stares. Sometimes, I put my blinders on and it's okay. Other times, I try to educate people about adoption. But today, I just didn't have the energy to be out there, and so I stayed home."

Let's talk about what we mean by "society." To most of us, society includes members of our country as well as our community, encompassing acquaintances, teachers, health care workers, strangers, and the media. In other words, society exists on a personalized and a depersonalized level. One striking example of a depersonalized media message received radio play in the southwestern part of the country recently. An international carmaker ran the following radio ad:

"What does getting a used car make you think of?
Adopting a problem child, perhaps?
Maybe it's more like a leap of faith.
A scary leap of faith."

A top ad agency marketed this advertisement based on a $90 million account with the automaker. Needless to say, the company was bombarded with angry calls and pulled the ad prior to national play. When contacted, the company was apologetic and dumbfounded as to how this ad had been approved. Yet this ad and the reactions it sparked after it aired speak volumes about how adoption is perceived in America today. And like it or not, those perceptions influence our expectations of society.

your expectations of society

"Society will respect the intimacy of my family."

"Conspicuous families," or those who by physical characteristics greet society with obvious differences, are met with stares and questions. But when acquaintances and strangers understand that any child—whether conspicuous or not—is adopted, they often ask questions that, while innocent, violate the intimacy of the family:

> *"Do you know anything about the real mother and father?"*
> *"How much did you pay for her?"*
> *"What language does she speak?"*
> *"Who are your real children?"*
> *"Is she okay?"*
> *"Why did you decide to adopt?"*

Lee Anne, mother to Erika, who was born in Haiti and Steven, a child by birth, explained how people's violation of her family's boundaries slowly eroded her feelings of mastery and control over her family life:

> *It's hard for adoptive parents to be intimate because you don't have the privacy when you cross racial and cultural lines. We are continually asked questions about adoption and where Erika is from or how did the adoption happen or why didn't the birthparents keep her. My son never gets asked those questions regarding his life. He gets questions about his sister's life. I think, "How can people out there not realize that the intimacy of a family is lost when a transracial adoption happens?" Society is taking away this intimacy because it's asking you*

these private questions, and they are also continually reminding you that you aren't like everyone else.

In some ways, I like to take the approach of educating people to make things easier for the next kid down the line. Sometimes I try to ask myself, "What can I do in these situations so that my grandchild will profit from this?" In other cases, I work hard on what I call the "tunnel vision," making absolutely no eye contact. I use it during times when I don't want to be approached, when I just don't want to have contact with others. Then there are times when I feel really sad because I can walk away from those people, but Erika can't because she is a person of color in this country.

While the family that crosses cultural and ethnic lines may be more conspicuous, no adoptive family is exempt from questions that are unreasonably personal. This familiarity—from strangers and acquaintances alike—stems from the notion that once you have adopted, you are "fair game." You have gone outside of birth to bring a child into your family, and therefore you have signed away certain inherent rights that a family that does not reach into society for a child retains. In other words, you have been given a child from society and as such, you owe society an explanation. The child is common property between society and you. By signing up for adoption, you relinquish privacy, intimacy, and the ability to remain silent.

At the root of society's questions is the notion that perhaps, just maybe, this isn't a real union of parent and child. Mother and father and child look so different. This child was not born to this mother and father. What society discounts is the power of unconditional love and the ability of adoptive parents to live this love seamlessly on a daily basis.

thoughts from an expert

ignorance isn't uncommon

You would think people would understand adoption by now. The world judges adoptive parents differently. We've had so many clients come to us and say, "We went to a psychologist, and he said to give her back." I said, "Give her back to whom?"

These parents say, "She's my daughter. How am I supposed to give her back? I found out that she was sexually abused and I didn't know that, but she's my daughter. If I had a birth daughter and she had been sexually abused, I wouldn't give her back."

Most of the parents who come to our clinic are very happy because we believe them and empower them and tell them it's not their fault, and we can help.

Regina Kupecky, L.S.W., coauthor of Adopting the Hurt Child *and* Parenting the Hurt Child

"My community will offer a peer group for my child and me."

The majority of the parents we spoke with were not "young" parents. They were in their fourth and fifth decades of life. Some had raised families and others had begun their families later in life, perhaps adding a child to existing birth or adopted children. As such, their peer group is often mismatched. Those in their age group are gearing up for retirement and those that have small children are 20 years younger than they are.

The lack of a peer group can create feelings of aloneness and the perception of difference. With no group to relate to, the empathy received from others in similar circumstances is absent. There is no one to share your experiences with. Your social support group is missing and this can further exacerbate feelings of panic and sadness.

"Society will support my decision to become an adoptive parent."

On a personal level, adoptive parents may be faced with friends' and acquaintances' comments, such as, "You didn't have to do this." And a second message they receive is, "You got what you wanted: a baby. Why are you still unhappy?" These comments revert to the higher plane on which adoptive parents are supposed to be operating as saint and superparents. But these standards provide a platform of backlash, as well. When we complain or seek support from others, members of our personal society cannot process the two conflicting views of you: You were a saint to do this, and now you're complaining? Saints do not complain.

Karen mentioned to a teacher at school that she felt very tired. She had been up all night with Annie, who had been suffering from a cold. The teacher turned to her and said, "Well, yeah. But you didn't have to adopt her. You kind of asked for this when you signed up to adopt a baby." Karen was amazed at the lack of empathy and the stark contrast between the treatment she had received as a birthmother and her treatment as an adoptive mother.

Society also assumes that we should have thought through every aspect, every contingency, and every possibility of parenthood prior to adopting. And when we're hit with unexpected events, well, then we should have known better. Sophie, a first-time mother who adopted from China, expressed it well:

peer group

Adoptive parents can feel isolated because most of them are out of sync with their peers. Parents who adopt are often 40, and they have a toddler. They may have been supportive of their friends and played with their friends' kids. Now their friends are busy with soccer and stuff, and they're not necessarily interested in playing with a toddler. The adoptive parent goes to "mommy and me" playgroups, and they are with a bunch of 27-year-olds. And maybe that's fine and they are like them, but they're probably not going to be their friends.

Or a lot of people who adopt from foster care are 50 or 60, and they adopt a 10-year-old. Well, the other 50- and 60-year-olds are planning their retirements. Who are their peers?

Or the child's peers ask questions. People are asking, "Is that your grandma?" The child answers, "No, that's my mother." And we have in foster care, especially, single moms and single dads adopting. The child gets asked, "Why don't you have a mom? Why don't you have a dad? Why aren't your names the same?"

Regina Kupecky, L.S.W.

I remember the first question people asked me when I was stressed was, "Didn't you think about this?" I thought, "Well, actually, no." I was totally surprised when I felt these feelings—we went through this wonderful agency. But there was no information about the possibility of struggling after adoption.

I felt like the World's Biggest Jerk. I felt like the dumbest thing on the face of God's green earth for not having thought this through. I couldn't believe I was so stupid. She was as cute as can be. I kept looking at her and going, "I can't believe I did this to you." But you finally realize you can't think it through. There's no dry run for this. The decision is at such an instinctual level. My husband and I said that maybe we should have borrowed someone's kid. But I said, "No, we would have said, 'It'll be different when it's ours.'"

So when people said to me, "Why didn't you think about that?" I felt like a jerk. I don't know. I'm not sure that I could have. I'm not sure that adoption is set up to think about it. When you're pregnant, you have 9 months to think about it and you have to think about it because your stomach gets bigger and bigger and bigger. You can't miss it. You can't ignore it. But in adoption, you lose that whole idea of preparing to be a mom.

families of a lesser god

Suddenly you've come home. You think you've gotten all of this in control and you find that the general population sees you as a Family of a Lesser God by the questions they ask. And suddenly, at a time when you think everyone is going to be supportive, you find out that they deem an adoptive family to be not as real a family as a birthfamily. So then, you start drawing in. Whereas if you'd given birth and you had an issue, you would reach out to friends and family. It's that lack of understanding that this is a real family. This is a real child. This is my child. I love this child.

One of the things I try to tell families—and a lot of my families that I work with are upper-middle class, well-educated people who wouldn't know what the word minority was if it sat down beside them—is that they become a minority by becoming an adoptive family. People have to understand that they are a minority in some sense. All of us who were mainstream majority, are suddenly the minority. You get into that loss of control that you thought you had just conquered. You begin to think it's never ending. You don't have support for it.

June Bond,
executive director of Adoption Advocacy of South Carolina

So once you find that you are struggling, the underlying beliefs held by our society get in the way of your ability to seek out support. First, you're berating yourself for not having "thought it through," and second, you have made a freewill, conscious choice that society believes you didn't have to make.

"Society will include my family and me as equal members."

Adoptive parents are a minority. What does this mean to us as parents, to our children, and to our family unit? It means our differences will count for as much as, if not more, than our similarities with other families.

Minority means the potential for more isolation and less support. It means that people's frames of reference don't include the choices we made to become a family. The driving forces behind these frames of reference are benign/malignant ignorance, innocent rudeness, irate accusations (regarding your inability to have thought all this through), or apathetic dismissal.

Already a minority within society, the adoption community can be further subdivided into the different adoption factions: the adopted child, the birthparents, and the adoptive parents. During Veronica's difficult transition into embracing her role as a mother, she used online support sites to describe her feelings and emotions. This is how she described the feedback she received:

> *I found a forum and posted a question. The responses shocked me. People wrote: "You don't deserve to have frustrations with the birth-mother because she gave you that baby." Other people online said, "Adoptive mom? No. You're not a mom. You're an 'adopter.'" Isn't it sad that we have to be so careful?*

When our family is out in public, Karen receives different looks when she is alone with Annie and the boys versus when John is with the family. People's stares and comments are much more tolerant and even overly solicitous when all members of the family are together. When Karen is alone with Annie, people seem more cautious, curious, and even judgmental.

On a depersonalized level, our media's objectivity and function come into question at times. An age-old communication question is: Does the media reflect society's values or does it create a new reality? Probably both. In newspaper and magazine articles, adoption is often mentioned when it is not of any newsworthy value.

"Professionals will treat adoptive families just like other families in society."

Physicians, nurses, teachers, and others in the "helping professions" are guided to do just that: help. However, adoption is woefully skimmed over in educational curriculums and because adoption itself is considered somewhat mysterious to others, professionals can be insensitive or unaware of issues that face adoptive and kinship families.

Constructing a family tree or writing an

---

thoughts from an expert

media bias

When a child gets in trouble and they are featured in newspapers, it's always the "adopted child" or the "adoptive parents." Usually, there is some sort of discrimination that implies that somehow this child is different, set apart, more vulnerable, and more likely to get into trouble. There is a bias in the equation. I tend to think it goes in the negative direction rather than the positive.

Barbara Rila, Ph.D.,
private practitioner

autobiography in school can force the child and family to answer questions they may or may not be prepared to deal with. The age of the child and rites of passage that he or she has progressed through impact how these assignments are faced. Nancy, mom to Vincent, who came home as an infant, commented on how his fifth grade autobiography assignment was approached:

> *He came home one day after getting the papers for the assignment and became very quiet. He said, "Mom, I have a problem." I asked what it was. He said, "What am I going to put down about myself? My birth? My history? What can I do?" His assignment instructions had examples and let's face it, a good percentage of these kids that do these autobiographies are not adopted.*
>
> *I said, "How do you want it to be?" I think that took some of the pressure off of him because the assignment wasn't rigidly structured.*

Sara talked about issues that surfaced when her son, Keith, was asked to prepare a family tree at school. Keith came to the family through a domestic adoption that was arranged by a private attorney when he was 2 days old. When he was in seventh grade, he was able to complete the assignment and advocated for himself as a child of adoption:

> *Keith had to do a family tree and I thought, "How do you deal with that?" Keith was very comfortable with it and he told his teacher, "I want you to know that I am an adopted child." His teacher said, "Well, how do you want to handle this assignment?" Keith told her that he would do his adoptive mom and dad's family tree, but he didn't know what his family tree is.*
>
> *My mother told him to just tell them that he's Finnish and English. You can't do that. I told her it was important to him. There is that hole there.*

Healthcare professionals interface with patients—people in normal states of physical changes (pregnancy and birth) and in the crises of illness. As an adoptive parent, your exposure to the healthcare system is lessened because of this. There is no need for you to go to postpartum checks or attend lactation classes. Physicians and nurses are called upon to take care of those in physical and mental need. As such, the time of labor and delivery, when both the birthmother and adoptive parents are present, is a vulnerable time, especially for those who do not understand adoption. When the professionals present are ignorant of adoption, both the birthmother and adoptive parents can be put through needless pain and suffering.

Veronica, her husband, and Cindy had arranged an open adoption. Cindy had contacted Veronica directly and had known that Veronica and her husband were struggling with infertility. In the early stages of the relationship, Veronica had insisted that Cindy obtain prenatal care and this is what she related happened at their first visit:

I think Cindy just picked a physician's name off a list. She and I were so excited. She was finally going to the doctor and I had all these expectations: I was going to hear the baby's heartbeat. The baby would be more of a baby to me, more than a lump inside another woman's tummy. I think from all those years of infertility, I was thinking, "Is it real? Is it real?" I was looking for evidence of a baby. I know I was naïve. I expected to hear birds singing.

Bring in the Doctor from Hell. The physician was very rude. I was seen as an interloper in the doctor-patient relationship. I was just the observer. I didn't open my mouth. The birthmother spoke up and said, "I'm going to give this child up for adoption, and this is the woman I'm going to give him to. I want her to come to my doctor's visits with me. I just wanted to let you know that she's going to be with me when I come here." The doctor shook my hand, but remained silent. Cindy added, "I'd really like her and her husband to come into the delivery room and experience the whole birth experience."

That's when he kind of gave me a dirty look and said, "They don't need to be in there at all. You shouldn't have them in there." She said, "But I really want them to experience the birth, and I want her husband to cut the cord for their baby."

He said, "What—are you crazy? You don't even know this man and you want him to see you naked?" I thought that was completely inappropriate. We tried to explain that we were attending preadoption counseling together and were spending a lot of time together. But the bad things didn't stop there. He kept telling her we didn't need to be there, and she needed someone there that was going to care about her. I took offense because I really cared about this woman.

After he left the examining room, Cindy and I just stood there in the little cubicle and started crying. He made her feel bad and made

*me feel like a baby-stealer. I told my husband, "Why did this sud-
denly get ugly? This was supposed to be a positive thing."*

The physician continued to make inappropriate comments leading
up to and throughout the actual labor and delivery. Veronica and her
husband thought that after the baby was born, things would ease up
for them. But then the nursing staff intervened:

*We were getting glares from the nursing staff. Cindy was put in a room
about four doors down from us. She wasn't actually in the maternity
ward. She was in a sleep-testing area, but on the same floor as we
were. The doctor had a fit and tried to get her discharged that night.
Fortunately, she refused and I told her she needed time to recover.*

*The whole night in the hospital and the next day, there were times
when the birthmother would try to come down to our room and the
nurses were shooing her away. We said, "Hey, she can come in here any-
time she wants to." Cindy went from taking baby-steps into our room
to finally holding our son and talking to him. She needed that time.*

*We continued to receive dirty looks when Cindy would come into
our room. Some of the nurses who had seen the birthmother in the
room would come in and make comments such as "Doesn't that make
you feel bad for the birthmother, holding her baby and knowing that
you're going to take the baby home instead of her?" I wanted to cry.
I'm not sure why they said it or what their motivation was.*

In reaction to the ignorance of the staff and because of the pread–
option counseling, Cindy, Veronica, and her husband were able to
form a stronger bond. Still, emotions were intense and the pain and
grief for Cindy was very real. Finally, in the middle of the night, support walked into the room:

*About 2 o'clock in the morning, an angel from heaven came in. She
was a night nurse who had adopted five children. She came in and
the baby was having a lot of gas and was crying a lot. She said, "I
know how you feel, honey. I've done this five times. I want to apol-
ogize for the attitude from the other people here because I know a
lot of them are antiadoption. They just don't know how to treat
adoptive parents in this situation." She was very calming and having someone say that she understood how I felt meant a lot to me.*

The card on the bassinette read: "BUFA." All of us were trying to figure out what that meant. The night nurse finally explained to us that it stood for "Baby Up For Adoption." Why couldn't they give the baby his first and middle name and the birthmom's last name, because the birthmother had let us name him?

common reactions to unmet expectations

Our first emotional reactions need to be examined so that we take charge of them. This is the first step toward moving forward and not getting stuck in the destructive emotions that come naturally but must be worked through.

anger

You may feel an incredible invasion of privacy by the questions posed to you. You may feel that others simply have no right to ask those things. There may also be anger at the anti-adoption folks who choose not to understand adoption and its beauty. Your anger is justified and needs to be felt, but don't let it zap your emotional energy.

self-imposed isolation/avoidance

Sometimes, it's all right to find solace in our own private worlds. You need to reenergize in the safety of your home and familiar surroundings. But realize that avoidance won't make the stressors go away. Use the time spent at home to regain your inner strength by recognizing the integrity of your family.

coping strategies

Given the myriad of expectations of our society, we need to have ways to cope with unanticipated and off-putting encounters. It helps to categorize the source. Is it personalized or depersonalized? Someone you know or a stranger? Once you've answered these questions, you can take actions that best suit your needs and those of your child. By keeping encounters from feeling like personal attacks on you, you can cognitively deal with the message rather than wasting emotional energy on it.

Separate your need for a peer group from your need for friendship. It's important to realize the differences between a peer group and the people we are friends with. Sometimes these two groups overlap, and they often do when your life circumstances are similar to those in your peer group. However, close friends don't have to be experiencing the same milestones you are, such as marriage and childrearing. Close friends need not be part of a playgroup or other peer group.

Stella, a single kinship parent who adopted her niece, struggled with finances, working evenings, and finding sitters for Sally. To work through Sally's alleged sexual abuse by another family member, Stella and Sally went to counseling for several years. But Stella had this to say about the point in time when she realized her daughter's needs and how she gained a peer group as well as a social support group:

> God is very important in my life. I don't see how people can live without Him. Since I have God, I have time to myself. When I would pray, I would focus on what was right for my daughter, Sally.
>
> Because she was older when she came to live with me the second time—almost 12—it was too easy for her to walk next door and get into trouble. She was just a normal preteen who wanted friends. But I felt we needed a new start where life was less complicated and just smaller, easier to grasp. So I moved to a safer place . . . less temptation. I moved from a larger city to a smaller country town because of the environment and because of the school system. We moved just before the adoption was finalized.
>
> I switched churches at the same time we moved and switched schools. So we went to a smaller town but a larger church. I had gone to a little country church all my life, but I knew that the opportunities would be better for Sally in a bigger church. There would be more kids. I wanted her to see that the church would be a support in her life.
>
> Later an adoption group was formed at the church. It's been going on for 3 years. When we started, there was only a handful of people, and then we opened it up to the rest of the community. What I've no-

ticed being a member of the group is that every person who attends comes for something a little different.

As the above passage articulates, the environment you live in is critical to you and your child. Moving to a new environment, one that better suits your family's needs, may provide you with the support network you need.

Prepare your personal story. When you're in public—at the grocery store, the library, or school—and you're engrossed in your children, a normal reaction to questions is to answer them. You may be caught off-guard by the intrusiveness of the question. Indeed, the intrusiveness may occur to you *after* the fact. And after you've answered the questions, you may be critical of yourself for answering them.

So be prepared. Know the likelihood of questions that are often asked. If you are part of a transracial family, know that the stares may be more frequent and the questions more plentiful. And when you prepare your responses, critique those responses with one criterion in mind: What is in the best interests of my child? What will she hear and how will she hear it?

You are a minority when you expand your family through adoption. How much, then, is owed to society and how much is owed to your child and family? Or to the world? In international adoptions, parents often feel a sense of debt to the country that has allowed them to adopt this child. Political events in countries can reflect that some nationals do not favor the idea of Americans adopting "their" children. Americans are viewed as buying babies; we are seen as the wealthy elite. Many adoption agencies, in fact, place more children in their countries of origin than abroad. And many agencies

---

thoughts from an expert

answering questions

One of the things I tell families right up front is to get their own personal story together. Come up with a consistent story that you feel is comfortable enough for public knowledge. And decide how much you want to educate others. I think it's very important to make that personal story very consistent before the child is old enough to hear it.

My personal story includes some pretty tough times trying to have children. And most often, people knew this history. But after I adopted my son as an infant, they still made comments such as, "What do you know about his mom?" At that time, I felt compelled to tell them. After a while, I realized my son wasn't going to be 3 weeks old forever.

It's important to feel comfortable with what you're willing to share.

June Bond

ask for donations of supplies and funds to help the orphanages that care for the babies and children.

Clearly, boundary issues apply here. We have to set boundaries as members of a family unit and as members of a larger world. We believe that the lion's share of the responsibility when we set these boundaries should lean toward the family unit. However, this sense of maintaining the integrity of the family unit should be balanced by the child's need to discover who they are and what their heritage is.

Adoptive parents also owe their children respect of their individual boundaries. They should seek the child's permission to share the "adoption story." And they should not feel compelled to share based on the needs of others; the decision should be based on the needs of the child and her preference. One adoptive mother always seeks her daughter's permission before sharing with others. She further points out that adoption is a legal process that does not define who her daughter is and refers others to books on adoption if they are curious and want to learn more.

Respond to media messages. Our society is a democracy. Our media enjoy freedoms as granted by the federal government and espouse a sacred code of unbiased news coverage. While the media boasts an objective eye, human nature would point to the possibility of bias. The carmaker referenced earlier was flooded with e-mails and phone calls from parents, agencies, and people in the adoption community. The Internet played a key role in the call to rally against this advertisement. Bulletin boards and lists announced that the ad had been played and who was responsible. The ad was pulled very quickly in response to the reaction.

And reaction by whom? Consumers. Not only was the message pulled for its demeaning nature, but also because of its economic ramifications. People made choices to buy other cars based on this ad. Savvy callers put pressure on the carmaker, but also on the advertisement agency that wrote the ad, forcing the carmaker to rethink their alliance with the agency.

Adoption in the media also has a history of showing sensational stories of birthparents and adoptive parents being at odds over custody—sometimes years after a child was born. Adoption laws vary by state, and while no two adoptions are exactly the same, remember the context of these stories and the texts within these stories: one child, two sets of parents. An adversarial relationship has been set forth—a relationship that need not exist.

Educate and advocate. Earlier in this chapter we discussed

educating professionals

I've had birthparents have a staff person at the hospital make them feel so guilty (because they are choosing adoption) that they change their minds. Unfortunately, healthcare workers, especially those working in obstetrics, have lots of negative ideas about adoption. It's so different from their normal frame of reference.

But when I've gone to speak to nursing and other healthcare provider groups, other than the two that sit in the corner with their arms folded and who are gunning for bear, I think people have ultimately thought, "Now wait a minute. You're right. This is about the child. It's not about the other stuff." I believe people as parents make the best decisions when informed.

Here's another story about informing the community: I placed a little girl, who was about 7 years old at the time, and she has a full sister who doesn't live with her. She went to her first grade class and talked about her sister and said, "My sister doesn't live with me." All the kids thought she was totally nuts. So the adoptive mother went in to the classroom and spoke with them about open adoption and how even though her daughter and her sister had different moms, they were still sisters. It was great.

Dottie Boner,
L.I.S.W., A.C.S.W., M.S.W.

Nancy and Vincent, who were grappling with his fifth grade autobiography. Nancy finished her story like this:

I spoke with his teachers. "Look, he's got some problems with this. He wants to portray himself to his friends as who he is without focusing on being adopted or not being adopted. I need to respect that for him."

What we ended up with was a beautiful, beautiful compilation. There were certain skills that the teachers wanted the kids to meet in the autobiography. We made it whatever was comfortable for him and it turned out just fine.

Finally, he began saying to others, "See, I'm adopted." Then he found out somebody else was adopted. I feel he needs reassurance that it's okay. I'll tell him, "Yeah, it's okay."

As you educate those around you, you can also be an advocate for your child and for yourself. Continued passivity will increase your resentment and anger, and assertiveness may not result in any changes. But you may be pleasantly surprised.

Bonnie, Charlie, and Nathan

Bonnie is a 52-year-old kinship parent who has been raising her deceased son's children. While she began to parent the 5- and 2-year-old boys, she grieved the loss of her son, and overnight, experienced a dramatic change in her lifestyle. In the following months, she fought for custody of the boys and worked full-time. Although the boys' parents were divorced prior to Bonnie's son's death, her parental right to the boys was murky and unresolved: guardian ad litems were appointed, attorneys retained, and counseling sessions and court hearings attended.

Bonnie admitted that she has never been able to process her grief because of the boys' behaviors and the need to protect them. The boys' birthmother continued to fight for custody, which Bonnie believes was motivated by the boys' social security income. Bonnie knew no other grandparents who were raising grandkids.

To cope, Bonnie found comfort and balance in her work: "Those hours spent with people, laughing at times., totally forgetting what I had to deal with later in the day." She also brought structure into the boys' lives rewarding them if their behavior at school warranted it. If the boys received good behavior marks throughout the week, they received a small treat during a shopping trip. Honesty was important to Bonnie. In conversations with Charlie, the older son, Bonnie encourages the boy to talk about his father and his feelings of grief, loss, and uncertainty.

Partner with your child as is developmentally appropriate. Both Sara and Nancy sought feedback from their sons to understand what their needs were before they addressed the issue of how to create their autobiographies.

Call in the backup troops: your personal support system. There is no substitute for the love we share with those closest and dearest to us. Support offered from family and friends can help us feel the acceptance we desperately need when faced with an unfriendly or ignorant society. These people know us. They love our children. They allow us to feel a sense of belonging.

Veronica, her husband, and Cindy had experienced a traumatic hospital environment, one that tainted what should have been a wonderful experience for Veronica and could have begun the healing process for Cindy. Veronica took action: reporting the physician to her adoption

Bonnie also amassed a strong support network, including a nurturing daycare with caregivers who offered consistency. Bonnie's children were supportive, offering respite for Bonnie during special times, such as Christmas shopping. Even Bonnie's 74-year-old mother-in-law pitched in and watched the boys during a court hearing. The Serenity Prayer offered comfort to Bonnie, who had learned to accept events that were out of her control. Finally, she played piano at her church on Sundays, and the congregation helped make sure the boys stayed quiet.

The legal uncertainty lasted for over 2 years. Bonnie longed for resolution and said, "I don't know that I'm so angry as tired. I'm just so tired."

The court finally reached a decision: The children were returned to the custody of the birthmother, despite ongoing legal investigations. Today, Bonnie finds comfort in knowing that she "taught the boys how life is supposed to be." The children have the hope of success—they can now conceptualize a child-parent bond. Bonnie's maternal model can remain in the boys' hearts and minds, which may make them more resilient through any stresses they encounter.

By maintaining contacts through work, church, and extended family, the loss of the boys—although acute and painful—was mediated by her support system. By taking advantage of these supports, she will be able to be more emotionally available to the boys, and open to their needs in the future.

agency, warning them of his behaviors, and vowing never to use that hospital again. She also realized how having family nearby would have helped:

In a way we were afraid to tell my husband's family, "Yes. Please come." We didn't want to be responsible for their pain if the adoption didn't go through. Then we'd have to send them home empty-handed. Now, if I had to do it over again, I would beg them to come for support. I was scared just like most people are when their dream suddenly comes true. Because part of you is asking if it's real.

People who care about us can help keep us grounded in reality; they are more objective and less emotionally involved. That perspective can help us reframe the larger world's message and allow us to feel loved.

expectations of adoption professionals

As this book has illustrated, there are many different ways to become an adoptive family. It's adoption agencies, facilitators, caseworkers, and attorneys who make the formation of these families possible. Post-adoption stress and depression have been touched upon in the adoption community's conversations, but there is much more to be said by both parents and professionals. And there are still many questions to be answered, the most prominent one being: How do we talk about post-adoption stress and depression so that family health and functioning can be improved?

When we stop to think about the role of our adoption professionals, the relationship is marked by intensity: the decisions these professionals make affect our future and our family. We are asking them to help us find a new family member. What other profession in society has intimate knowledge of us (remember the home study and documents we've been asked to provide), information about how the whole process works, and negotiates with others to determine who our new family member will be? They are the "go-between" folks, the ones who reside between birthparents and adoptive families.

While it is realistic to expect our professionals to educate and support us during the adoption process, adoptive parents sometimes hold the following expectations, which can lead us to disappointment.

your expectations of adoption professionals

"They will prepare me for the challenges I might face."

Time and time again, parents who had adopted domestically, internationally, publicly, and privately—through all the potential paths—declared that their adoption professionals did not prepare them for the possibility of post-adoption stress and depression. From failing to completely disclose the child's needs to avoiding discussions of stress and depression after the child's placement, the parents felt their agencies and attorneys had fallen short of their needs. But we believe that the responsibility for preparation rests equally between parent and professional.

Sophie, mom to an infant girl from China, knew she needed help and she needed that help very quickly. The difficulty in bonding with her child and the lifestyle adjustment Sophie was going through had overwhelmed her immediately after returning home. The agency spoke with Sophie and ultimately helped guide her to a therapist. The agency social worker, Jennifer, and Sophie talked about her feelings. Sophie related the conversation to us:

Jennifer told me what she knew of "post-adoption depression" and handed me an article that cited the prevalence of this. She said, "Sophie, this is really common."

> thoughts from an expert

opening the conversations

I think there is some fear about discouraging people from adopting when we open this conversation. I clearly think that in some ways, the adoption community is concerned that if you say too many negative things about adoption, people aren't going to do it. Well, people are going to do it. They're just not going to be as happy if they don't know about it. The more enlightened agencies that I deal with agree that if a family is scared off by what you tell them about adoption, then they shouldn't be adopting.

Dana Johnson, M.D., Ph.D., professor of pediatrics, director of the Neonatology Division, and director of the International Adoption Clinic, University of Minnesota

I thought, "Now would not be the time to tell me this." In fact, I said, "Why the hell didn't you tell me this in the first place?" After I looked at the article, I said, "This prevalence—something like 64 percent—would make this a normal thing." I was really mad.

I will completely agree that if you told me that this would happen to me, I would have said, "No, this won't happen to me." But when it did, if I had known about it, I would have gone, "Oh. That's what they were talking about." Instead, I felt like a nut.

In the case of kinship parents or when custody issues are being decided in court, a guardian ad litem may be appointed to advocate for the child's best interests. The preadoptive and kinship parent have few agency supports to call upon. In fact, they may be fearful of the state's involvement. In essence, there is a void. No agency exists to help them. Agencies are considered "them." Sometimes, privately retained attorneys guide them through the maze. More often than not, though, they are left to themselves to sort through this time. Discussions of stress and depression fall on the ears of counselors and therapists sought out by the kinship and preadoptive parents, therapists who may or may not be knowledgeable about post-adoption stress and depression.

"They will help me cope with any challenge I face."

After the child is in the home, the agency may send representatives to do post-placement visits. However, in some instances, there are no such visits. Sara, mom to Tanya who came home as a toddler, spoke about the social worker who came for a post-placement follow-up visit:

Our agency didn't really prepare us. My aunt had adopted and so I had heard her stories about what she had encountered. The focus was on the child. We had the social worker come for our post-placement visit and she asked, "How are things going? What areas do you feel that you're struggling in?"

I said, "When Tanya doesn't want me to do something, she'll scream at the top of her lungs and you can't get her to stop screaming. For example, if I take her sippy cup away—because if I didn't take it away, she'd drink the whole sippy cup at one time—she screams and screams and screams."

The social worker said, "I perceive part of the issue as communication."

I had just told her that part of the issue was communication.

She said, "Well, maybe it would be a really good thing for you to seek out someone who can teach you sign language."

In my mind, I thought, "Oh my gosh, one more thing to have to learn." I know she was trying to help, but I was so overwhelmed. We had one post-placement visit.

In this example, the social worker and Sara missed some important cues from Tanya. Tanya, having spent the first months of her life in an Eastern European orphanage, may have been reacting to the fear that food and drink would be withheld from her. That fear caused her over-reaction to the drink being removed. Sara, trying to focus on the child, neglected to confide in the social worker how she was feeling. But could she have shared that with her? There is a real, perhaps irrational fear in most adoptive parents that the social worker will hold our imperfections against us and even take steps to remove the child from our home.

After placement, the focus is on the child. How is the child adapting to the home? How is the child coping with the loss and grief of being placed in new surroundings? These questions must be addressed, but the questions stop prematurely. Parents may or may not be asked how they are coping. And if the question is asked, you may not feel safe enough to answer in a forthright and genuine manner. All those old mental habits and thought patterns of wanting to be in control, of wanting to be The World's Best Parent, of having desperately wanted this child, override the need to disclose your true emotions. Your answers become pat. You may perceive this agency to be more of a threat than a

> **thoughts from an expert**
>
> # the power of the pen
>
> When I do post-placement visits, I notice that people are very cautious about telling their caseworkers about anything that isn't perfect. The social worker is perceived as having "the power of the pen." This power stems from being able to write in the legal documents their assessment and impressions of the family, assessments and impressions that will ultimately contribute to the last stamp of approval—or disapproval—on whether this child will stay with this family. That person may be one of the last you'll confide in if you're struggling.
>
> *June Bond,*
> *executive director of Adoption*
> *Advocacy of South Carolina*

support. You don't want them to know about your difficulties. It's too hard. And you think, "What will happen if I tell them the truth? What will they think of me? What will they do?"

One reason adoption professionals may avoid conversations about how the adoption is working is because of the fear of disruption (prior to finalization) or dissolution (after finalization). They may feel overwhelmed or unequipped to support you in these instances.

"They are there to get me a child."

"Get me a child." It is an unspoken plea of preadoptive parents as they begin the adoption process. And usually, parents feel, the sooner the better. But sooner may indeed be sooner than we anticipated. Sometimes, you may be caught off-guard by the speed at which events move. The child is placed and you haven't had time to adjust to this life-changing event. You may even think, "Is this all there is? Hold on. I wanted to enjoy this time a bit more. I needed this time to prepare."

In contrast, you may be disappointed by a birthmother who has changed her mind or by paperwork stalled in a court halfway around the world. The ups and downs become a roller coaster ride, making you feel as if you're never going to hit that lovely flat, smooth road again. But then a child does come, and you find that it *still* doesn't seem quite real.

Either way, the communication and rapport that you have with your adoption professional will have an impact on this time. Our natural tendency is to blame someone or something when things go wrong, especially when a life-changing event such as welcoming a child into our family is at stake. The agencies are fair game, to an extent. Who else is there to blame?

But is this realistic? It depends. Have you been kept up-to-date on the process? Have you been given a fair, reasonable, and accurate depiction of the steps? Does your adoption agency understand that you are an important member of this process? Many adoptive parents we spoke with said that they felt they were on the "lower end of the adoption food chain." Some parents felt that they were the last to know things and were given unsatisfactory explanations.

Annette had bonded with her daughter, Catherine, during a summer program that brought children to the United States for 6 weeks. Annette and her husband knew that this was their daughter.

The family believed that the contact over the summer would count as their first visit. It did not. So that pushed the adoption back to January. Six long months waiting for the child they'd fallen in love with to come home was a very long time:

The waiting period was definitely the hardest. Because we initially thought the summer visit would count as the first visit, we thought we'd be on a plane the next month to bring Catherine home. That Christmas was horrible. I was very angry. Angry. Helpless. I felt completely helpless even though I would call the adoption agency constantly. They were sick of hearing from me. It got to the point where there was no information coming back. And I finally said, "How do I know this child is even in the orphanage? I can't speak with her. I can't communicate with her. How do I know that her grandmother is not going to come back into the picture and say she wants her? How do I know she's going to be mine?"

The agency worker kept saying, "She's yours. It's just the process. We see slowdowns, and we're working on them. Hang in there."

All I remember was one day, my husband coming home and finding me in Catherine's bedroom on the floor with her Nadia doll, which was her favorite doll, and just crying. So he tells that story to me. There were times when I couldn't do it anymore.

For us it was really horrible because Catherine was old enough to know and understand and become part of our lives. Then it was hard to have her go back to the orphanage. She's your child in your heart, yet you have absolutely no control.

"They are there to give me a license to parent."

We look to the professional to give us a "license to parent" through approval of the home study and later, through post-placement reports. This approval is always on our minds. Without these approvals, we cannot adopt our child. On rare occasions, adoptions do not work, and the child may need to be removed from the home. When this happens before the adoption is finalized, it is called disruption. When it happens after the adoption is finalized, removing a child from the home is called dissolution. Depending on when the removal happens, the child may go back into the foster care system.

Often, parents aren't totally honest about their issues because they don't want to jeopardize the placement or they believe that things will smooth out with time. Then the parenting license comes and they're left with issues that they've missed the opportunity to explore.

Along with our need for a license to parent comes resentment. Teens become pregnant; children by birth are removed from homes every day due to abuse and neglect. Sometimes, you just get tired of the process, tired of having to complete the paperwork and stare at government workers who don't seem to understand that there is a life waiting at the end of the forms. You think, "Other parents never had to go through what we've had to go through." And secretly, you may feel more capable than these parents. So you think, "Give us the license. It's a formality." Or is it?

Have we reduced the home study and post-placement visits to necessary but superficial events in the adoption process that often aren't optimized? And does the responsibility lie with us or with our adoption professionals? We believe the responsibility lies with both parties.

"They will understand adoption and be competent in assisting me with the process."

the home study

I would like to see more attention paid to the psychological and psychiatric aspects of the adoptive family. Unfortunately, we still run into kids who are physically abused within an adoptive family. It doesn't happen very much—probably less than it does in the general population. Parents are scrutinized prior to adoption, but usually no one fails their home study. If one agency refuses to approve the home study, the family will find someone who does.

Dana Johnson, M.D., Ph.D.

As in any field of service, the competency of adoption professionals varies widely. Their goals and mission statements vary considerably. You have to educate yourself about the professionals you are considering. Where do their operating funds come from? How long have they been in operation, and are they licensed by the state? Can you speak with some of their former clients? These are just a few of the important questions to ask. Ultimately, it comes down to the quality of the staff that provides the services, how well trained they are, and how much experience they have with adoption services.

Also, consider whether the relationship you are entering into is one that will continue after the child comes home. If it isn't, focus on how competent the agency is in all areas up to placement, then make sure they will be able to refer you to other competent professional services for post-placement follow-up.

Just as important, ask whether the agency or attorney understands the dynamics of the parties involved. Do they understand the needs of the birthmothers and birthfathers? Do they appreciate the needs of the child when questions arise at age 8 or 18? Have they done everything they can to forge a relationship that will be healthy and natural for you, your family, and the birthparents 10 years down the road, not just 10 days?

Carmen, who is in an open adoption, talked about the services she received:

> My attorney was very indifferent, very calm, which was stressful for me. The whole, "Everything is going to be fine. Don't worry. Trust me," wasn't enough. I was like, "You just don't understand. I need answers now. I need to know how this is going to happen. How this is going to go. Don't call me back tomorrow. Call me back in 5 minutes, as soon as you hang up the phone with whoever it is you're calling." He was a specialist in adoption.

When we were exploring various types of adoption and adoption agencies, we knew we'd found a winner when the agency sent a list of clients to us—clients who had agreed to be phoned to provide references for the agency. We called, and the clients didn't paint an entirely rosy picture of adoption. There had been glitches with international laws or paperwork snafus. But they all stated that the agency had been there to provide support and answers.

coping strategies

During the process of adoption, the relationship that forms between you and your adoption professionals is intense. They have reviewed intimate information about you and your family. You are asking them to help place a child in your home, a request unequalled in society. And there is an economic side to it, as well. You pay for their services, or you're negotiating for subsidies after the adoption. Let's talk about how you can make this partnership work more effectively and how you can protect yourself and your family.

Engage in pre- and post-adoption counseling. People begin to entertain thoughts of adoption with varying degrees of commitment. Just as some people decide not to have children, some people decide that adoption is not right for them. Preadoption counseling can serve a variety of functions, from helping you decide whether adoption is the right choice for you, to determining which path to adoption best suits your needs, to clarifying your strengths and weaknesses as you enter into adoption. The counseling can also educate you on the potential needs of your child. In other words, it can help you align your expectations with the realities you'll face.

Veronica and her husband adopted an infant boy through an open adoption arrangement. She had this to say about the counseling:

I don't know if I would have been able to make it through this without the pre- and post-adoption counseling. I really don't. I think it should be mandatory. The counselor did validate my role, but it was also hard to keep that in mind when the birthmother would say to me daily, "I gave birth to this baby."

The counselor kept saying, "It's so good for the baby to keep the adoption open and have the visits. Your child will know that the birthmother cared about him and didn't just 'give him away.'" Having talked with the birthmother, the counselor felt her dependence would only go on for a short period of time and she would eventually break off the contact. She essentially did that.

I would advise others to definitely keep going to post-adoption counseling, or at least have a counselor that you can speak with over the phone because it's hard to leave the house with a new baby. It's important to have someone there that can validate what you're going through, to validate what you've experienced. It felt good to get it out of my system.

> thoughts from an expert
>
> # pre-adoption counseling
>
> The length of pre-adoption counseling depends on the situation. At least one visit and probably two or three would be helpful. I don't think most parents may be able to really hear it. It's like counseling parents during a pregnancy that there may be problems afterwards. No one wants to hear that. The most I think that families can absorb is that sometimes there are problems—and if there are problems, here is a resource for you.
>
> *Dana Johnson, , M.D., Ph.D.*

Introduce the topic of post-adoption stress and depression to your adoption professionals. Because adoption professionals traditionally focus on the child, questions of your well-being may seem superficial. However, these questions are vital to the health of the family. The effects of parental depression are real and well-documented through research. The questions your professional should ask include:

- How are you, the parents, coping in general? What lifestyle changes have taken place?
- Have there been discoveries about the child's background that you were not told about or that were unknown until the child came home? How have you coped with this? What supports are in place for you?
- Do you feel bonded with this child? What has been the most difficult for you?
- How have your children (the siblings) been coping? Do you sense family cohesion and unity?
- Is this what you expected? If not, how have your expectations differed from reality? What can we do to help you right now?

You may have attempted to call your adoption professional and your phone calls may not have been returned, or your questions may not have been answered to your satisfaction. This tepid response may have less to do with you than with the adoption professional. Post-adoption stress and depression may not be a topic that they feel comfortable addressing. Perhaps they feel that it's too negative or that it's outside their scope of practice to deal with. Or they may feel guilty for having helped arrange an adoption that they are afraid is not working.

While your job isn't to educate your professional on the topic of post-adoption stress and depression, it's okay to bring it up. It's all right to admit that you're having difficulties adjusting. You may even candidly admit that it's not their fault that you're struggling. But if you feel that some fault lies with the agency, then we believe it's appropriate to voice those concerns, too.

When we spoke with Elaine, who adopted 12 children through the public system, we asked her what she wanted us to convey to adoption professionals in this book.

counter-transference

Adoption professionals need to recognize post-adoption stress and depression, normalize it, and not run away from it. I think a lot of adoption professionals, as they see issues coming out, stop calling and stop returning phone calls. The professional should really increase contact. They decrease contact because they feel they don't have the skills to help. They don't know what to do. For example, they may think a disruption may occur. They're hoping to avoid a disruption, so they back away rather than going in there and working with the parent.

I think the professional feels guilty. I think part of it is, "What did I do to this child? What did I do to these people? I'm a failure." It's like a doctor who takes responsibility for a patient dying. After all, the surgery was supposed to be successful. People are supposed to be happier after adoption, and sometimes, it doesn't work. The professionals feel a counter-transference: "What did I do wrong?"

Regina Kupecky, L.S.W., coauthor of Adopting the Hurt Child *and* Parenting the Hurt Child

I want to tell them that we're not a Maximum Security Detention Facility. We are a family. We live in a home. It's not a prison. We're not an institution. We need to be treated like a family. We need to be treated with respect and integrity.

Advocate for yourself and your rights, as well as the child's and birthparent's rights. Part of advocating for your rights prior to entering into a relationship with an adoption professional is to understand their role and what part they will play in the adoption. Does an attorney have a relationship with social workers who can provide services such as pre- and post–adoption counseling? Does the facilitator hold a state license and work with reputable agencies? Is your professional doing all she can to make sure this is a healthy, natural relationship that protects everyone's rights? Are you getting the answers you need regarding the process, and are they coming in a patient, prompt, and professional manner? The answers to the above questions should all be yes. If they are, your adoption professional should be a strong advocate for your rights.

The field of social work is responsible, in large part, for the legitimization of adoption in America today. Licensed social workers are necessary to provide the documentation on home studies and post-placement visits. These professionals will be your first line of support throughout this process. In contrast to the assessment of her attorney, Carmen had this to say about her social worker:

There were post-placement visits. My social worker was phenomenal, both pre- and post-placement. She never pulled any punches, yet she was very

encouraging. There were a lot of people discouraging us from getting ex-
cited. And while she did express that we should have our reservations
until the papers were signed, she was very encouraging, emphasizing that
if this adoption didn't work out, there would be another one. That was
refreshing after hearing so much from people trying not to get my hopes up.

I still keep in touch with her. It was funny because after our last post-
placement visit, she e-mailed me and said, "Can I please have an open
adoption with your son? Will you please send me pictures?" She made
the whole process better.

When arrangements are vague in kinship parenting, it is critical that you line
up legal assistance. Most kinship parents
enter into the situation with an unclear
view of the future. What was entered into
as a temporary situation becomes more
permanent, especially as the child begins
to see the kinship parent as Mom or Dad.
Candice, kinship mother to her 7-year-
old granddaughter, Mallory, had no
formal arrangement to keep Mallory.
Candice had raised Mallory since birth
and suspected sexual abuse had taken
place when Mallory's mother, Amber, had
babysat her. When Mallory was 4 years
old, Candice and her husband decided
that legal protection was essential for Mallory's safety. When Amber was served
with custody papers, a crisis emerged.

Two days after Amber was served, the po-
lice came. They told me that by all rights,
Amber had the right to come and get her.
They couldn't do anything to stop her. I
called my lawyer and while the policeman
was sitting there, my lawyer said, "You
get your stuff, you get that baby, and
you get out of there. If she gets her hands

thoughts from an expert

the letter

I always ask birthparents to write a letter to their child in their own words about why they made the decision [to put them up for adoption]. It doesn't have to be long. Even with an open adoption, you never know what the future is going to hold, but if you can get a birthparent to do that, the child will have that forever. The big question is: What was going on in your life that made you decide to place this baby? I think that is so powerful for adoptive children to understand, that I try to get every birthmother to write the letter.

I would love it if the birthmom writes it during that time right after birth. But if I get it 2 years later, I've still got it. If I get it from the birthmom who has an older child who has been adopted and she said how the system did her in, that's okay, too. I think it is one more thing that the child has from that biological parent that says they were worthy enough and that they were good enough.

Dottie Boner,
L.I.S.W., A.C.S.W., M.S.W.

disruption/
dissolution

Disruptions and dissolutions are terrible situations, and occasionally, they'll happen rapidly. More commonly, it takes a while for the family to realize that they don't have the financial or emotional resources to parent a particular child. The grief and loss is horrendous, and they feel they aren't good parents or something is wrong with them. The shattered dream is just horrible. Obviously, we try to get them in to see a psychologist or psychiatrist who is aware of these kinds of issues.

Dana Johnson, M.D., Ph.D.

on Mallory, we'll never get her back."

I just said, "Yes, sir" and "No, sir" to the policeman and he finally left. I loaded up my stuff and borrowed my friend's vehicle and took off. I'm driving down the freeway not knowing where the hell I'm going. And that's a pretty scary thing. I stayed with a friend of my mother's for 3 days with Mallory. My lawyer went to court and received a judgment against Amber. She couldn't take the child out of the home.

Remember to expand your support as necessary. Let your agency network for you and connect you with the services you or your child might need. These services could include psychiatric and psychological services. Many of the parents we spoke with had sought counseling for themselves and for their children. At times, some of them had taken medication to help ease their anxiety and depression.

If a disruption or dissolution has occurred, don't let shame or guilt prevent you from seeking help. All of our experts agreed that a disruption or dissolution of an adoption was a tragic occurrence. But, they were quick to add, support was necessary for the parents. Society's judgments can be greatly tempered by the adoption professional. The interview with one of our experts was cut short because a mother had called in crisis, wanting to disrupt because her child had struck her again. The expert emphasized how uncommon it was for an adoption to fail.

Many, many times, when a disruption or dissolution has occurred, the parents' guilt is enormous. And many, many times, so is their relief and tragic sadness. Some experts we spoke with believed that parents often process what has happened before the child has left the home. The parents had done all they could to make the situation work. Parents who have experienced losing a child this way need to be able to come to support groups and professionals who will meet them with open, kind, and receptive ears.

a **closer** look

the father, the family

The roles of father and mother are heavily influenced by our culture. While both parents work in many households today, some families choose to have the mother stay at home with the children. The opposite is also true—increasingly, many households rely on the father to remain in the home while the mother works. This chapter's discussion of the father's role is embedded within our cultural value system—what we see as mainstream. Yet we do not wish to perpetuate stereotypic roles. Many parents are in single-parent households; many partner with significant others to raise children.

In order for us to examine these issues in-depth, let's explain the foundation of the discussion. First, although mothers have often been seen as the primary caregivers, both mothers and fathers are nurturing, loving parents. Society's roles, driven by economics, have shaped our family roles. But economic roles do not define the extent of parental love. Economic realities do shape family dynamics and, at times, which parent is cast as the primary disciplinarian. Second, both parents are influenced in their parenting decisions by their experiences with their family of origin. Often the father's most challenging period of personal development will spark parenting issues. These issues are revived as the child reaches the age the father struggled with.

For too long, fathers have been at the periphery of society's discussions of parenting. The focus has been on the mother and her relationship with her children. Both birth and adoptive fathers have been excluded, and we have paid the consequences—stifled feelings, less than optimum fulfillment of the father role, and discord within the marriage. This exclusion can rob our children of what they desperately need to parent the next generation: solid knowledge of the role of the father.

Definite patterns emerged through our conversations with both experts and parents. Within these patterns lay the dynamics we wish to address, the problems that surface and that you react to as a family. Below are what we have assessed to be common unspoken thoughts of the father in the post-adoption period.

what fathers think

"I'm not sure I can be a good dad. I'm not sure I'm ready."

Some fathers are the "foot dragger," the hesitant one, the cautious one. For many fathers, there is a "fork in the road," according to Jerry Dillon, M.S.W., co-founder of Dillon International and pioneer in international adoption. The caution and hesitation may exist at an unconscious level; the father is unsure of why he is not embracing the role. But ultimately, once at this crossroad, he will decide whether he will draw from his history with his own father or carve out a new path that reflects his own fathering style and goals. Sometimes this decision is delayed until the child hits the teenage years, when issues are more prevalent.

Sometimes the father may feel he has prepared himself to assume the fathering role. But the reality of a screaming child throwing a temper tantrum can be very stressful for a father who thought he was well prepared and he now finds he's not quite sure what to do. Where he turns for support and answers is critical to owning the fathering experience.

He may also feel overwhelmed as he realizes that this child is dependent upon him. The child has so many needs, and these needs last a lifetime. That realization may be overwhelming to the father and very difficult for him to admit to others.

As the adoptive mother thinks about the birthmother, so too does the adoptive father think about the birthfather, although these thoughts may come later in the child's life. When birthfathers are excluded, important questions will never be answered: Why did the birthfather place the child? What was happening in his life that made parenting the child impossible? What was his relationship with the birthmother?

"I'm feeling down, but more anger than sadness."

While women tend to talk about their feelings with friends and other social support people, men often lack these supports. Depression manifests itself in different ways in men. Men are more likely to report fatigue, irritability, loss of interest in work or hobbies, and sleep disturbances *rather than* feelings of sadness, worthlessness, and excessive guilt. They tend to feel angry, frustrated, or discouraged, and they may act out violently. Other men may throw themselves into their work, attempting to hide their depression from themselves, their family, and their friends, or they may take on reckless, high-risk behaviors.

During our conversations with fathers we heard their anger, particularly at the "system," a system they felt was responsible for not fully disclosing all of their children's needs, and a system they felt was irresponsible for not providing adequate educational and healthcare resources for their children. They were quieter, more subdued, and less trustful than the mothers we spoke with—at least initially.

Fathers were focused on problem solving and tasks, even to the extent of denying their own feelings. Fixing the problem and working toward a solution were ways of helping their family. Often the father took action rather than dwelling on the emotional side of events. By "doing something" they felt less helpless and hopeless. Adopting this mindset was how they coped.

They loved their children, and they believed the therapists and

left out of the loop

Continually, birthfathers are left out of the loop because it's just easier. That's terribly unfortunate. Needless to say, it comes back to haunt us. I would encourage as much as participation with the birthfather as possible. That's that child's father. That's 50 percent of the biological heritage that you can obtain for the child. Again, that's what's best for the child. I think it's worth the effort. But continually, I see that. I see that with agencies, too. It's just too hard to chase these guys or to make these kinds of efforts you have to make in order to get them involved.

Dottie Boner,
L.I.S.W., A.C.S.W., M.S.W.

caseworkers who told them that with love, "Everything will be fine," or "Give it 6 months and she'll grow out of this behavior." But of course, the behaviors often didn't stop, and the fathers were robbed of critical time that they could have used to help their children. They felt stranded and alone, given more responsibility than they could cope with.

Emotions experienced by fathers often go ignored. In one 1998 study, however, Kirby Deater-Deckard, Ph.D., and colleagues found that men and women experienced similar patterns of and relationships to depression after the birth of a child. The research emphasized the adjustment period for men and women after the birth. Another study found that fathers' postnatal depression was associated with their own history of depression as well as the presence of depression in their wives or partners during pregnancy and soon after the child was born.

Do fathers react more to the mother's depression rather than experiencing their own depression? More research is needed to answer that question and to thoroughly understand the dynamics of post-adoption stress and depression in fathers.

"My wife is too dependent on me. My work is suffering."

If the mother is struggling, her partner—the father or significant other—may represent her only lifeline. He is often the one person whom she feels is safe to confide in. That responsibility is an incredible charge for one person, and the father is left unsure of how to handle the needs of his wife. The wife may call him repeatedly at work or demand that he come home to help. When Karen was struggling with feelings of anxiety after Annie's arrival, she paged John frequently just to hear him tell her that things would be okay. Many of the couples and experts we spoke with echoed this pattern.

When this specific pattern emerged, the father was usually the parent who had bonded with the child and the mother was the parent who was struggling emotionally. The mother may look at the father and wonder at how easily he has bonded with the child. Her guilt may be compounded and her confusion increased by seeing the ease with which father and child have fallen in love. She witnesses their bond and knows that he has something she desperately wants.

"We tried so long to have a baby. Why is my wife so unhappy?"

As we'll talk about again in the next chapter, resolution of fertility loss and pain is not instantly healed upon receiving a child—either by birth or by adoption. In fact, the issues are very separate. The father cannot understand at times how the mother may be processing the past, which is now brought to the forefront by the presence of the adopted child. The pain his mate is feeling—and she may not even be aware of this fact—is indeed only related to the adopted child's *presence*, rather than the unique, wonderful child she is. The couple needs to process this earlier grief for the child's sake.

The adoptive parents may resent the birthmother during this time just because she is a person who is biologically able to carry and give birth to a child. The family's happiness depends on uncovering those feelings and honestly addressing them.

"I'm enjoying this more than I thought I would—but my wife is struggling."

The mother may be feeling the disconnect herself: Why aren't I happy? Even without a history of fertility issues, she may suddenly find her world in disarray, filled with a little person whom she is not prepared to parent. She has little comprehension of her emotions and cannot explain them to her partner. The father, on the other hand— the parent who may have been initially hesitant—has embraced his role and is enjoying his new daughter or son. The husband enjoys the newfound balance in his life: being able to work and come home to enjoy the child.

But he sees his wife's behaviors start to affect him and their child. He sees his wife coping poorly, and he is at a loss as to how to help. The husband becomes frustrated because what he thought his spouse wanted has finally come true and yet now, no one seems happy.

"My wife tells me how poorly behaved our child is. But I don't see it and so my wife gets mad at me."

Children can split the most cohesive couples. They sense the disso-nance between the discipline styles, roles, and temperaments of the parents as much as the parents sense the temperament of the child. The mother—if she is at home—will spend the majority of the time with the child. The father, when he comes home, may be seen as the play-mate, the "fun" parent, the parent the child will demonstrate her most charming behaviors to. The mother tries to explain that this angelic child isn't the child she cares for during the day.

The father looks from mother to child: Whom should he believe? He wants so very much to have a happy family, a united family. He has trouble believing that this child is capable of the behaviors that his wife describes to him. He decides to be lenient with the child, and his wife explodes, withdraws, or becomes tearful.

The stay-at-home mom may even be jealous of the husband being able to go to work. The husband is mystified because leaving for work every day is hard, and in some ways, he may envy his wife for being able to stay home.

"My wife and I never have any time to ourselves anymore. I feel abandoned."

Just as the birth of a child can change patterns of intimacy between partners, post-adoption feelings and the presence of a new child can alter the couple's physical and emotional bond. The mother may be preoccupied with the child's needs. She may be withdrawn and overwhelmed, unable to accomplish household tasks that used to be routine. The father may feel cheated and neglected. He may ex-perience feelings of ambivalence toward the child that has changed his wife's affections. The lifestyle change has left the father feeling frustrated.

One father said, "My wife and I haven't been intimate for months. Our little girl seems fine, but some of the other families we traveled with have had problems with their children. My wife is so tense. It's changed our whole family. I'm feeling resentful and guilty at the same time. I just thought it would be different."

If she has bonded with the child, the mother may be having many of her physical and emotional needs met. She may have shifted her en-ergies to the child and away from her mate. Suddenly, the child is her whole world.

"The adoption process was so intense. Now our child is home and I feel this letdown, like, 'Is that all there is?'"

Adoption is just as heady an experience as having a birthchild. While different, adoption is just as intense and just as beautiful. And as a birth child's arrival marks an end to the gestation period, the arrival of your child marks the end of the pre-placement wait. And boy, what you have been through! Completion of paperwork that takes a fairly compulsive person to keep track of; opening one's heart to others to justify your wanting to parent; and the longing, the aching for this child to come to you. And she does.

Now you think, What next? What am I supposed to do? We've been so acclimated to achieving step after step of the adoption process, there hasn't been much left of us to concentrate on the child. The letdown can be quite intense. And as with achieving any great life event, the letdown can shadow the event itself.

"My wife wants us to start raising the grandkids, and I'm not for it," *or* **"We need to take steps to protect our grandchildren, but my wife's not for it."**

If you've raised your children and seen grandchildren come into the family, you may have been thinking of retirement, of finally being able to stay at home and rest after many years of hard work. You never anticipated taking on a second family, a family you don't have the resources to take on. Yet your spouse tells you there's no choice. It's either you take the children or they'll be placed in foster care or neglected by their parents.

These children may not be your biological kin. Perhaps this is a second marriage and they are children from your wife's prior marriage. You're at a loss as to what to do. You feel you're being realistic, but your spouse sees you as heartless and uncaring. Your marriage is suffering.

Or you may see your wife holding out hope that the birth parents will start to parent again. You see your situation and the children's as extremely vulnerable. You love these children and want to know that they are protected legally in your care. But your wife is hesitant to make drastic changes for fear of alienating other family members.

"Just because I'm silent, don't assume I don't care."

Many men will be emotionally engaged in the adoption process even though they operate from the privacy, the shadows, of the couple. Often, the fathers bond more quickly than the mothers; fathers tend to be "doers," more task-oriented and less verbal about the process. Often, fathers seem to internalize the process and support the family by working and providing for their economic needs, while loving with an open, yet often quiet, heart.

coping strategies for fathers

As we've discussed, men use action-oriented problem solving skills when faced with stress. The following strategies may offer you productive alternatives as you process your fathering role and reach for the future.

Explore your motives and reasons for adoption. The ability to be honest, to open up regarding your readiness to father, is critical before adoption. The mother may be the one motivated to pursue adoption. In that case, it is all the more necessary to deal with hesitancy from the father. In other words, if you're hesitant, don't take the approach that once you see the child, all your concerns will be overcome. The underlying issues may still be there.

Also, be specific about why you're hesitant. If an open adoption is being arranged, do you feel that your feelings have been heard? Do you think your concerns are being addressed? Do you feel pressure to go along with the plans? Has the birthfather been contacted? Do you worry about the future of your child and her relationship with her birthparents? Be sure to speak up—now is the time!

Kinship parents may have the decision to parent thrust upon them, either over time or abruptly during a crisis. Make sure you've looked at all sides of the situation and asked the questions for which there are no easy answers: What are the alternatives? Why is this so important to your spouse? Why is it so important to you? What are you most fearful of? What can be done to temper those fears? Have you had the opportunity to openly discuss these fears with your spouse? Do you feel you have a choice? Or does your caution stem from the unknowns of a long-term commitment? Is it a lack of confidence or is it a lack of feeling that the resources are available to you? Does your spouse express fears or do you perceive her as demanding? Communication with your spouse is imperative, and a counselor may be able to help you see the situation from all sides.

Seek support. Often, the mother will drive the adoption process. She is the one to speak with the licensed social worker the majority of the time. She is the one who keeps track of the paperwork and appointments. Yet there are opportunities for the father to become involved in the support offered by the social worker in the home study and post-placement visits.

Still, many fathers simply do not feel comfortable sharing with a social worker. That's when a buddy system or a support group for fathers could be helpful. Both of these avenues will help you work out your hesitancies and offer companionship as you embrace the role of fatherhood.

In the course of our research, we had the honor and privilege to be guests at a long-standing adoptive parent support group. John was able to lead the fathers in a discussion while Karen met with the mothers. There was something unique and astounding about the safety that surrounded the fathers that night. They were able to share in a forum that provided them with a sense of sameness, of blessed familiarity, of not having to explain quite so much because the empathy was immediate and often unspoken. We believe that such a support group is a powerful medium for mothers and fathers alike.

Arrange for activities that encourage attachment. Although some adoptive mothers choose to breastfeed their babies, adoptive

> thoughts from an expert
>
> ## adoptive father advantage
>
> Adoptive fathers have an advantage over biological fathers. They have significant time to determine their motives and readiness for adoption. Having participated in pre-adoptive conferences with adoptive fathers, I have found that they question their ability to father, if they're very honest about it. Usually, they will mask it with other issues and deny it, because who doesn't think he can be a father?
>
> It's a very important issue to address up front: Why are they interested in adoption and how do they feel about their own abilities? I see differences between those fathers who have adopted [before] and those who are first-time fathers. Their confidence level is up [if they've adopted before]. They feel much more capable if they have good health insurance to take a child with some risks.
>
> *Jerry Dillon, M.S.W.,*
> *co-founder, Dillon International, Inc.*

a buddy system for fathers

We use a buddy system, and we're moving more toward a model similar to Alcoholics Anonymous. The father has a sponsor. We like adoptive dads, particularly new adoptive dads, to have a buddy that they can go through the process with. Throughout the year, we have many social and cultural occasions for families to come to, and we bring potential adoptive couples to meet and observe the events. During that time, we see those men meeting other men and those natural relationships are formed. We try to create many of those opportunities for them to meet other dads so we don't have to arbitrarily assign them to others.

If they don't connect, we help get several men together in a group and just ask them to see if there is someone within the group that they feel comfortable talking one-on-one with about fathering issues. Multiple phone calls occur; having coffee or lunch, or going fishing or playing golf happens.

Feeling a sense of comfort and safety with another father is critical. This relationship can offer support, acceptance, and acknowledgement.

Jerry Dillon, M.S.W.

children are usually bottle-fed. This provides an opportunity for the father to share in the physical care of the baby, an opportunity not as available to some birthfathers.

If possible, take time off work. The first months are full of wonderful times, full of opportunities that you will never be able to anticipate or duplicate. There is no substitute for time. Family leave from work is an opportunity to provide a transition for the child from pre-placement to your home. Many couples who are teachers try to bring their children home during the summer, when they have a break from their busy schedules.

Pay attention to your marriage. Our society often views the woman as the individual able to express emotions, and men are viewed as "stuffing" emotional feelings or denying them. A husband may assume the woman is more emotional. A wife may assume he is quiet and stoic. These assumptions are not productive, and they don't lead us to a greater understanding of our partners.

Mutual understanding of how love is demonstrated and received can help. Do you demonstrate love in your relationship? Is this love demonstrated through spending time with each other? Gifts? Physical affection? Words of encouragement? Is your style of demonstrating love the same as your spouse's?

"Couple time" is essential. After an adoption, the focus moves from the couple to the child, and this dramatic shift can create disharmony. Understanding, honoring, and respecting the foundation of your relationship will ease much of the pressure on the family. Children sense unified parents. They seek security from this union, and their behavior will reflect this security.

Arranging for a "date night" or having someone come over for a short time in the evening to allow the couple to go for a walk can give parents the time to begin to reconnect. After the child has gone to sleep, make plans to watch a movie or cook dinner together. Thwart the temptation to do chores or give in to other distractions. If you don't make these plans, you can easily miss the opportunity to communicate with your partner, even when the child is not in the immediate environment.

Many parents said that they were blessed with spouses who understood when they needed a break from the child and would often "spell" each other. Many fathers were sensitive to when their partner had reached her limit with the child and would literally hand her the car keys and her purse so she could take a drive or run errands. This sensitivity toward each other enabled them to maintain control and feel supported in the process.

Think about your family realistically. The father who is a high-achiever or who insists on a tidy home will have to adjust his thinking after a child comes home—at least initially. His expectations of the child, a child he may have envisioned as ideal and completing his family, may need to be adjusted. Families, we have found, are messy, complicated, and loud. We encourage fathers to carve out their role with care and to be an active, equal parent with their significant other. This role defines part of who you are and who you want to be.

Recognize imbalances in behaviors and bonding. If a child has traveled with a parent, often the child will attach first and intensely to that parent. If the child spends the day at home with mom, then that child may test those limits more than with the parent who is at work. If the child has needs and the mother is involved with those needs, the father may also feel less involved.

Purposeful time spent with the child often equalizes the bonding, although the child may persist in showing a preference for one parent. Look beyond what may appear to be a preference. One mother told us that her husband was the favorite parent, but upon further conversation, admitted that the child sought her out when hurt or tired.

Consistent discipline is essential to avoid "splitting" of parents. There are many fine disciplinary approaches described in parenting

a father's influence

Fathers have more influence on our children than we deserve. The power of a father figure is so profound in how it affects all aspects of a child's life, be it faith, work ethic, how they treat their wife, issues of discipline, politics, and attitudes on racial issues—so much. The power of the father figure is so significant.

We never outgrow our need for a father and a mother.

Jerry Dillon, M.S.W.

books. We look for a balance between nurturing the child and ensuring that they realize the parent is in charge and in control. We also look for an approach that takes the context of various situations into account, thus allowing for flexibility (a rigid system won't work). The parents have to be diligent and consistent. John has counseled many parents who, after being instructed on a behavioral modification schedule for their child, complained it didn't work. Inconsistency in the program—enforcing the rules in an unreliable fashion—had occurred. The child hadn't failed, but rather the parent had allowed the program to fail through poor implementation.

There are situations when a child has learned socially and emotionally inappropriate behaviors that worked either in an orphanage or in multiple placements. The parents must be unified in their approach with this child, even though the child may not be demonstrating the same behavior to both parents. A counselor may be able to provide situations in therapy that will show the charmed parent the child's other side. This isn't setting the child up to fail, it's allowing the child to reveal to both parents what she normally saves for only one.

Use the Internet for help and support. We emphasize our earlier caveat: The Internet is great for information, but it should be used with the utmost caution when obtaining placement services. That being said, because we believe fathers have been excluded from society's conversations for too long, we can recommend some very helpful sites that provide great ideas, information, and opportunities to create support groups (see the Resources on page 232). In addition, grandparents and kinship parents are finding increasing support and information on the Internet, one of the first forums to acknowledge this growing part of our society.

chapter 12

post-adoption stress and depression

I *was chronically sad.*
  I felt panicked. Total fear.
  I gained 30 pounds.
  I couldn't sleep.
  The guilt was horrible.
  I didn't know what to do.
  I paced back and forth.
  I stopped eating. That never happens to me.
  I felt melancholy.
  I didn't feel depressed, but I felt a lot of anxiety.
  I felt angry.

When we asked parents how they felt during the post-adoption period, these were some of the responses we received. And while none of the parents expressed thoughts of harming their child or themselves, their stress and depression were very real. Aside from a few articles dating from 1995, there is no literature that specifically addresses post-adoption stress and depression—until this book. In this chapter we'll show how post-adoption depression relates to general depression and postpartum

Relationship Between Depression, Postpartum Depression, and Post-Adoption Depression

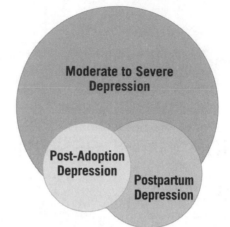

Post-adoption depression exists within the larger context of generalized depression, while sharing risk factors with postpartum depresson. However, post-adoption depression also has unique characteristics, such as its effect on fathers.

depression. We'll also look at the unique characteristics of post-adoption depression that set it apart from other forms of depression.

when depression strikes

Our research has shown that post–adoption depression can be classified as mild, moderate, or severe, with the majority of cases falling within the first two classifications (see figure above). Our research also indicates that depression after adoption shares characteristics and risk factors with postpartum depression, as well as risk factors and characteristics unique to the post-adoption experience.

Approximately 13.1 to 14.2 million American adults or 6.6 percent of the population have a clinically significant depressive episode in a given year. More than 16 percent of us will suffer from a major depressive episode during our lifetime. Think of 10 people—acquaintances, friends, and family—that you spoke with this week. One or two of those people may be depressed. Depression often goes unrecognized and it frequently goes untreated, only to manifest its symptoms through physical complaints or other mood impairments. The figures are astounding and troubling. The cost to society is great, not only in terms of loss of quality of life, but also in terms of loss to the workforce due to illnesses secondary to depression. The cost to the family unit has also been well documented.

Women report a higher rate of depression than men, and this rate increases during a woman's reproductive years. Women who suffer from post-adoption depression seem particularly likely to have had depressive episodes in their past. Infertility is a common factor among many adoptive mothers. This experience brings with it feelings of loss and grief, memories of physical pain, and other emotions. If the loss of what June Bond calls the "dream of a birth child" hasn't been resolved, then the mother is particularly at risk for depression after adoption.

Theoretical perspectives present a compelling case. Ellen Olshansky, D.N.Sc., RNC, professor and chair, department of health and community systems, University of Pittsburgh School of Nursing, found that women with a history of infertility who have "experienced repeated and sustained interferences with significant relationships,"—such as those losses experienced with miscarriage and the inability to conceive—may develop postpartum depression despite the new role of being a mother. In other words, a child by birth in the home does not necessarily diminish the pain of those past losses. Infertility's history and legacy need to be emotionally dealt with and separated from the presence of a child in the home.

When you're depressed, your body responds with physical symptoms. You may feel unable to sit still or you may be paralyzed with panic. Getting out of bed may seem impossible. Women report physical symptoms associated with depression—sleep disturbances, fatigue, or appetite disturbances—at twice the rate of men. Just as interestingly, over two-thirds of people suffering from depression complain of pain with or without reporting the symptoms of depression. Pain is often overlooked as an indicator of the presence of depression.

When depression strikes, it either begins to destabilize the family or is itself triggered by a downward spiral of the family. At this point, it's impossible to say what came first, the chicken (depression) or the egg (the challenges). But we do understand that when depression develops, it impacts the child's developmental and emotional progress. Mark Appelbaum, Ph.D., professor, School of Psychology, University of California, San Diego, and his colleagues at the National Institute of Child Health and Human Development (NICHD) found that children of depressed mothers performed more poorly in areas such as school readiness, comprehension, and expression. The mothers were found to be less sensitive to their children, and the children were less cooperative. In other words, the depression experienced by the mother influenced the well-being of her child.

More recent research validates this effect. Adopted children between 4 and 8 years old whose mothers reported feelings of insecurity had children who completed stories (as prompted by partial stories supplied by the researchers) with higher levels of aggressiveness compared with children whose mothers reported feeling secure. Similarly, mothers who reported unresolved mourning of past losses and traumas had children who completed stories with themes of the parents appearing childlike. Based on this study, it seems that children in early-to-middle childhood make sense of their mothers' insecurities by offering aggression to end scenarios. Children also saw their parents as less mature and the children, in turn, felt less secure.

The duration of the depression appears to be a predictor for the long-term effects on the child. Constance Hammen, Ph.D., and colleagues found that prolonged *mild* depression predicted children's risks for depression by age 15 more so than relatively brief, *major*, maternal depression. At an intuitive level, we know that maternal and paternal depression affect a child, but more research is needed to understand how this depression impacts the child's future as well as what factors add to resiliency in a child.

Adoptive parents aren't the only individuals at risk; kinship parents are also vulnerable. In an ongoing study funded by the National Institute of Nursing Research, Carol Musil, Ph.D., is studying the effects of child-raising on the health of grandmothers. According to the U.S. Census 2000, almost 1 million grandmothers in the United States are responsible for raising their grandchildren. Many grandmothers provide care for their younger and older generations' needs. Given their responsibilities, this study is exploring how grandmothers are meeting their own healthcare needs, which are at risk of being overlooked.

postpartum depression

Our research revealed that postpartum depression and post-adoption depression share some common underlying themes. First, let's explain what we mean by postpartum depression. The postpartum blues or "baby blues" are mild and transient, and they usual resolve without help from outside the family. The baby blues are common, with 70 to 80 percent of all mothers saying they felt "blue" after delivery. This sadness can be traced, in part, to the hormonal changes a woman's body experiences after childbirth.

At the other extreme is postpartum psychosis, which alters the mother's ability to see reality. For example, the mother may believe her child is possessed by the devil. The mother is in immediate need of help and should be separated from the child. It is estimated that postpartum psychosis occurs in 1 in 500 to 1 in 1000 deliveries, or about 0.2 percent of cases.

In the middle is postpartum depression (PPD). Estimates of the number of women with PPD vary, with most researchers finding an incidence rate of between 5 and 20 percent. This is no small number. A study by Cheryl Tetano Beck, D.N.Sc., professor of nursing at the University of Connecticut School of Nursing, found 13 risk factors or predictors of PPD. These significant predictors of postpartum depression are described below (in descending order of significance):

1. Prenatal depression (depression during pregnancy)
2. Childcare stress (stressful events such as infant health problems and infant difficulties eating and sleeping)
3. Life stress (both positive and negative changes related to relationships, jobs, and/or crises)
4. Lack of social support (both instrumental and emotional support)
5. Prenatal anxiety (unease over a vague or unspecified threat)
6. Marital dissatisfaction (how happy a woman feels in her relationship)
7. History of previous depression (previous depression prior to pregnancy)
8. Infant temperament (infant disposition or difficulty)
9. Maternity blues (begins within days after delivery and can last 1 to 10 days longer)
10. Low self-esteem (feelings of self-worth and self-acceptance)
11. Socioeconomic status (factors such as income, occupation, and education)
12. Marital status
13. Unwanted/unplanned pregnancy

It is plausible—even likely—that all the predictors except maternity blues and unplanned/unwanted pregnancy could apply to adoptive mothers, as well. The *Diagnostic and Statistical Manual-IV-TR* (*DSM-IV-TR*), a book used by the medical and mental health community, legitimizes postpartum depression by including its description as a "specifier" for mood disorders. In other words, it's a sub-type of depression. At present, there is no medical definition or description of post-adoption depression in the *DSM-IV-TR*.

We spoke with Dr. Beck, who has devoted two decades of research to understanding postpartum depression (See "Postpartum Depression Screening Scale," on page 210). She stated:

> *For the majority of women (with PPD), it's hard to disclose this problem because of our society and the stigma we attach. The problem with postpartum depression that I've learned through my research is that there isn't a typical profile. There are about seven different categories of symptoms and each mother takes on a different constellation of those symptoms. For one mother, for example, anxiety may be much more of a problem than the depression. For another mother, it's what I call "Loss of Self." They don't know who they are anymore. They're not the same person; they don't feel real. So while there are these seven constellations of symptoms, every mother experiences a different grouping of them so they don't present with the same symptoms.*

The seven constellations of symptoms discovered by Dr. Beck and Robert K. Gable, Ed.D., Professor Emeritus of Educational Psychology, Neag School of Education, University of Connecticut, are:

1. Sleeping/eating disturbances
2. Anxiety/insecurity
3. Emotional lability
4. Guilt/shame
5. Cognitive impairment
6. Contemplating harming oneself
7. Loss of self

The adoptive parents we interviewed reported feelings in six of the seven constellations identified. None of the parents reported thoughts of harming themselves, however this was not a question we asked. Another striking similarity between postpartum and post-adoption depression is that the symptoms varied considerably with parents, some reporting more guilt, others more anxiety, and still others more melancholy.

However, the onset of depression seems to differ between postpartum and post-adoption. Postpartum depression—when women feel depressed after childbirth—starts within 4 weeks after birth and lasts about 1 year. After this, the depression is referred to as maternal depression. Based on our research of post-adoption depression, the onset can occur years after the child has been adopted and last for years, as well. There are also peaks and valleys (remissions and reoccurrences), and the depression can evolve from an acute depression triggered by an event to a chronic, ongoing depression.

post-adoption depression

June Bond first coined "post-adoption depression syndrome" in the Spring 1995 issue of *Roots & Wings Adoption Magazine*. This groundbreaking article was a critical step toward identifying this depression. Adoption magazines have picked up on the need to bring awareness of post-adoption depression into the community. Adoption conferences and seminars also reflect an increased sensitivity; there has been an increase in scheduling speakers on the need for post-adoption services. There are also several theories that offer ways to explain post-adoption depression.

attachment theory

One theory in the postpartum literature that may help us understand more about post-adoption depression is attachment theory. This theory proposes that when a mother's attachment needs are not met by her partner—whom she sees as unresponsive or inaccessible to her—postpartum depression is triggered. Styles of attachment can be categorized as secure, ambivalent, or avoidant. Secure attachments refer to the child's ability to expect a response from her caregiver and her own ability to elicit such a response. This leads to the development of an attachment style used in close relationships. Adults who use anxious-ambivalent attachment styles emphasize romance, suffer jealousy, and have a high divorce rate. Adults who use an avoidant attachment style are not invested in relationships, tend to withdraw from conflict, and fear intimacy. Adults with secure attachment styles demonstrate investment in relationships without fear of rejection or much possessiveness. Attachment theory contends that the anxiety-filled transition to parenthood demands that the mother and father rely on each other. When spousal attachments are not secure or are avoidant, fearful, or dismissive, there is a greater likelihood of depression.

While we are not convinced that this model fully explains the dynamics of post-adoption depression, we do see attachment between members of the family as a common denominator in cases where it is present. Reactive attachment disorder is a broad disorder that refers to the child's disturbances in her ability to relate socially to others. But often, we think of reactive attachment disorder as the impairment or inability of a child to form an attachment and bond with a parent. Some of our parents confessed to experiencing this with their child.

Can we use postpartum theory and apply the attachment "styles" of secure, avoidant, and dismissive to help us understand the dynamics of the adoptive family? Can we examine how adoptive family members connect with each other and with others in their social worlds to uncover where the attachment difficulties lie? Further studies are needed to uncover not just whether attachment has occurred in adoptive families, but what the *styles* of attachment are.

control

In some cases, attachment theory may explain post-adoption depression, but in other families, attachment is not an issue. However, control was a central issue for many of the adoptive families we spoke with. They reported feeling that they had lost control over their lives and futures, as well as control over how to raise their adopted or custodial child.

Again, postpartum research has given us preliminary insight into what dynamics may be found in post-adoption depression. Dr. Cheryl Beck found that loss of control was the "basic social psychological problem" in 12 in-depth taped interviews. The mothers reported going through four stages to solve this loss of control issue:

1. Encountering terror
2. Dying of self
3. Struggling to survive
4. Regaining control

These stages are amazingly similar to the reports of Harriett McCarthy, the first individual to explore post-adoption depression through research.

pioneering research

Harriet McCarthy has devoted her time and energy to supporting mothers who are in the midst of depression. She is also the first individual to conduct exploratory research into the disorder. While not a psychologist or therapist by training, she has intimate insights into post-adoption depression. Over several years, she experienced post-adoption depression to varying degrees as she and her husband adopted three older children from Russia.

McCarthy offers help to mothers and fathers through the Eastern European Adoption Coalition (EEAC), which now has over 5,000 subscribers. The EEAC was originally called the A-Parent-Russ list for adoptive parents with children from Russia (Eastern European children). It traces its roots back to 1993, when it began as a group of people who reached out to each other over the Internet. McCarthy is now the administrator of the Parent Education Preparedness List, or PEP-List (which is part of the EEAC), which was also established to help with parental adjustment.

An extremely pervasive type of depression, McCarthy characterized post-adoption depression as being a recurrent and persistent issue in all her support experience. She admitted that her interest in this type of depression grew out of her own feelings, and she joined the EEAC after her oldest son was brought home in 1993. Due to age restrictions outlined by Russian adoption authorities, there had to be a 40-year age difference between the parent and the child at the time she and her husband adopted. When they were both 46 years old, the McCarthys brought their first son home.

McCarthy's empathy and knowledge stems from her memories of the shock she felt as she realized the needs of her first child. She cites a lack of stimulation in the orphanage, places she calls "eerily quiet," for contributing to her son's issues. He didn't want to be touched and was "sensory-defensive to a remarkable degree." He suffered from auditory processing disorder—an inability to make sense of sounds or process sounds correctly. He had phobias, including fears about water and his own shadow.

Wanting to help other adoptive parents, McCarthy decided in September of 1998 to launch the PEP-List with the endorsement of the list owners. With over 2,000 members who struggle with post-adoption issues, this list includes individuals who have newly adopted children in the home or who will receive them within the next 2 to 3 weeks. McCarthy told us about the hours she has spent connecting people with resources and validating their feelings:

> *I see people hit the list in a panic mode. And they quickly find that it's an extremely supportive environment, and I keep it that way. I see people in crisis. They don't understand what's happening. Once they get stabilized, then they start exploring more common issues that are seen in these children. They start to talk about the children's post-traumatic stress disorder, sensory integration disorder, and learning disabilities. Those are the three biggies.*

survey tool and prevalence

McCarthy conducted an exploratory study in the fall of 1999 to examine the vast unknowns about post-adoption depression. She solicited feedback from the Eastern European adoptive community via an online survey. In order to assess post-adoption depression without bias, McCarthy invited participation from individuals who were not experiencing feelings of depression. While she did not use the standardized and commonly used Beck Depression Inventory-II (BDI-II), she did use the DSM–IV-TR discussion on depression to compose a tool. After comparing the two surveys, McCarthy found them to be very similar. Please remember that this research is based on parents who adopted children internationally, specifically from Eastern Europe. These findings may not be applicable to others in the adoption community.

Of the 145 respondents, over 65 percent reported that they had experienced post-adoption depression. After years of supporting parents, McCarthy believes this prevalence rate to be accurate. However, it could be argued that this is a high-risk group of mothers. Only eight individuals said that they had been advised by social workers that this syndrome existed. However, 61 percent of the respondents reported that knowing about post-adoption depression would have been helpful.

McCarthy's survey also described the details of the depression:

These mothers aren't immobilized. They did have sleep problems. They had eating problems. Most slept too much. Most ate too much. They had sadness. They had feelings of despair. They believed that they had ruined their families' and their own lives. And most said that this was definitely more than feeling blue. But I look at a major depression as something that requires hospitalization, and most of these mothers had a more moderate intensity to their depression. They were still functioning in the home.

characteristics

McCarthy believes that post-adoption depression has a higher incidence than postpartum depression. She also sees post-adoption depression as having a delayed onset, meaning it doesn't begin immediately after the child enters the home. She said, "I think most of what happens initially is in sort of a panic, like the parents have been hit on the side of the head with a boat oar. The onset of the problem is different than the 'blues.' It's actually depression."

McCarthy reported that post-adoption depression started about 1 month after the child came home, and the duration of the depression was much longer than the "blues." People admitted to having this type of depression for over a year and feeling that it was not abating. McCarthy realized that she was depressed after adopting her first son. She videotaped a family member's wedding and heard the woman's voice—her own voice—speak on the tape. The incredible difference between the buoyant voice and how she felt inside motivated her to seek help. The wedding occurred a year after her first son came home.

McCarthy summed up the characteristics of post-adoption depression that have been reported to her:

> *What I see is that post-adoption depression is more serious than the postpartum blues. It's longer in duration; the onset is later; and early on, it may be closely tied to the parents having feelings of utter panic and shock. The outlook seems pretty bleak. I remember taking an eyebrow pencil and writing on my mirror: "Tomorrow will be better." I left it up there for a long time.*

relationship to the child's behaviors

McCarthy asserts that the development of post-adoption depression isn't dependent on the age of the child. Mothers of infants and toddlers, of school-age children, of older children—children of any age—can experience depression. McCarthy said these findings surprised her, but she found that the severity of the child's needs had a direct and critical impact on the depressive episode. She also found that the needs seemed to influence the severity of the depression. In other words, the intensity of the child's needs—both qualitatively and quantitatively—made the presence of post-adoption depression more likely. McCarthy advises mothers to see every adoptive child as a special needs child. The idea is implanted into the mother's mind that what she is doing is very difficult, and this prepares her for what she might be facing. If parents start with this set of expectations, the image of the "healthy child," the "dream child," will match the real child more closely.

bonding, reactive attachment disorder, and disrupted adoptions

McCarthy believes there is a definite pattern to the bonding that occurs between the adoptive mother and child—if bonding does indeed take place. She is quick to point out that most children are able to bond with their parents. However, this bonding may be postponed if the child is sick when she arrives. An ill child may be fairly easy to care for, docile, and compliant. After the child recovers, her full personality and issues become more apparent, and the parent is left wondering what happened.

According to McCarthy, who has identified this pattern through her years of support and has validated it with many other parents, the first 6 months are perhaps the biggest challenge, and the stressors increase as the 6-month mark draws near. After this time, bonding starts to pick up again, with breakthroughs occurring at approximately 12 months. Another downturn in the parent-child bond happens at about 18 months. After approximately 2 years in the home, McCarthy states, "things really start to congeal." The bonding process can't be seen as one straight, upward-sloping line, but rather as jagged ups and downs.

McCarthy sees this pattern across the age range, for toddlers through mid-childhood. The pattern applies to children that come with their own personalities already formed, who are not totally helpless when they arrive, and who have substantial orphanage skills already in place. (Orphanage skills include socially unacceptable ways ways to get attention—such as yelling, kicking, hugging every adult in the environment—becoming very independent at an early age, and learned helplessness.) And these children, can also bring with them other medical and learning disorders and difficulties along with the signs of institutional life.

McCarthy believes that the diagnosticians can lump the various neurological or communicative problems of this community of children under reactive attachment disorder. While she cautions against this, she sees its allure:

> It's so attractive to look at a child who is very complex and say, "Oh, I know what's wrong with him, and this is how we're going to fix him." When in fact, it can be 20 things that are wrong, all of which are going to take individualized therapy. People have to know that they can't take an easy out. It's going to take a lot of work with these kids.
>
> I know reactive attachment disorder really exists, but the way I see it, it exists in very small numbers. It certainly isn't untreatable, especially when you catch it fairly early. What I do see is a lot of women who just give up, and they are no longer willing to try. If mom doesn't dance, then nobody dances.

serial adopters and post-adoption depression

McCarthy has coined the term "serial adopters" for those individuals who adopt multiple children, one after the other. But she has found that some of the children actually adapt better to this type of large family environment because it has some of the characteristics of the orphanage, with the addition of significant nurturing and consistency. These adoptive mothers appear to be able to welcome child after child into the family with little disruption.

McCarthy told us about an experience she'd had with a mother she counseled:

> *The mom was on her ninth child when she became depressed. She and I used to go head-to-head off-list because she was so Pollyanna-ish. I didn't want to rain on her parade, but I also wanted new mothers to feel comfortable describing their feelings. Finally, she told me, "I got it. I got it on the ninth child. I was so surprised. I thought it would never happen to me."*
>
> *She and her husband had adopted a little boy who was really close to death, a very, very, very sick kid. He was starving to death. He was a mess. It was way harder for her than with her other kids. What helped her was that she already knew about post-adoption depression from the fact that it was being openly discussed. She felt much better about it and knew that it would pass, and that her feelings weren't uncommon or unnatural.*

support

The adoptive community is incredibly supportive of its members, tied together as we are by the choice of taking a child that was born to another into our lives. McCarthy stated:

> *I feel compelled to do this, and obviously if there's a higher power— and I think there is—that factors into it, too. I have no doubt that I am helping people, and I'm hoping I'm helping a lot of children, too.*

I realized that I was not going to help the kids left behind in the orphanage. I wanted to do as much as I could for the kids who did get here.

longitudinal research

Some long-term research has been conducted with international adoptive parents. Spanning 3 decades of adoption, parents—most of whom had received children from Korea (78.9 percent)—were surveyed. Ninety-four percent of parents reported that if they "knew at the time of adoption what they now know about the children," they still would have adopted the child. Only 2.3 percent said they would not have adopted.

Other preliminary research into the Eastern European adoptive parent population has been conducted. Sharon Judge, Ph.D., examined the child's health, developmental issues, and perceptions of attachment, and reported on the stress levels of parents who had children from Eastern Europe. In general, the findings are positive. Developmental delays plummeted between the time the parent first met the child and the time of the interview (within 6 months after placement), although approximately one-third of the children remain at risk for atypical behavior, particularly in language-related services. Scores on the parenting stress index for both fathers and mothers, as well as scores on family functioning, were "within normal ranges when compared with normative data for each measure."

So while Harriet McCarthy's research helps us understand adoptive mothers' reactions to the unforeseen challenges in adoption, these longitudal studies suggest that parents and their children do somehow find ways to move forward despite the challenges. Indeed, it has been our experience, and we strongly believe, that parental depression does not indicate a lack of parental love. Instead we believe that the post-adoption period is an evolutionary process, a joyful, rewarding journey with vulnerable moments that overwhelm us, as well as happy years that sustain us.

chapter 13

assessment of post-adoption stress and depression

Many scales are designed to assess for depression. We'd like to present a basic format for social workers and therapists to use when assessing a generalized mood disorder (depression). This format has proved successful for John in his practice, and he has used this method to evaluate thousands of patients in his 15 years of psychiatric medicine. We will then discuss one scale that we believe has the specificity to measure depression in women after a child is introduced into the home. While the scale was conceived for use after childbirth, you'll see that many of the issues it addresses are common to the adoption process.

assessing depression

John has had great success with his patients by approaching their situation with a deceptively simple set of questions. These questions are derived from Aaron Beck's work in the 1960s. Called the cognitive triad, these beliefs pertain to the patient's view of himself, his view of the future, and his view of the world. John relies on the following method to provide a crude yet accurate picture, which may then point to the need for a deeper follow-up to determine whether the person is depressed. He asks the client just three questions:

> *What do you do?*
> *What do you love?*
> *What do you look forward to?*

By asking yourself these questions, you can begin to identify aspects of your life that may need more attention or professional care.

what do you do?

Embedded within this question is the goal of finding the day's structure. What time do you get up in the morning? What time to you eat? Go to bed? What work do you do in your life? How much time is taken up with work? How much leisure time is in your day? In your week?

Do you feel you have a balance between work and leisure? If you are not satisfied, what would you change about your day? How can you change it? What would happen if it changed? Is it feasible to change it now? Is this structure temporary or permanent? Do you feel a sense of control over your day? If not, why? (This question taps into whether or not a person has a sense of helplessness.)

By looking at what you do, you can begin to understand how structure and work impact how you're feeling. If a child's presence has created a dramatic shift in the structure of your day, or if you feel overwhelmed by the responsibilities of daily life, then the risk of stress and depression increases. Similarly, if you are unable to institute a routine or daily structure in your life, this could be a symptom of depression.

The lack of support systems available to you can also be uncovered by asking, "What do you do?" By looking at what you do, you'll also see with whom you do it.

what do you love?

This question reveals what it is in your life that you feel passionate about, that you enjoy doing. It pinpoints a person that you love or a thing that you adore. What motivates you? When was the last time you did the thing you enjoy the most? When was the last time you found pleasure in life? When did it stop? Why? Why have you been unable to do the thing you enjoy most?

Who do you love? Do you feel that they love you back? Has this changed? When did it change? Did you once feel loved? Did you expect to feel loved?

When was the last time you had fun? Laughed really hard? Did nothing during the day and didn't feel guilty? Paused to reflect on a spiritual basis? Took time to assess your life?

These questions provide you with a sense of how much pleasure your life brings you. Americans believe in and live a hard-working lifestyle. We often forget—or, because of circumstances, are unable to find—enjoyment in our lives. Truly, being able to plant your tomatoes or read a book or play the piano or have a "date night" with a significant other—anything that gives you a sense of enjoyment—serves an important purpose. Look at this as your "work."

what do you look forward to?

This question probes for hopelessness regarding the future, and it can also offer information about the past. What is there in your future that fills you with hope or a sense of anticipation? When is that event? Weeks away? Months? Years? What are you doing to make that event happen? Do you feel control over that event? What will you do if that event doesn't happen?

Do you see your situation as hopeless? As never-ending? Do you feel trapped in the present and future? Do you have intense regrets over your decisions? Do you feel guilty or blameworthy? How much control do you feel over your future?

Do you feel angry about your future? Do you think that life has been unkind to you and will continue to be unkind? Who do you feel anger toward? What do you do about your anger?

By looking at what is possible versus what is "set in stone" in your future, you may realize that hope is needed to survive in the world— at least in a mental world without depression.

the postpartum depression
screening scale

In addition to understanding the nature of generalized depression, it's important to look at the nature of depression in homes where children have just arrived. Based on our research, the formal depression screening scale that has the greatest potential to assess for depression in the post-adoption population is the postpartum depression screening scale (PDSS) by Cheryl Tatano Beck, D.N.Sc., and Robert K. Gable, Ed.D. This scale has documented validity, reliability, and specificity. (Note: The scale is intended to be used for *mothers* at this time.) Written at a third-grade reading level, the 35 items that make up the scale are brief and easy to understand. Unlike general depression rating scales, PDSS specifically addresses those issues faced by mothers who are struggling after a child is introduced into the home.

The scale can be used across disciplines, including nursing, social work, family therapy, obstetrics, pediatrics, psychology, and psychiatry. Post-placement visits by social workers and post-adoption counseling sessions by therapists provide excellent opportunities for administration of this scale. When introducing the tool to the mother as described in the manual, the professional may suggest that the mother infer the word "child" in instances where "baby" appears. In just 5 to 10 minutes, the PDSS identifies mothers who need a more complete evaluation for depression and assesses the presence of moderate to severe depression. The scale is published by Western Psychological Services (www.wpspublish.com). Examples of the PDSS items by its seven dimensions or symptom areas appear on page 210.

Postpartum Depression Screening Scale: Selected Items By Dimension

During the past 2 weeks . . .

Sleeping/Eating Disturbances

#1: I had trouble sleeping when my baby was asleep.
#8: I lost my appetite.

Loss of Self

#19: I did not know who I was anymore.
#5: I was afraid that I would never be my normal self again.

Anxiety/Insecurity

#23: I felt all alone.
9: I felt really overwhelmed.

Guilt/Shame

#20: I felt guilty because I could not feel as much love for my
baby as I should.
#27: I felt like I had to hide what I was thinking or feeling
toward the baby.

Emotional Liability

#3: I felt like my emotions were on a roller coaster.
#31: I felt full of anger ready to explode.

Suicidal Thoughts

#14: I started thinking I would be better off dead.
#28: I felt that my baby would be better off without me.

Mental Confusion

#11: I could not concentrate on anything.
#4: I felt like I was losing my mind.

intervention and treatment

This book has provided coping strategies and other interventions aimed at alleviating post-adoption stress and depression. We want to add a short general discussion of antidepressant therapy and "talk" therapy. Many of the individuals we spoke with agreed that pharmacological intervention with antidepressant therapy had proven to be very helpful.

We applaud these individuals for seeking out help and recognizing that, for the sake of themselves and their families, they needed assistance. Research has thoroughly documented the chemical changes that take place in the brain when depression occurs, as well as the chemical and neurological receptors of the various medications. It has been proven that depression has a physical presence within us.

We do want to emphasize that parents suffering from post-adoption depression should not rely entirely on a pharmaceutical agent to "take the problems away." A diabetic who takes a pill to control her blood sugar also has to take responsibility for her diet, exercise, and health. Similarly, an adoptive parent who realizes her depression and seeks out medication also has to realize that the other issues won't solve themselves without work, which usually includes communication with family, friends, or a counselor.

We see post-adoption depression as very amenable to treatment. Most of the parents who spoke with us said that they were able to get back on track and enjoy their children. But we want to stress that if you are *ever* fearful of hurting your child or yourself, it is an urgent situation that requires you to seek out help. Calling a mental health hotline or 9-1-1 can prevent a tragedy.

Part of this book's purpose is to decrease the stigma attached to post-adoption depression. The other part now rests on the shoulders of the adoption community. We challenge the researchers and educators to continue this journey into fully understanding the dynamics of post-adoption depression, identifying the risk factors associated with it, and refining diagnostic tools so it can be recognized and treated early. The next challenge is to bring this knowledge to parents by opening the conversations at the first home study and post-placement visits, at the first pediatrician's visit, or when it's time for the court hearing to decide parentage. Those moments are our opportunities to help.

empowering parents

Parenting is a tough job, full of events, emotions, and evolutions that are—to some degree—out of our control. Adoptive parenting has the added challenge of a child who may not have been in our home since birth, but who has come to us as an older baby or child. Such children have experienced life for months or years outside our parentage.

What we'd like to do in this chapter is to present a brief overview of some of the issues that you need to be aware of as you prepare for your child or welcome her home. We'll discuss a family inventory to help you become more aware of your family's dynamics, strengths, and weaknesses. But first we'll give you a blueprint for navigating the system in which you may suddenly find yourself a player.

searching for support

As we've heard from parents, the medical needs of a child may be unknown or undisclosed. Yet the experts all agree that you should expect the possibility of medical, psychological, or social needs. But exactly how do you go about learning what to expect?

First, be a careful consumer. Our current healthcare environment has to be navigated with savvy and as much knowledge as possible. These strategies apply to kinship parents, as well. The majority of the kinship parents we spoke with had identified their children's struggles, such as attention deficit/hyperactivity disorder (AD/HD). These children need appropriate evaluations of needs. Listed below are some tips on how to go about the critical process of accessing information.

preadoption (and post-referral) support

- Utilize the services of clinics and physician practices that offer review and feedback on videotapes of children and their medical documents and case records. For example, international adoption clinics can provide you with medical opinions based on your referred child's videotape supplied by your adoption agencies.
- Understand what feedback will be offered after the tape and records have been viewed.
- Take notes on what is said and refer to them when you realize the questions that are still unanswered.
- Make sure you receive clear and adequate explanations of the feedback you're receiving. Are these short-term or long-term issues? Are these treatable or chronic problems? What are the treatment options? Are there grounds for a second opinion?
- Understand your own issues: Are you hearing what is being said? Did your significant other hear what you heard? Have you discussed these issues?
- Explore the "what-ifs"? What if this is the case? Could we handle this? Do we have the information we need, or are there gaps? Can we deal with those gaps, those unknowns with this child?
- Find out how many people have information about this child. Can you speak with them? Can they tell you about the child's environmental history, or how many caregivers she has had since birth?
- Look at the quality of information: What is it really telling me? Is it dates and facts or more about the child's personality, development, and temperament?

■ Find out whether you will have an opportunity to meet the child. For how long? Under what conditions? What supports will be there for you after meeting the child?

post-adoption support

■ Hopefully, you will have established a relationship with a physician prior to your child coming home. Be sure that you've given the child's physician copies of all her health records. Inquire about your doctor's experience with adopted children. Our physician, while not greatly experienced with the medical needs of adopted children, networked with a major children's hospital and consulted with an expert there.
■ Be aware of all the dimensions of your child's health and well-being that need to be assessed:

1. Physical, including gross motor movement, allergies, nutrition
2. Emotional (her ability to bond and attach to you, to express the loss and grief of her previous life and surroundings, and so on)
3. Social, including her ability to communicate with her world
4. Processing, including her ability to process the sensory stimuli from her environment with her auditory system, her tactile processing, and her visual processing
5. Developmental, including comparisons of where she was when she came home and where she is now. Understand the normal milestones and what her environments have offered her
6. Cognitive, including her abilities in language versus her abilities on "performance items" of IQ tests. A gap between the two may indicate a learning difficulty. Understand the impact that culture plays when assessing a child using American-based tests.
7. Cultural, including her spoken language and her belief system, and dependent on the age of the child. One family's child believed that walking was for the lower class in her country, yet her American family enjoyed walks for the physical activity.
8. Spiritual, including how she makes sense of life, loss, and separation. Is she able to express how placements and loss of a known or unknown birthparent has affected her?

the **whole** child

The list on the opposite page takes a child and divides her into segments. While this approach can be informative, we believe an additional step is necessary in order to understand the whole child, a step that is often overlooked. Let's assume you've collected enough information to give you an understanding of your child's needs. You may even have been offered several diagnoses. You may feel overwhelmed and mystified, as if suddenly you're expected to understand terms and tests that are as foreign to you as another language.

Take a moment and regroup. Look at your child and see more than those terms and labels. To emphasize the importance of this larger picture, we'd like to share one boy's story with you.

At 3 years old, he could barely utter his name, and then it sounded more like "Be" than "Ben." The language test results of both receptive (what he could understand) and expressive (what he could say) showed delays in months and years. His eye contact with those unknown to him was averted and downward-focused.

In new situations, he often refused to engage with others. His parents realized these behaviors stemmed from his anxiety, but were unable to understand the root cause of his anxiety. Tolerance of foods and textures was poor. Ben insisted on eating only certain foods and wearing only soft clothing. Often distracted, he seemed to have difficulty staying on and completing tasks. He fell more often then usual for his age and required stitches twice due to falls.

Ben was affectionate and kind and relaxed at home. He interacted with his environment in others ways besides language—through gestures and utterances with inflections. He was loving toward his sibling. Once familiar with the situation, he formed bonds with his therapists and cooperated well in therapy.

Three years later, after countless speech and occupational therapy sessions, his parents received the correct diagnoses for their son: Auditory processing disorder, expressive and receptive language disorder, and sensory integration dysfunction.

This child, our older birth son, was severely delayed, and many people who tested him in his early years implied that he was autistic. He was not. Had we not looked at the whole child, we would have missed

Ben's real deficit and arrived at a conclusion that wasn't accurate, a conclusion that would have assigned him to a different path of treatment.

The whole child can tell us more than the sum of his diagnoses.

learning the professionals' roles

Being thrust into the healthcare maze can be quite daunting. "Who
Does What: The Roles of Professionals" on page 218 gives a brief
overview of the professionals who treat children and what each professional's role is. As with any decision as important as choosing a caregiver,
be a careful consumer. Important questions to ask if you're unsure:

1. What is your area of practice? What types of patients do you
    evaluate and treat?
2. What interventions do you normally recommend: medication,
    therapy (if so, what kind)? What other interventions are used to
    treat this diagnosis? Why don't you provide those in your prac-
    tice? Can you refer me to clinicians who do provide this type
    of therapy? What are the costs of these therapies? What success
    have you had with managed care payment of these services?

    The issue of candidacy is a critical one: Based on the assess-
    ment and test results, will your child's needs be addressed with this
    therapy? Is she a good candidate to be helped by this treatment?
    Is it likely that your child will benefit from this therapy? What are
    the candidacy criteria for this type of therapy? In other words, let's
    say a locked door represents your child's need. You need to find
    the key to that door. There may be lots of keys and even more
    than one lock on the door. The key may be a very new, shiny key
    that is research-based, but it has to be the right key for your child.
3. If you have been offered a diagnosis of your child's problems,
    be sure to ask what behaviors, tests, and examinations were
    used to arrive at this diagnosis. What behaviors does my child
    have that would not lead you to this diagnosis? Are there
    other diagnoses that may address these behaviors? Why did
    you not arrive at any of those diagnoses?

    We offer this example from our own experience: Auditory
    processing disorder (APD) can mimic attention deficit/hyperac-

tivity (AD/HD) disorder. The superficial signs are almost identical: The child is easily distracted, unable to stay on or finish a task, and has an inability to follow directions. Yet the two disorders are very different and require different management tools. Also, the two disorders can coexist. A child can have both AD/HD and APD. These questions will help you tease out whether all avenues have been explored by the professional.

4. May I have a copy of my child's tests and reports? Ask that those tests and reports be explained to you. If you are not satisfied with the explanations, remember that you have paid to have these tests done, and part of the professional's responsibility is to make sure you understand them. Remember, you are the most important member of your child's treatment team.

family survey

We'd like to expand on a strategy offered by Barbara Rila, Ph.D., whose private practice specializes in adoption. She employs this strategy in her practice: the family's self-assessment.

characterizing the family

Family Identity. What is your family's identity? Who does your family include? How will this identity change once your child is home/How has this family identity changed since your child has been home? How do you encourage the family to see itself in a unique and proud way?

Family Cohesion. Do you sense that your family is close? Do they share an intimacy that protects them in society? How will that cohesion be influenced with a new child? What is the relationship between your children? How would you describe your family to others: close, neutral, or distant?

Is your family a parent-centered family or a child-centered family? Whose needs take priority, the parents' or the child's? How is the partnership/marriage honored in the family? Do children tend to split the parents as decisions are made? How cohesive a bond do you enjoy with your significant other?

Who Does What: **The Roles of Professionals**

A s you enter into the healthcare system, the titles and roles of various providers can seem overwhelming. This is a general overview of some of the professionals you may encounter. What follows is meant as a guide; your state may have different designations and titles, as well as different professionals available.

Physicians

Physicians hold either a medical doctor (M.D.) or doctor of osteopathy (D.O.) degree. They can prescribe medications and are held to high ethical, legal, and practice standards by state licensing boards and national organizations such as the American Medical Association.

Family practitioners are physicians who practice in general medicine. Pediatricians are specialists who treat children, usually up to the age of 18. Pediatric developmental specialists, pediatric neurologists, and child psychiatrists are medical doctors who treat children's specialized needs in development, neurological functioning, and mental health disorders. There are a variety of certification examinations that physicians can take, and if passed, the doctor can become "board certified" in her field of expertise.

Psychologists

In addition to the child psychiatrist, psychologists and social workers also provide behavioral health (mental health) services. Psychologists have doctoral degrees, holding either a doctorate of philosophy (Ph.D.) or a doctorate of psychology (Psy.D.) degree. Psychologists do 1 year of full-time predoctoral internship and a postdoctoral period of supervision prior to getting their Health Service Provider in Psychology (HSPP) designation. The HSPP means that they can independently diagnose and treat mental illness; do not have to rely on physician referrals; can bill third-party payers (such as insurances); and do not require the supervision or signatures of an M.D. While there is some movement toward granting psychologists the authority to write prescriptions, this is still somewhat controversial in most states.

Psychologists also differ from others in the mental health field in that they can conduct a variety of tests, including intelligence, personality, and psychometric evaluations. As with other professionals, psychologists specialize in various specialties such as education, pediatric, and other areas.

Social Workers

As we've mentioned, adoption in the United States was defined and evolved by social workers. A social worker may be baccalaureate (BSW)- or masters (MSW)-prepared. A social worker counsels and educates individuals, families, and groups to improve or restore their ability to function at their capacity. Licensing credentials determine which social workers provide clinical social work services. Usually, the licensed social worker (LCSW) is able to bill third-party payers (insurance) for counseling.

Other Disciplines

An occupational therapist (OT) assesses and treats a variety of fine motor and sensory difficulties. This professional will assess for sensory integration dysfunction (SID). Occupational therapists can also specialize based on treatments and age groups (for example, pediatric and geriatric populations).

A speech-language pathologist (SLP) assesses and treats a variety of speech, language, and listening disorders. The terms receptive (what a child can understand) and expressive (what a child can verbalize) are terms used in many assessments and treatment plans. The Certificate of Clinical Competency (CCC) is used to designate those masters-prepared professionals who have completed a 9-month period of supervision and passed a certification exam. This designation is awarded by the American Speech-Language-Hearing Association (ASHA).

An audiologist is a trained specialist who assesses how well your child can hear and can recommend educational interventions as well as equipment to aid in hearing. This professional is also the one charged with testing for auditory processing disorders (APD), an inability to process sounds efficiently. You may see CCC after their educational degrees as well (see speech language pathologist, above).

The pediatric optometrist is the professional who assesses visual acuity (how well your child is able to see) and formulates a treatment plan for visual disorders such as tracking. The sense of sight is often overlooked when looking at your child's learning needs, but to ensure your child gets the correct diagnosis, it is vitally important that it be assessed.

Nurse practitioners and clinical nurse specialists are registered nurses who have received advanced training and education. These individuals may have prescription privileges, and based upon education, they may also be able to bill third-party payers for therapy and treatment.

Discipline. Who is the disciplinarian? How is discipline carried out in the family? Is it effective? Is it carried out consistently? Is it fairly carried out among the children? Is there a child who is considered "good?" Have your children been "easy" to raise? How would you deal with a child whose needs were disruptive?

Roles within the Family. Is your family patriarchal? Matriarchal? Are the roles dependent on the situation—does Dad take the lead in some instances and Mom in others? Who owns the idea of expanding the family through adoption? Is there a person who is more cautious? Has that person been able to fully express her or his feelings?

Who is the income producer, or is this responsibility shared? Are there contingency plans in place if something happened to one or both jobs? Do you have goals for the future? Where do you see the family in 1, 5, and 10 years?

dimensions of family

Social. What is your support network? List three-to-five people you could call no matter what time of day (or night) for a favor (such as running an errand, emergency babysitting, or picking up a child). Are both parents comfortable with these people? Do you feel your friends and family support your decision to adopt? How do you communicate that support or lack thereof to others or to your partner?

If you could have more social support, what form would it take? Have you told others what you might need after your child comes home? Have you arranged for a trusted individual to provide short respite childcare while you and your significant other have time alone?

Financial. Is there enough money to meet the needs of the family? Are there emergency plans a crisis for? Do you have adequate health insurance? Have you made plans to ensure coverage for your child? Does your will or estate include your new child?

Cultural. What are the cultural assumptions made in the family? Has prejudice been discussed? How comfortable are you bringing a child of a different race or culture into the home? Have you discussed these issues openly and with your children? How will heritage issues be integrated into the family? Remember, the child isn't merely adding a new culture to the family, she is merging her culture into the family. *You* will be part of that culture, and part of the adoption culture, for the rest of your life.

If you're a kinship parent and a child has been brought into the family with a racial background that you weren't anticipating, how will you handle that? How will you accept this child? How will you feel around your friends and neighbors? How will you communicate your feelings about your grandchild to your son or daughter? What is your history of racial acceptance?

Emotional/Psychological. How are emotions dealt with in your house? How is affection shown? How is conflict handled? Who is seen as having the most influence in the family? Why? Who has the most power to affect the family's decisions? Why?

What steps have you taken to prepare for the adoption? Have you networked through your agency to meet and interact with other parents? Have you attended seminars to educate yourself on the possible needs of your new child? What are your expectations of yourself? Your spouse or partner? Your family and friends? Your child? Your child's birthparents? The society you live in? Your adoption professional? Are these realistic?

Physical. How old are you? How old do you feel? How healthy are you? Are you prepared for the change in lifestyle (this applies to parents of all ages) such as getting up in the middle of the night, lack of privacy, and 24-hours-a-day, 7-days-a-week responsibility? Are you up-to-date with your own preventative health exams (general health, eye, and dental)?

Are you facing menopause in a few years? How old will your child be when you reach this milestone? What types of healthy behaviors can you start practicing now to help prepare for the physical demands of a child?

Spiritual. What are your beliefs? How do you integrate them into your daily existence? How do you, or will you, teach those beliefs to your child? How does holding those beliefs influence your choices as a family? What rituals surround your faith? How does adoption and parenting fit into those beliefs?

strengths and weaknesses

After discussing the above dimensions, the heads of the household and the children (if any) need to list five strengths and five weaknesses of your family—concerning anything that they perceive. Compare your answers and discuss each list.

a call to action

We wrote this book for three reasons. The first was to describe the dynamics of post-adoption stress and depression. The second was to offer coping strategies that work. And the third was to make adoptive and kinship parents' needs known to a wider community. Ultimately, we wanted to help families. We have sought to honor adoption and those who have chosen to build their families in this manner.

While differences do exist within the adoption community, its strength lies, and will continue to lie, in its love of children. Society at large may view adoption as being for the faithful or the flawed; but we view adoption simply as being about family, the sanctity of that union, and how we as a society need to do more to foster and protect that precious foundation.

Toward that purpose, we want to acknowledge that our work is but another step toward understanding, legitimizing, and addressing post-adoption stress and depression. More needs to be done. Adoptive parents need support—emotional, social, physical, financial, and spiritual support. They need this support just as any new parent might, but more so because society has yet to fully embrace the adoptive and kinship family, and because the children we unconditionally love as part of those families come to us with specific needs that have to be addressed.

our invitation to you

Because of this, we would like to call our readers and those with whom they would share this book to make adoptive families even stronger and better prepared to face the future. There are specific and simple ways you can make a difference in the lives of these families.

parents

- Get involved in organizations that further the awareness of adoption as a legitimate part of our society and culture. Support their efforts. From subscribing to adoption magazines to attending seminars, these efforts help adoptive families.
- Share your feelings about post-adoption needs with others, in whatever forum or with whatever audience or group is comfortable to you. The bottom line: We adoptive parents have a right to our emotions. We're not being disloyal to our children or families to feel the way we do.
- Realize that you need to turbocharge your astoundingly beautiful, unconditional love of your child with real, practical resources. What this means is that you're going to have to acknowledge the problems that exist and actively seek out the help you need. You may not find the right counselor the first time; you may hit many obstacles trying to locate services. Keep trying. It's imperative that you keep trying.
- Give what you're experiencing a name: post-adoption stress and/or post-adoption depression. We believe that giving this constellation of emotions a name legitimizes it, offers direction for treatment, and takes into account the specific needs of your family You are not crazy, and you are not alone.

friends and families

- Your daughter, son, or friend needs your support now. They need you to accept their role and their children.

- Empathize with what the adoptive parents and children have experienced. You may not understand it completely, but they will understand your support.
- Examine your own feelings about having a child by adoption in the family. By being honest, you can separate your apprehensions from the real child who is now a family member.
- Stop and realize how very much your acceptance means to your family member. Withholding love and acceptance ripples into the extended family and can polarize family loyalties.

professionals

- Whether you're a physician, nurse, social worker, teacher, court official, or member of some other field that brings you in contact with adoptive families, allow adoptive and kinship parents the right to feel as legitimate as any parent. Be sensitive to the parents' needs in different settings: the hospital, the courts, their homes, the classroom.
- Educate yourselves on what defines adoption. It *is* about parenting. It's *not* about second choices. It's not about taking another person's child without the consent of that birthparent. It's the ability to care for and love a child that was not born to you. It's about fulfillment.
- Health professionals who come in contact with adoptive and kinship parents have multiple opportunities to forge an easier path for these individuals. Make it safe for parents to speak openly and freely about their feelings. Put aside unnecessary questions that violate the intimacy of the family (such as, "Why did you adopt?"). Push for professional understanding of post-adoption stress and depression by acknowledging that, while it's not part of the *Diagnostic and Statistical Manual-IV-TR,* this depression is a real experience and support is needed by those who seek your services.

researchers

- Pursue ways to formally answer scholarly questions about post-adoption stress and depression. Seek out and apply for grants to fund research into this social reality. There are so many questions left to ask, and complacency will not fill this void of knowledge. Efforts toward theory building (understanding the "why" of post-adoption stress and depression) and applied research (what to do about it) are open to you. It is truly unmarked social territory.

elected officials

- Enact legislation that is adoptive- and kinship-family friendly. Recent years have seen much legislation enacted that is pro-adoption, from adoption tax credits to encouraging permanent placement for children in foster care to citizenship laws. These laws have made a real difference in many lives. But laws need to be enacted to provide the post-placement supports that are so desperately needed. The issue becomes one of money and allocation of resources to the domestic system of social workers, caseworkers, foster care, and permanency initiatives. Laws that enforce the historical and legal boundaries that cut off adopted individuals from their birth information also stand in the way of adoption becoming a secret-free institution in our society.

our wish for you

While much of our work focused on the challenges of adoption, through it all, over and over, we found ourselves returning to our core belief of how extraordinarily beautiful unconditional love of a child truly is. The unifying factor in speaking with parents and experts is that the parent's love of this child is a love that fights, keeps trying, and refuses to die. It is also a love that, at times, knows pain. It's a love that comes to realize that its rewards are often hidden or postponed. It is a love that has to rely on education and sharing, a love that is adaptable and enlightened. It is our heartfelt wish for you to experience that love, to have that love grow deep roots within your soul and to lead you and your child to become more than you ever thought you could be.

glossary

adoptee: An individual, adult or child, who is adopted.

adoptive parent: A parent who legally adopts a child not born to him or her.

attention deficit/hyperactivity disorder (AD/HD): A behavioral/neurological disorder whose defining symptoms include impulsivity, inattentiveness, distractibility, and hyperactivity. There are three types: 1) AD/HD, combined type (inattention and hyperactivity/impulsivity); 2) AD/HD, predominately inattentive type; and 3) AD/HD, predominately hyperactive–impulsive type. Both children and adults may have AD/HD.

auditory processing disorder (APD): Jack Katz, a pioneer in APD research, defined APD as "What we do with what we hear." APD occurs when there is a jumbling or distortion in the processing of sounds. APD impacts learning, language, and listening.

autism (autistic disorder): A developmental disturbance characterized by impaired social interaction and communication and an abnormally narrow range of activities and interests. This disorder usually is evidenced before age 3. Individuals with autistic disorder have restricted, repetitive, and stereotyped patterns of behaviors, interests, and activities.

birthmother/birthfather/birthparent: Preferred term over biological parent, which some consider to be scientific and not nurturing.

closed adoption (confidential adoption): An adoption where the parents and child are not given access to birthparent information. There is no contact between the birthparents and the adoptive parents, either before or after the placement of the child. The adoption records are sealed after the adoption.

developmental delay: A delay in achieving developmental milestones in which children are normally able to achieve proficiency or accomplishment. The delays may be in specific academic, language, speech, or motor skills.

developmental learning disability: A disability evidenced by the child's inadequate development of specific academic, language, speech, or motor skills. These disabilities are not due to physical or neurological disorders, a pervasive developmental disorder, mental retardation, or deficient educational opportunities.

disruption: When the child is removed from the home prior to legal finalization of the adoption.

dissolution: When the adoption is reversed or voided after legal finalization. The child is placed outside the home or in foster care when a dissolution occurs.

expressive language disorder: A disorder evidenced by the child's inability to verbally express herself. Examples include identifying objects by the wrong names, jumbling the order of words, or having a limited vocabulary.

fetal alcohol syndrome: A syndrome of children born to mothers who drank heavily during their pregnancy. The syndrome, in its full-blown form, can include severe mental retardation, a small head, diminished physical size, and facial abnormalities.

guardian ad litem (GAL): A court-appointed adult whose role is to provide an independent assessment that ensures that the interests and legal rights of the child are given adequate consideration.

home study: A written report that summarizes the social worker's findings based on several meetings with the prospective adoptive parents and other immediate family members who reside in the home. Other information in the report includes the adoptive parents' health, medical, criminal, family, and home background findings. The home study report aids the court in determining whether the prospective parents are qualified to adopt this child based on state laws.

international adoption: An adoption in which children who are citizens of other nations are adopted by American families. (Preferred term over "foreign adoption.")

kinship parent: A family member who takes on the parenting role of the child. This role may be defined through legal adoption or through an informal agreement between the birthparent and the kinship parent.

learning difference: A disorder in one or more of the basic physiological processes involved in understanding or in using language, spoken or written, which may manifest itself in an imperfect ability to listen, think, speak, read, write, spell, or do mathematical calculations. (Preferred term over "learning disability.")

open adoption: An arrangement that can have many gradations and which provides for contact between the birthparents, adoptive parents, and child. A birthparent may be seen as an extended family member who has frequent contact with the child, or the birthparent may be only an occasional guest or correspondent.

post-adoption (time period): Traditionally, this has been defined as that time after finalization of the adoption. In this book, we use post-adoption as the time from placement onward. Post-adoption is an active, rewarding, and challenging time of living as a family.

post-adoption depression: A mood disorder that occurs post–placement or post–adoption of a child. Post-adoption depression can be classified as mild, moderate, or severe. The etiology is unknown, but predictive factors include impaired parent-child bonding, lack of social support, and lack of parental preparation. The onset of the depression can occur days or years after the child joins the family. Prevalence is unknown. Duration is greater than 3-to-12 months. Post-adoption depression may be episodic, with remissions and reoccurrences. More research is needed to fully describe this mood disorder.

post-adoption stress: A diverse set of events encountered by the adoptive parents either post-placement or post-adoption of a child. These specific events can trigger anxiety or depression.

post-finalization (period). See *post-adoption (time period)*.

post-placement (time period): The time after the child has been placed in your home, but before finalization. A social worker will visit your home for post-placement visits during the 6-to-12 months between placement and finalization, to provide support for you and your child. During these visits, the social worker will gather necessary information in order to write a report to the court. The social worker is also there to help you obtain other professional assistance, if needed, to make the placement successful. The court requires a certain number of visits before the adoption can be finalized. See *post-adoption (time period)*.

reactive attachment disorder: A disorder demonstrated by a child's inability to form appropriate bonds and attachment. Behaviors include: 1) the inability to initiate or respond to social interaction by showing ambivalence, avoidance, and resistance to comfort, or 2) the formation of indiscriminate social attachments, such as excessive familiarity with strangers or lack of choice to attachment figure.

receptive language disorder: A disorder that is evidenced by the child's inability to understand, make sense of, or comprehend certain words or sentences. Their ability to hear may be normal.

respectful adoption language (RAL): A vocabulary about adoption that strives for respect, responsibility, and objectivity about the decisions made by birthparents and adoptive parents and the discussions that surround that. First introduced by social worker Marietta Spencer 2 decades ago. RAL begins with the concept of family.

semi-open adoptions: A combination of confidential and open adoption, with the emphasis on privacy versus confidentiality. Communication before and after placement usually takes place through a third party, usually an adoption agency or an adoption attorney.

sensory integration dysfunction: A child's inability to correctly process information brought in by the senses; the child may have unusual responses to touch and movement. Children may be hyposensitive (seeking sensory stimulation) or hypersensitive (avoiding sensory stimulation).

selected readings

Bennett, S. S., and P. Indman. *Beyond the Blues: A Guide to Understanding and Treating Prenatal and Postpartum Depression.*. San Jose: Moodswings Press, 2003.

Callander, J. *Second Time Around: Help for Grandparents Who Raise Their Children's Kids.*.Newberg, OR: Bookpartners, Inc., 1999.

Cline, F. W., and J. Fay. *Parenting with Love and Logic: Teaching Children Responsibility.* Colorado Springs: Piñon Press, 1990.

Crumbley, J., and R. L. Little. *Relatives Raising Children: An Overview of Kinship Care.* Washington, D.C.: CWLA Press, 1997.

Eldridge, S. *Twenty Life Transforming Choices Adoptees Need to Make.* Colorado Springs: Piñon Press, 2003.

Eldridge, S. *Twenty Things Adopted Kids Wished Their Adoptive Parents Knew.* New York: Dell Publishing, 1999.

Federici, R. *Help for the Hopeless Child: A Guide for Families (With Special Discussion for Assessing and Treating the Post-Institutionalized Child).* Alexandria, VA: Dr. Ronald S. Federici and Associates, 2003.

Foli, K. *Like Sound through Water: A Mother's Journey through Auditory Processing Disorder.* New York: Atria Books, 2002.

Hallowell, E.M., and J. J. Ratey. *Driven to Distraction: Recognizing and Coping with Attention Deficit Disorder from Childhood through Adulthood.* New York: Touchstone Books, 1994.

Hamaguchi McAleer, P. *Childhood Speech, Language, and Listening Problems: What Every Parent Should Know.* New York: John Wiley & Sons, Inc, 2001.

Hopkins-Best, M. *Toddler Adoption: The Weaver's Craft.* Indianapolis, IN: Perspectives Press, 1997.

Houtman, S., and B. Rowland (Ed). *To Grandma's House We...Stay: When You Have to Stop Spoiling Your Grandchildren and Start Raising Them.* Northridge, CA: Studio 4 Productions, 1999.

Jernberg, A. M., and Booth, P. B. *Theraplay: Helping Parents and Children Build Better Relationships Through Attachment Based Play, Second Edition.* San Francisco: Jossey-Bass Publishers, 1999.

Keck, G. C., and Kupecky, R. M. *Adopting the Hurt Child: Hope for Families with Special-Needs Kids.* Colorado Springs: Piñon Press, 1998.

Keck, G. C., and Kupecky, R. M. *Parenting the Hurt Child: Helping Adoptive Families Heal and Grow.* Colorado Springs: Piñon Press, 2002.

Kornhaber, A. *The Grandparent Guide: The Definitive Guide to Coping with the Challenges of Modern Grandparenting.* Contemporary Books: Chicago, 2002.

Kranowitz, C. S., and L. B. Silver. *The Out-of-Sync Child: Recognizing and Coping with Sensory Integration Dysfunction.* Perigee Books: New York, 2002.

Levine, M. *A Mind at a Time.* New York: Simon and Schuster, 2002.

Melina, L. R. *Raising Adopted Children: A Manual for Adoptive Parents.* New York: Perennial. 1998.

O'Malley, B. *LifeBooks: Creating a Treasure for the Adopted Child.* Winthrop, Massachusetts: Adoption-Works, 2001.

Peacock, C. A. *Mommy Far, Mommy Near: An Adoption Story.* Morton Grove, IL: Albert Whitman & Co, 2000.

Perkins, P., and D. Slorah. *Grandparents' Rights: What Every Grandparent Needs to Know.* Bloomington, IN: 1st Books Library, 2003.

Poe, L. M. *Black Grandparents as Parents.* Berkeley, CA: LMP Publications, 1992.

Schooler, J. *The Whole Life Adoption Book: Realistic Advice for Building a Healthy Adoptive Family.* Colorado Springs: Piñon Press, 1993.

Van Gulden, H., and L. M. Bartels-Rabb. *Real Parents, Real Children: Parenting the Adopted Child.* New York: Crossroads Publishing Co., 1993.

Viorst, J. *Necessary Losses: The Loves, Illusions, Dependencies, and Impossible Expectations That All of Us Have to Give Up in Order to Grow.* New York: Free Press, 1998.

Welch, M., M.D. *Holding Time.* New York: Simon & Schuster, 1989.

resources

support for adoptive parents

Adoptive Families of America
24-Hour Helpline
(1-800-372-3300)

magazines

Adoption Today
Subscription Department
541 East Garden Drive, Unit N,
Windsor, CO 80550
(888) 924-6736
www.adoptinfo.net

Adoptive Families
42 West 38 Street, Suite 901
New York, NY 10018
(800) 372-3300
www.adoptivefamilies.com

organizations

Ethica: An Adoption Advocacy
  Group
www.ethicanet.org
This organization seeks to be
an independent voice for the
improvement of adoption and
child welfare practices. Offers case
advocacy and crisis management
to families.

Jewel Among Jewels Adoption
  Network, Inc.
Sherrie Eldridge, President
(317) 849-5651
www.adoptionjewels.org
mail@adoptionjewels.org

Learning Disabilities Association of
America (LDA)
4156 Library Road
Pittsburgh, PA 15234
(412) 341-1515
www.ldaamerica.org
This nonprofit organization's purpose is to "advance the education
and general welfare of children of
normal or potentially normal intelligence who have learning disabilities of a perceptual, conceptual, or
coordinative nature."

North American Council on
Adoptable Children
970 Raymond Avenue, Suite 106
St. Paul, MN 55114
(651) 644-3036
www.nacac.org
Contact: Dina Martin-Hushman,
NACAC Parent Support Group
Coordinator, for information about
existing and new parent support
groups.

The Evan B. Donaldson Adoption
Institute
525 Broadway
New York, New York 10012
(212) 925-4089
www.adoptioninstitute.org
info@adoptioninstitute.org
Offers lawmakers, the media, and
others education, research resources, and information about
adoption. The Web site offers
some publications that may be
downloaded for free.

The National Adoption Information
Clearinghouse (NAIC)
330 C Street, SW
Washington, D.C. 20447
(703) 352-3488
(888) 251-0075
http://naic.acf.hhs.gov/index.cfm
naic@calib.com
The NAIC is a comprehensive resource on all aspects of adoption.

support for kinship parents

AARP
AARP Grandparents Information
Center
601 E. Street, NW
Washington, D.C. 20049
(202) 434-2296
www.aarp.org/grandparents
gic@aarp.org
This organization includes information and referral assistance to
local support groups, as well as referral assistance to legal services,
including access to the AARP
Legal Services Network benefits
for AARP members.

GrandsPlace
154 Cottage Road
Enfield, CT 06082
(860) 763-5789
www.grandsplace.com
Kathy@grandsplace.com
This site offers extensive resource
listings, including information on
adoption, legal services, support,
and chats.

The Foundation for Grandparenting:
   The Grandparent Foundation
108 Farnham Road
Ojai, CA 93023
www.grandparenting.org
gpfound@grandparenting.org
Arthur Kornhaber, M.D., president
and founder of The Grandparent
Foundation, offers extensive support
and information for grandparents
through this site. Dr. Kornhaber is
the author of *The Grandparent
Guide: The Definitive Book to Coping
with the Challenges of Modern Grandparenting.* Online support group for
parents who have adopted or who
have custody of grandchildren or
other family members. Message
boards and chats are available.

In-Family Adoptions:
   http://groups.msn.com/
   InFamilyAdoptions/_homepage.
   msnw?pgmarket=en-us
Online support group for parents
who have adopted or who have
custody of grandchildren or other
family members. Message boards
and chats are available.

publishers

Perspectives Press, Inc.
P.O. Box 90318
Indianapolis, IN 46290
(317) 872-3055
www.perspectivespress.com

Tapestry Books
(800) 765-2367
www.tapestrybooks.com

Western Psychological Services
   (WPS): Postpartum Depression
   Screening Scale
12031 Wilshire Boulevard
Los Angeles, CA 90025-1251
(800) 648-8857
U.S. and Canada: (310) 478-2061
www.wpspublish.com

web tools and sites

www.adoption.com
Popular Web site that includes information for adoptive parents,
birthparents, and adoptees. The library and glossary sections are full
of wonderfully specific information.

www.adoptionlawsite.org
Released by the National Center
for Adoption Law and Policy at
Capital University Law School in
Columbus, Ohio. This site provides free access to adoption-re-
lated statutes and regulations, key
cases, and articles from every U.S.
state and territory, as well as federal
and international materials.

The National Center for
   Fathering: www.fathers.com
Founded in 1990 by Ken Canfield,
Ph.D. A wealth of information for
fathers—including adoptive.

The Theraplay Institute: Therapeutic
   Play for Children and Their Parents
www.theraplay.org.

U.S. Census Bureau: Special
   Report on Adopted Children
   and Stepchildren: 2000
www.census.gov/prod/2003pubs/
   censr-6.pdf.

notes

introduction

page 2 ...*children in that age group...* Krieder, R.M. (October 2003). *Adopted Children and Stepchildren: 2000 (Census 2000 Speical Reports)* United States Census Bureau, retrieved from http://www.census.gov/prod/2003pubs/censr-6.pdf

page 2 ...*more education, than birthparents...* Census 2000.

page 4 ...*born in other countries...* Census 2000.

page 4 ... *one or more grandchildren...* Census 2000.

chapter 10

page 174 ...*in America today.* Melosh, B. (2002). *Strangers and Kin: The American Way of Adoption.* Cambridge, Massachusetts/London, England: Harvard University Press

chapter 11

page 181 ...*reckless, high-risk behaviors.* National Institute of Mental Health. 2002. Men and depression. Retrieved from http://menanddepression.nimh.nih.gov/infopage.asp?id=16.

page 182 ...*after the birth of a child...* Deater-Deckard, K., Pickering, K., Dunn, J. F., and J. Golding. (1998). Family structure and depressive symptoms in men preceding and following the birth of a child. *American Journal of Psychiatry,* 155:818-23.

page 182 ...*after the child was born...* Areias, M. E., Kumar, R., Barros, H., and Figueiredo, E. Correlates of postnatal depression in mothers and fathers. *British Journal of Psychiatry,* 169:36-41.

chapter 12

page 192 ...*in a given year...* Kessler, R.C., Berglund, P., Demler, O., Jin, R., Koretz, D., Merikangas, K. R., Rush, A.J., Walters, E.E., and Wang, P.S. (2003). The epidemilogy of major depressive disorder: Results from the National Comorbitity Survey Replication (NCS-R). *JAMA, Journal of the American Medical Association* 289:3095-3105.

page 193 ...*a woman's reproductive years...* Kornstein, Susan G. (Supplement 24, 2001). The evaluation and management of depression in women across the life span. *Journal of Clinical Psychiatry,* 62:11-17.

page 193 ...*of being a mother...* Olshansky, E. (2003). A theoretical explanation for previously infertile mothers' vulnerability to depression. *Journal of Nursing Scholarship,* 35:263-268.

page 193 ...*twice the rate of men...* Silverstein, B. (1999). Gender differences in the prevalence of clinical depression: The role played by depression associated with somatic symptoms. *American Journal of Psychiatry,* 156: 480-482.

page 193 ...*the symptoms of depression...* Stewart, D. E. (2003). Physical symptoms of depression: Unmet needs in special populations. *Journal of Clinical Psychiatry,* 64: 12-16.

page 193 ...*comprehension, and expression...* Appelbaum, M., and the Steering Committee of the NICHD Study of Early Child Care. Maternal depression linked with social and language development, school readiness. *NIH News Alert,* September 3, 1999.

page 194 ...*parents appearing childlike...* Steele, M., Hodges, J., Kaniuk, J., Hillman, S., and Henderson, K. (2003). Attachment representations and adoption: Associations between maternal states of mind and emotion narratives in previously maltreated children. *Journal of Child Psychotherapy,* 29:187-205.

page 194 ... *major maternal depression...* Brennan, P.A., LeBrocque, R., and Hammen, C. (2003). Maternal depression, parent-child relationships, and resilient outcomes in adolescence. *Journal of the American Academy of Child and Adolescent Psychiatry,* 42:1469-77.

page 194 ... *National Institute of Nursing Research, Musil...* Musil, C. M. (2003). Bringing up grandchildren: Ohio study examines effects of child-raising on the health of grandmothers. *Reflections on Nursing Leadership,* 29:40-41.

page 195 American Psychiatric Association. 2000. *Diagnostic and statistical manual of mental disorders, Fourth Edition, Text Revision.* Washington, DC, American Psychiatric Association.

page 195 ... *predictors of PPD...* Beck, C. T. (2001). Predictors of postpartum depression: An update. *Nursing Research,* 50: 275-285.

page 195 ... *Unwanted/unplanned pregnancy...* Beck, C.T. 2002. Revision of the postpartum depression predictors inventory. *JOGNN* 31:394-402.

page 196 ... *Loss of self...* Beck, C. T., and Gable, R. K. (2001). Comparative analysis of the performance of the Postpartum Depression Screening Scale with two other depression instruments. *Nursing Research,* 50:242-250.

page 197 ...*1995 issue of* Roots & Wings Adoption Magazine... Bond, J. (1995, Spring). Post adoption depression syndrome. *Roots & Wings Adoption Magazine.*

page 197 ... *into the community...* Gonzalez, H. (2003). Post-adoption depression syndrome: How to get through a time of difficult transition. *Adoption Today,* 6:32-33. Also, Page, S. (2003). After the bliss. *Adoptive Families,* 36:365-38.

page 197 ... *secure, ambivalent, or avoidant...* Ainsworth, M. D., et al. (1978). *Patterns of Attachment: A Psychological Study of the Strange Situation.* Hillsdale, NJ: Erlbaum Association.

page 198 ... *greater likelihood of depression...* Johnson S. & V. E. Whiffen (eds.). (2003). *Attachment Processes in Couple and Family Therapy.* Guilford Press. New York.

page 198 ...*12 in-depth taped interviews...* Beck, C.T. 1993. Teetering on the edge: A substantive theory of postpartum depression. *Nursing Research* 42:42-48.

page 200 ... McCarthy, H. (2000). Post-adoption depression: The unacknowledged hazard. Retrieved from: http://www.eeadopt.org/home/services/research/pad_survey/

page 205 ... *would not have adopted...* Serrano, S. (2002). Three decades of adoptive families share parenting experiences. *Adoption Today,* 5: 32-34.

page 205 ... *children from Eastern Europe...* Judge, S. (2003). Child and family outcomes for children adopted from Eastern Europe. *Adoption Today,* 5:19-21.

index

Underscored page references indicate boxed text. **Boldface** references indicate illustrations.